DEPARTMENT OF THE NAVY
HEADQUARTERS UNITED STATES MARINE CORPS
WASHINGTON, D.C. 20380

24 February 1967

FOREWORD

1. PURPOSE

This publication, NAVMC 2614, PROFESSIONAL KNOWLEDGE GAINED FROM OPERATIONAL EXPERIENCE IN VIETNAM, 1965-1966, is a compilation of material that has previously been published in the Fleet Marine Force, Pacific, publication titled, TACTICAL TRENDS AND TRAINING TIPS, and in Marine Corps Bulletin 3480 (Professional Knowledge Gained from Operational Experience in Vietnam). The purposes of this publication are:

a. To acquaint Marines with the Republic of Vietnam, its people and their enemies.

b. To enhance the professional knowledge of Marines as to the tactics and techniques being employed by military units in the Republic of Vietnam.

c. To serve as a nondoctrinal reference publication for commands training Marines for duty in the Republic of Vietnam.

2. SOURCES

Although the major part of this publication is based on Marine Corps experience in Vietnam, liberal use has been made of the experiences of the U.S. Army, U.S. Navy, U.S. Air Force and the armed services of the Republic of Vietnam.

3. REQUISITIONING

Additional copies of this publication, not in excess of 50, may be ordered directly from the Commanding General, Marine Corps Supply Activity, 1100 South Broad Street, Philadelphia, Pennsylvania 19146.

4. CERTIFICATION

Reviewed and approved this date.

L. F. CHAPMAN, JR.
Lieutenant General, U.S. Marine Corps
Chief of Staff

DISTRIBUTION: "CA" plus 7000-42(200)

TABLE OF CONTENTS

Chapter		Page

Chapter		Page
VI	COMMUNICATIONS (Continued)	

Chapter		Page
VIII	CIVIC ACTION - PSYCHOLOGICAL OPERATIONS	

Chapter | Page

Chapter I: INTRODUCTION TO VIETNAM

1. BACKGROUND OF THE WAR

Much of Vietnam's history is the story of its relations with China, its vastly larger and more powerful neighbor to the north. The Vietnamese for many centuries have both admired China for her culture and feared her for her power. During the thousand years that the Vietnamese were ruled by China (Second Century B.C. to Tenth Century A.D.), they adopted much of the Chinese culture but were not absorbed into the Chinese race as were the people of the Canton area. Ridding themselves of Chinese control in 1038 A.D., the Vietnamese maintained their independence for the next 800 years with the knowledge that it was held more or less at the whim of China. Varying degrees of Chinese influence prevailed throughout these years until the French military takeover which began in 1858. By 1900 the French had consolidated what are now North Vietnam, South Vietnam, Laos and Cambodia into French Indochina, but armed insurrections by nationalist-oriented Vietnamese prevented a real peace from settling over the new French colony.

During the years of French rule, many nationalist-inspired political groups formed which had one primary purpose in mind, the freedom of Vietnam. Hidden among these groups was the communist inspired League of Vietnamese Revolutionary Youth founded in Canton, China in 1926 by a man known today as Ho Chi Minh. For the next 20 years, considerable infighting occurred among the various political groups. Finally the upper hand was gained by the Communists. In 1940, the strategic control of Indochina was passed from the French to the Japanese while internal affairs remained with the French. This was done by an agreement struck between Japan and the Vichy Regime, a puppet government set up by the Nazi's to rule France during World War II.

The old saying that "War makes strange bedfellows" was never as true as during the Second World War. Ho Chi Minh offered to provide intelligence information from his sources in Vietnam on Japanese activities to the Allied Forces in exchange for money and arms. This offer was accepted and a small amount of aid was received from the U.S. and Nationalist China which was used to mold and strengthen the Communist "Viet Minh" as it was now called. The Viet Minh also began waging limited guerrilla warfare under the leadership of Vo Nguyen Giap against the Japanese. Increasing numbers of patriotic non-communists joined or at least supported the Viet Minh as the true independence movement of Vietnam. Capitalizing on the anticolonialist propaganda organized by Moscow, the Viet Minh claimed to be fighting only against economic misery and for national liberation. They were not recognized by the Vietnamese as representing an alien force.

When it became obvious in March 1945 that they were losing the war, the Japanese interned all French officials and troops bringing an abrupt end to French rule in Indochina. Following this, the Japanese set up a Vietnamese named Bao Dai as Emperor of Vietnam. He proclaimed Vietnamese independence under Japanese "protection." Bao Dai failed to form an effective government as a result of differences of opinion among his subordinates and the outside pressure of the Viet Minh. Bao Dai felt that the only means of preventing the return of French control was a united and independent nation. Recognizing only the nationalistic character of the Viet Minh, he decided to abdicate in its favor and, on August 23, 1945, handed over his imperial seal and other symbols of office to Ho Chi Minh.

The French, however, had no intention of giving up Indochina and prevailed upon the Allies to allow their reoccupation of the former colony. In late September 1945, French troops landed in Saigon at about the same time Nationalist Chinese troops entered Vietnam from the north to disarm the Japanese. Vietnamese of every political persuasion rose up in defense of their newly won independence, but with British assistance, the French managed to gain control of all strategic points in the South. In the North, the Chinese were dealing directly with the provisional government which had been established by Ho Chi Minh in August of 1945. In February 1946, a Franco-Chinese agreement was concluded whereby China supported France's return to Indochina in exchange for the surrender of all of

France's extra-territorial rights in China. Faced with the loss of Chinese support, the Viet Minh were forced to negotiate with the French. In March 1946, French troops landed in the North. Immediately differences developed between the French and Viet Minh forces. Although an attempt was made to settle the difficulties that arose between the two forces, it was destined for failure as neither side was willing to submit to the other. Ho Chi Minh decided to risk a long war of liberation and on December 19, 1946, the Viet Minh launched the first attack. The war, touched off by this attack, lasted for eight years and caused the Vietnamese unending misery. It was financially disastrous to France, still suffering from the destruction of World War II, and cost them 35,000 killed and 48,000 wounded. The battle of Dien Bien Phu, at which the French suffered a heavy defeat both psychologically and militarily, brought an end to the fighting.

The cease fire negotiated at Geneva on 20 July 1954 ended the war and partitioned Vietnam at the 17th parallel with the Communist Viet Minh in the north and the non-communists in the south. It further provided for a total evacuation north of the 17th parallel by the forces of the French and the State of Vietnam (now the Republic of Vietnam), as well as the evacuation of the south by the Viet Minh. In addition, an understanding supplementing the conference agreements provided for free elections in 1956 to reestablish the unity of the country.

Final negotiations for the armistice were made directly between the French High Command and the

Viet Minh. The truce agreement was reached over the objections and without the concurrence of the State of Vietnam which advocated United Nations control until such time as free elections could be held. The United States refused to sign, but agreed to observe the substance of the agreement and stated that a grave view would be taken of any attempt to use force to upset it.

Despite the terms of the Geneva Agreement, the Viet Minh had other ideas for the newly established government of South Vietnam. Caches of arms and equipment and groups of the best guerrilla fighters (estimated at 2,500 men) were left behind in the remote jungles of the delta and in the highlands. When the State of Vietnam, which had signed none of the Geneva Agreements, objected to holding elections for unifying north and south in which more than half of the population would go to the polls subject to Communist coercion, Ho ordered these guerrillas into action. Propaganda and terrorism campaigns began in late 1956 to persuade the people to oppose the Government of the Republic of Vietnam. This marked the transition of the Viet Minh to the Viet Cong.

The Viet Cong--remaining Communist guerrillas, Party members, and their supporters--unlike the Viet Minh who had struggled to defeat a colonial power within its own boundaries, now launched a campaign to topple the Government of a free nation. Open admission of Communist ties and acceptance of Communist aid from both elements of the Chinese-Soviet bloc also marked this transition.

Viet Cong propaganda, terrorism and guerrilla activities increased in tempo throughout the late 50's, and by 1960, battalion size operations were being conducted. Infiltration of military reinforcements and materials from the north were stepped up and by 1962, the Viet Cong numbered about 25,000. Terrorism, sabotage and armed attacks reached new heights despite vigorous governmental efforts at control. Any official worker or establishment that represented a service to the people by the Government in Saigon became fair game for the VC.

Between 1963 and 1965, internal political struggles in the government of South Vietnam gave the VC invaluable opportunities which it fully exploited. Their agents did all they could to encourage dissatisfaction and organized demonstrations in Saigon and elsewhere. In the countryside the VC consolidated its hold over some areas and enlarged its military and political apparatus by increased infiltration and penetration of other areas. It expanded its various campaigns against the people and the Government. In 1965 alone, 230 South Vietnamese hamlet chiefs and other government officials were killed in bombings and other acts of sabotage, and at least 10,225 civilians were kidnapped by the VC.

Today the war in South Vietnam has reached new proportions with the outright participation of thousands of North Vietnamese regular troops as well as weapons and equipment provided by the Communist bloc. Although the facade of nationalism remains in the Viet Cong insurgency, it is clearly being directed by Hanoi and Peiping. The tiny Republic of Vietnam has been publicly singled out by communist leaders as the next to submit to them in their program of attempted world domination.

The United States has honored its commitments to support the Geneva Agreement and has aided the fledgling government of the Republic of South Vietnam in its struggle to establish peace. However, to the Peiping leaders, a new dimension has been added to the conflict, that of proving the United States a "Paper Tiger." It has been said in Peiping that the objective in South Vietnam is the capitulation of the United States. The United States is not going to capitulate and will continue to meet its commitment of assisting the Government and people of South Vietnam in preserving their independence.

For this purpose, and this purpose alone, United States Marines were landed on the shores of South Vietnam on 8 March 1965.

# # # # #

2. INDIVIDUAL BEHAVIOR AND VIETNAMESE CUSTOMS AND TRADITIONS

a. Individual Behavior

Winning and maintaining the friendship and cooperation of the Vietnamese civilians living within the operational area is an essential step in reducing the effectiveness of the local Viet Cong guerrillas--they cannot operate effectively without civilian support.

256-290 O-67—2

The Viet Cong attempt to separate Marines from the local civilians by showing that they are cruel, unthinking, and not concerned with the welfare of the local people. The Viet Cong can be defeated in these efforts by the strength and generosity Marines show in their daily life. The "NINE RULES" for the military man in Vietnam provide the guide for doing this. They are:

→ Remember you are a guest. Make no demands and seek no special treatment.

→ Get to know the people: Understand their life, use phrases from their language, and honor their customs and laws.

→ Treat women with politeness and respect.

→ Make friends among the soldiers and the common people.

→ Always give the Vietnamese the right of way.

→ Be alert to security and be ready to react with your military skill.

→ Do not attract attention by loud, rude or unusual behavior.

→ Avoid separating yourself from the people by a display of wealth or privilege.

→ Above all else, remember that we are members of the U.S. military forces on a difficult mission, responsible for all our official and personal actions. Reflect honor upon yourself, the U.S. Marine Corps and the United States of America.

b. The People

The Vietnamese appear at first glance to be quite different from us and in many instances his reasoning and actions do not appear "rational" to an American. However, the geographical, economical, cultural, religious, and political factors that determine how the Vietnamese think, act and live are vastly different from our own. We must be careful not to judge the Vietnamese by our own standards and way of life, but to respect him in his own cultural environment.

There are certain areas in which mistakes have often been made by Americans that resulted, at best, in embarrassment. Here are some tips on how to get along with the Vietnamese as provided by long term residents of the country:

→ Basically, the American in Vietnam will usually find that his naturally forthright approach will have to be curbed if he is to make friends among the people he has come to help. The Vietnamese, in common with other Easterners, seem to us to often beat around the bush conversationally. Ask a direct question and you're likely to get either an evasive answer or the response it is assumed you want to hear whether it is correct or not. This is often the case when you request

agreement and the other party is too polite to disagree directly. It is considered rude to make a request of an individual. Hint that you would like something done and let the Vietnamese volunteer to do it.

→ The American use of first names among people they have only recently met can cause resentment among Vietnamese, who are more reserved in their personal relations. Stick to Mr. and Mrs., and let the Vietnamese get on the first-name basis when they are ready. This same reserve applies to introductions. It is much better to arrange an introduction through a mutual acquantance than to introduce yourself to a Vietnamese.

→ In conversation with a new Vietnamese acquaintance, stick to small talk. Don't discuss politics, and don't use the words "native," "Asiatic" or "Indochina."

→ Even when talking to Vietnamese whom you know fairly well, it is wise to avoid giving outright advice. Don't push your ideas; act on your ideas when possible, and let the Vietnamese observe the benefits to be derived by following your example.

→ Public displays of emotion are considered vulgar by Vietnamese. So control your anger, affection and other emotional impulses, and try to speak quietly at all times.

→ Don't pat a Vietnamese acquaintance on the back or on the head. In fact, "hands-off" is the rule, since such personal contact may be considered an affront to dignity.

→ If invited to eat in a Vietnamese home, let the older people begin the meal before you do. Eat every bit of the food put on your plate--as a compliment to your hostess' cooking, but don't clean the platter from which everyone is taking food since this would make your hostess feel she hadn't prepared enough food to satisfy you.

→ When visiting Vietnamese in their home, remember to keep your feet on the floor. Putting feet up on a table or chair is considered arrogant behavior, and pointing your feet at someone (such as sitting with an ankle on the opposite knee) is considered extremely insulting.

→ However much you may admire an object in the home, it's bad manners to ask what it cost or where it was bought.

→ After a visit to a Vietnamese home, an American can repay the hospitality by inviting his friend to a restaurant--but make it an expensive restaurant, even though the food is better at a cheaper place. The knowledge that he is being entertained expensively will please a Vietnamese more than a good meal could.

→ Incidentally, the Vietnamese don't believe in "Dutch Treat." The older person is expected to pick up the tab after joining someone by chance in a restaurant.

→ When sending a gift to a family that has entertained you, send something for the children rather than to the wife, and avoid sending just one item since odd numbers are frowned upon. Send two inexpensive presents to a child rather than a costly one. This holds especially true for wedding gifts; one present is seen as an omen that the marriage won't last.

→ Observing social customs such as these, even when they seem strange to Westerners, goes a long way toward creating good relations with people of a different culture.

→ Also of importance is the willingness to learn at least the basics of the Vietnamese language. It's a hard one, but learning enough to conduct simple conversations pays off in smoother work relationships.

"A fool lies here who tried to hustle the East," wrote Kipling, and things have not changed much in this regard since his days east of Suez.

The Vietnamese, in common with the other people of Asia, usually have a far different concept of time than do Westerners. Timetables, appointments, schedules hold little interest for them. Getting the job done is of second importance;

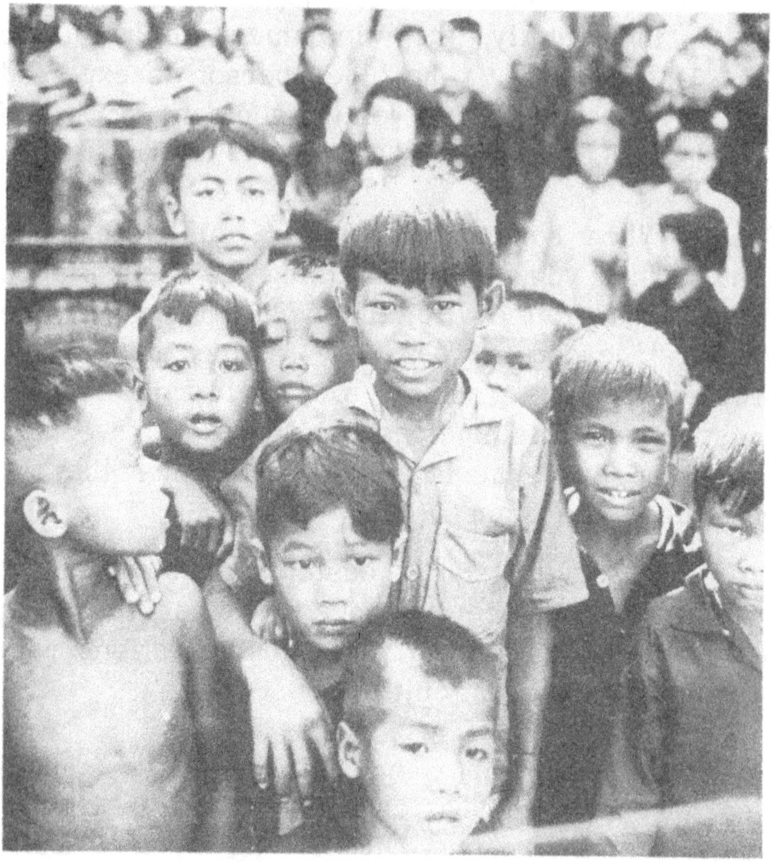

what matters most to them is to strive for perfection regardless of the amount of time required.

The disinterest in the passage of time is a basic part of the Easterner's general attitude toward life. Unlike Americans, who have become known as people who change the physical world to suit their needs and desires, Easterners believe that the world around them is their fate and that it is necessary to strive for harmony with their surroundings. Many try to reduce their needs to the minimum necessary to sustain life, and are amazed by the "needs" of Americans. Also, considering the fact that the average income of Vietnamese peasants is slightly over $120 a year, it is hardly surprising that American needs are luxuries in their eyes.

A particular point for all to remember is that most Vietnamese are deeply motivated by their religion. A great significance is attached to religious places and things. Temples, shrines and religious artifacts should be accorded respect. A careless act on the part of a Marine can create considerable ill will that is most difficult to overcome.

In regard to the oriental respect for the dead, a reverence is shown for burial sites. The Marine must pay particular attention to ensure that he does not violate this ground that the Vietnamese hold sacred.

Looking at the Vietnamese as a man, we see him in a hamlet in the country side supporting his family with what he can grow in his rice fields. His house is small but he makes do with what he has. He has very little education but he is by no means ignorant. His hamlet is run by the hamlet chief and in turn, depending upon the number of hamlets in the village, the hamlet chiefs are controlled by the village chief. When any problems arise the man seeks advice from his hamlet chief. This life, although humble, is extremely orderly.

The Vietnamese people, much the same as the Marine Corps, have a chain of command.

Before you have anything to do with the people, you must first contact the village and hamlet chiefs. They speak for their people and know all that occurs in their areas, and would be embarrassed and indignant if bypassed.

If these points are held in mind by the Marine, they will undoubtedly serve him well during his stay in Vietnam. They will help to make his job easier and most likely will lead to a more enjoyable tour.

c. Customs and Traditions

"If you know the enemy and know yourself, you need not fear the results of a hundred battles.. If you know neither yourself nor the enemy, you are a fool and will meet defeat in every battle."

Sun Tzu (500 B.C.)

If you turn that ancient saying around a bit, you can say you certainly know yourself and you can always learn something about the Vietnamese. It is a matter of knowing your friends equally as well as the enemy. Some of the Vietnamese customs and traditions are discussed here to increase your knowledge of your Vietnamese friends.

THE CALENDAR

The Vietnamese observe the lunar calendar year (354 days) rather than that of the solar calendar year (365 days) in which the year begins on 1 January. The apparent movement of the moon around the earth (lunar year) is shorter than the earth's movement around the sun (solar year). Thusly the lunar year has fewer number of days than the solar year.

FESTIVALS AND HOLIDAYS

FIRST DAY OF THE FIRST LUNAR MONTH

The first day of the first lunar month is also a national holiday in memory of Le Van Duyet (1763-1832) who unified Vietnam through his courage and military skills. He founded schools, built roads and canals, and refused to mobilize an army against his people. Several large Vietnamese cities have streets named after him.

TET NGUYEN DAN (NEW YEAR CELEBRATION)

This celebration, usually called TET, marks the end of one lunar year and a harvest season, and the beginning of a new lunar year. It is traditionally the time when many Vietnamese try to return to the village of their birth to visit the family tombs. The beginning of TET corresponds to the appearance of the new moon. Traditionally it should last one month, for January used to be regarded as the month for rest and amusement (following the harvests). Now, most Vietnamese celebrate TET for just three days. The first day is devoted to ancestor worship; the second for visiting parents, relatives, elders and friends; and the third day is spent honoring the dead. Special TET meals may be served especially to mark the final day of celebration. It is considered a great honor to be invited to share a TET meal and participate in the family's celebrations. During TET, workers have a holiday and no work is normally required. A TET bonus, in the form of money, is usually paid to civil servants and workers.

A number of religious ceremonies may be performed prior to and during TET, all of which generally celebrate the end of one year and beginning of the new year with a clean slate.

HAI BA TRUNG DAY (6TH DAY, 2D MONTH)

This day commemorates the anniversary of the death of the Trung sisters who led a revolt against the Chinese in 41 A.D. and won freedom for Vietnam. But three years later the Chinese recaptured the country and according to the heroic legend, the two sisters drowned themselves rather than surrender. Often they are shown riding elephants into battle.

HUNG VUONG DAY (17TH DAY, 4TH MONTH)

The first ruling family of Vietnam was founded by Emperor Hung Vuong. A number of customs such as the wedding ceremony, chewing betel nuts, the offering of special rice cakes, and the enameling of teeth all date from the period of Hung Vuong.

TRUNG THU (15TH DAY, 8TH MONTH)

This is sometimes called Childrens' TET and celebrated mainly by them. For some weeks before this day, sweets, fruits, lanterns, paper dragons and unicorns are sold along the streets in cities and villages. Moon-shaped cakes of rice are made and filled with peanuts, sugar and melon seeds. Every family prepares for the festival and children light their lanterns and parade through the streets on this night. This is an especially good time to present a small gift to a Vietnamese child. It is considered in good taste to give two minor gifts rather than a single more expensive one.

TRAN HUNG DAO DAY (20TH DAY, 8TH MONTH)

In 1285, a Vietnamese prince, later known as Marshal Tran Hung Dao, drove out the army of the Mongol leader Kublai Khan from North Vietnam. One of the decisive tactics used by the Vietnamese was the installation of long, pointed stakes driven into the river which, at low tide, pierced the hulls of the Mongol ships. This same tactic is used by the Viet Cong today.

LE LOI DAY (22ND DAY, 8TH MONTH)

A century after the death of Marshal Tran Hung Dao, the ruling power of Vietnam was assumed by the Minh dynasty. Le Loi, the son of a rich farmer in Thanh Hoa, led a 10-year struggle to recover the national independence from the Minh emperor. Principal streets are often named after these two Vietnamese.

BIRTHDAY OF CONFUCIUS (28TH DAY, 9TH MONTH)

The confucian doctrine as practiced in Vietnam upholds the family as the ideal and the father as the head of the family. The year 1967 is the 2510th year of the Confucian period.

26 OCTOBER, VIETNAM NATIONAL DAY

This is the anniversary of the proclamation (1954) of the Republic of Vietnam (RVN).

# # # # #

3. REPUBLIC OF VIETNAM ARMED FORCES

VIETNAMESE
MARINE CORPS EMBLEM

ARVN CAP BADGE

a. History

The Vietnamese pride themselves on the courage and fighting ability of their men, and they look back on a long history of both offensive and defensive wars - all of them bloody. In the tenth century, they expelled the Chinese who had ruled them for nearly a thousand years. From that time on, except for a brief period of Chinese occupation, they resisted both Chinese and Mongol invasion.

Many of the Vietnamese generals distinguished themselves in successful defensive actions against more powerful enemy forces. Special pride is taken by Vietnamese historians in the forces which stopped the armies of Kublai Khan in 1285. In three successive campaigns before they were formally defeated, more than 500,000 Mongols attempted to crush a Vietnamese army of less than 200,000. The Mongols invaded and occupied what is now North Vietnam in 1281. In 1285, Marshall Tran Hung Dao regrouped and retrained his forces, defeated the invaders and killed their commander.

During the 17th and 18th centuries the Vietnamese engaged in two intermittent wars with the Chams and Khmers, who then lived in what is now Central South Vietnam. Eventually the Vietnamese eliminated these nations and drove them out. There are still small elements of Cham and Khmer descendants living in South Vietnam.

A cult of military heroes naturally developed and their adventures are celebrated in songs and stories. Temples and monuments have been created in their memories.

As it exists now, the Army of the Republic of Vietnam (ARVN) grew out of a militarized police force which was formed in 1947 and operated until 1954 as part of the French Union Forces. The Vietnamese Marine Corps was officially established in 1954 and organized into four infantry battalions. Since then it has grown to six infantry battalions, an artillery battalion, a support battalion and a brigade headquarters. The Vietnamese Marine Brigade along with the Airborne Brigade and selected other ground units form the general reserve force of the Vietnamese Armed Forces and as such are employed throughout the four Corps areas. Needless to say, the Vietnamese Marines enjoy a high reputation as a tough, well-trained fighting organization.

Shown below are the rank insignias for the Vietnamese Marines and Army. The Regional Forces and Popular Forces use the same insignia as the ARVN.

b. Organization

Political power in the Government of Vietnam (GVN) is concentrated at the national level; most important decisions and major programs originate and are directed from Saigon. The Prime Minister is the real head of the Government and is assisted in the development of policies by the heads of the various ministries. These policies, decisions, and programs are then passed to the lower echelons of the Government--corps, division, province, district, village and hamlet--for execution.

The first command level of government below Saigon is the corps--each of the four corps commanders acts as the government representative in his Corps Tactical Zone (CTZ). Not all instructions originating at the national level pass through the corps headquarters. Routine administrative instructions from the various ministers in Saigon normally go directly to the province

256-290 O-67—3

VIETNAMESE ARMY (INCLUDING RF/PF) AND MARINE CORPS RANK INSIGNIA

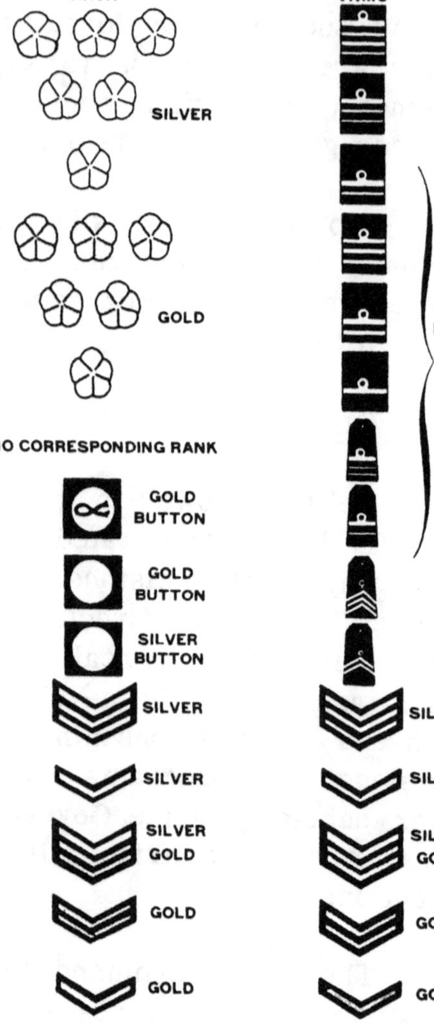

RANK	ARVN	VNMC
COLONEL DAI TA		
LTCOL TRUNG TÁ (TRUNG TA)	SILVER	
MAJOR THIÊU TÁ (TEA-YOU TA)		BLUE & GOLD
CAPT DAI UY (DIE WEE)		BLUE & GOLD
1STLT TRUNG ÚY (TRUNG WEE)	GOLD	BLUE & GOLD
2DLT THIÊU ÚY (TEA-YOU WEE)		BLUE & GOLD
CWO CHÛAN ÚY NHẤT (CHOW-AN WEE NYUT)	NO CORRESPONDING RANK	BLUE & GOLD
WO CHƯAN ÚY (CHEW-AN WEE)	GOLD BUTTON	BLUE & GOLD
SGTMAJ THƯƠNG SĨ NHẤT (TOO-UNG SHE NYUT)	GOLD BUTTON	
MSGT THƯƠNG SĨ (TOO-UNG SHE)	SILVER BUTTON	
SSGT TRUNG SĨ NHẤT (TRUNG SHE NYUT)	SILVER	SILVER
SGT TRUNG SĨ (TRUNG SHE)	SILVER	SILVER
CPL HA SĨ NHẤT (HA SHE NYUT)	SILVER GOLD	SILVER GOLD
L/CPL HẠ SĨ (HA SHE)	GOLD	GOLD
PFC BINH NHẤT (BEEN NYUT)	GOLD	GOLD
PVT BINH NHÌ (BEEN KNEE)		

chief, by passing the corps and division headquarters which are primarily concerned with tactical operations. There are 43 provinces in the country. Below the province, the next subdivision of government is the district, which is similar to our county. Districts are divided into villages, with an average of 8-12 per district. Villages normally consist of 4-6 hamlets. Historically, the village has been the most important organization for local government, and even today it retains many essential legal and tax collecting functions.

The Armed Forces: The Republic of Vietnam Armed Forces (RVNAF) consists of the Army of the Republic of Vietnam (ARVN), the Vietnamese Air Force (VNAF), the Vietnamese Navy (VNN), the Vietnamese Marine Corps (VNMC), and the Regional and Popular Forces (RF and PF). Each of these elements has a specific role in the overall strategy for defeating the VC and the North Vietnamese Army (NVA) main force units, the VC local force units, and the guerrillas.

Army of the Republic of Vietnam: ARVN, the Vietnamese regular army, is primarily an infantry force, consisting of 10 infantry divisions plus separate infantry, airborne, ranger and armor units. ARVN is normally committed against the VC/NVA main force units in search and destroy or clearing operations. When not employed in offensive operations, ARVN units are often committed to securing areas where civilian police or

Revoluntionary Development teams are operating and defending key installations or supply and communication routes. ARVN operations are closely coordinated with the local GVN province officials to ensure that they support the local efforts and do not endanger local government forces.

MACV advisory teams work with all ARVN forces, normally down to battalion level, but in certain instances even at company level. These advisors provide a ready point of contact in coordinating combined operation.

The Vietnamese Air Force: The Vietnamese Air Force (VNAF) includes five tactical wings; each is organized differently and may include any number of fighter, helicopter, and transport squadrons. Fighter squadrons can engage designated targets with a combination of general purpose, fragmentation, concussion, incendiary, delayed action and fire (Napalm) bombs, rockets and 20mm cannon fire. The transport squadrons provide a capability for air dropping troops, equipment and supplies, flare drops for illumination of target areas in support of offensive airstrikes and ground operations, and for air movement of troops, equipment, supplies and officials. The liaison squadrons are capable of performing forward air control, visual reconnaissance and liaison operations. Helicopter squadrons, equipped with H-34 aircraft, furnish a limited capability for air movement of troops, equipment and supplies throughout RVN.

MACV advisors work with the VNAF at all echelons often accompanying them on missions. They provide a ready point of contact for liaison or coordination.

Vietnamese Navy: The Vietnamese Navy (VNN) is primarily a defensive force, consisting of a small sea force for offshore counterinfiltration surveillance along the coast from the 17th parallel to the Cambodian border, a coastal force--the junk fleet--for patrolling of inshore coastal waterways, and a river force for inland waterway operations. The river force is organized into seven River Assault Groups (RAGs). Each RAG is capable of transporting by water a battalion of RVNAF and supporting them for 10-14 days. MACV advisors work with the VNN sea, coastal and river forces; they are a coordination contact for combined and joint operations.

Vietnamese Marine Corps: The Vietnamese Marine Corps consists of one brigade of six infantry battalions, one artillery battalion, and one amphibious support battalion. U.S. Marines attached to the Marine Advisory Group (a part of MACV) work with the Vietnamese Marines and accompany them on all operations. The brigade is stationed in the Saigon area and conducts operations in that area as well as joint operations with the U.S. Marines in I Corps.

Regional Forces: The Regional Forces (RF) are a nationally administered military force assigned to and under the operational control of the sector commander (province chief). The basic combat unit of the RF is the light infantry company, though in certain provinces there are also a number of RF mechanized platoons, intelligence platoons and squads, and river patrol companies.

Normally RF units are recruited locally, placed under the operational control of the sub-sector commander (district chief), and habitually employed in the same general area. The primary missions given to RF units are to secure key installations and communication routes, to protect the local government officials and key people loyal to the Government, and to provide a sub-sector reserve for assisting village or hamlet defense forces under attack. When ARVN or Free World Military Assistance Forces (FWMAF) units are operating in an area where RF are located, the RF can often contribute to the success of the operation through their detailed knowledge of the local terrain and people.

Popular Forces: The Popular Forces (PF) are a nationally administered military force organized and operated at the village level and consisting of light infantry squads and platoons. The PF units are commanded by their own noncommissioned officer leaders who are responsible, through their village chiefs, to the district chiefs. PF members are full-time volunteers recruited within their native villages and hamlets to protect their own families and property. Though legally this force may be supplemented with draftees, its primary motivation stems from the fact its members are recruited from the villages and hamlets in which they are stationed and in which their families live.

Because of their small size, light arms, and limited training, the combat capability of PF units is restricted to local defensive and counterattack operations. The basic concept of employment is for village platoons and hamlet squads to defend their own area with the inter-village platoons providing responsive reinforcement. Occasionally PF units may participate in operations with other forces. In such operations, which are normally undertaken to reinforce, support or relieve a village or hamlet under attack, the PF are employed to act as guides, lay ambushes, protect flanks, or provide a rearguard for the main body.

The Vietnamese have paid heavily in their long struggle against the Communist insurgents. Despite the costs, they retain their determination to be victorious. We are assisting them in all their efforts--militarily, economically, and politically--wherever we can, in the field, with the rural peoples, and at the governmental and military headquarters. Success will ultimately depend on the effectiveness of our joint and combined programs and operations.

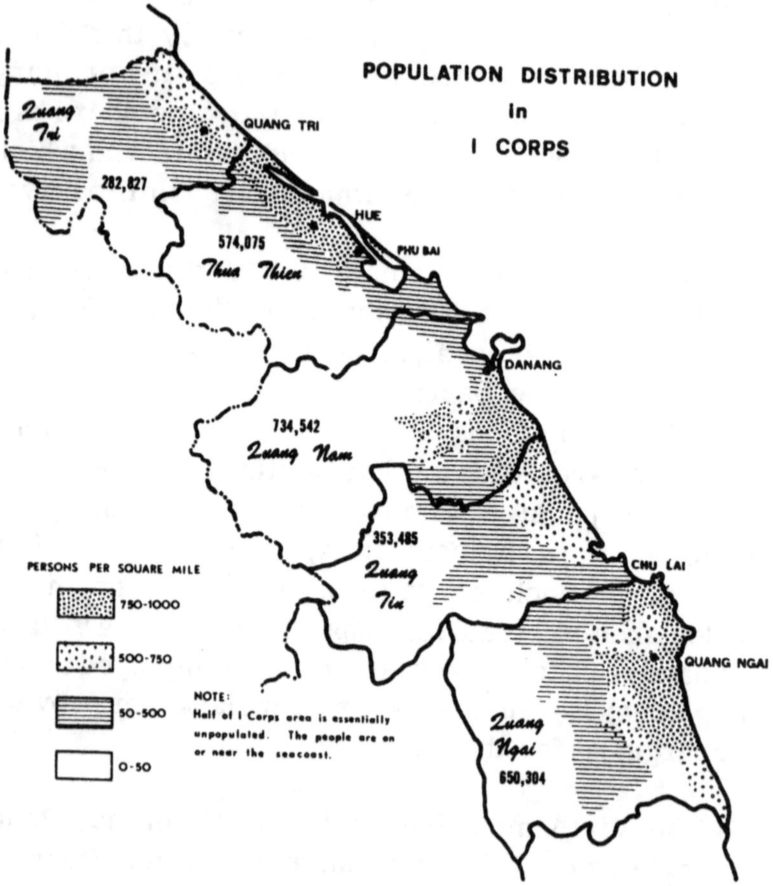

# # # # #

4. TERRAIN IN I CORPS

The I Corps area as shown above is approximately 200 miles long and varies in width from 30 to 80 miles. The I Corps area can be divided into four geographic regions as follows: the coast, lowlands, piedmont and the jungle highlands.

a. Coast

The I Corps area, as is all of South Vietnam, is bounded on the east by the South China Sea. No general statement can be made to typify this coastal region as it varies considerably from place to place. In some locations, high cliffs rise up from the edge of the ocean while at others, low, sandy beaches extend inland to the area known as the lowland. For example, in the Northern Coastal region of I Corps, lagoons and tidal channels run parallel to the coast and are separated from the sea by a narrow sandy belt, while around the Danang area, mountain spurs from the highlands extend out to the sea giving a considerable variation in terrain over a short distance of coastline.

In the flat areas along the coast, the beaches extend inland usually about 100-150 meters but can extend much farther as is the case at Chu Lai where the soft sands reach inland some 4000 meters. Beyond these dune areas, one moves into the hinterland which is actually the edge of the lowland areas. Generally the drainage is poor. Construction of dikes for rice raising has compounded the drainage problem. The various rice paddies in any given part of the coastal lowland region are flooded at different times; consequently there is no one period during which all of the land is dry

and movement overland made easy. This surface water is either salty or contaminated by the human wastes used for fertilizer in the fields.

Fishing is the main source of income for the people living on the coast, but most families have their own rice paddy. Numerous fishtraps, some quite elaborate, will be found throughout the bays, rivers, lagoons and canals of the coastal and lowlands areas.

Fishtraps like these are found throughout the rivers and inlets in the coastal area. These should not be harmed if at all possible. The income of most of these coastal people is comparatively higher than the people of the other regions. This fact, coupled with the need to have ports through

which supplies from North Vietnam can be imported, makes the coastal area a desirable target for Viet Cong control.

b. The Lowlands

The lowland region of I Corps is made up of a narrow coastal plain stretching the entire length of the Corps area and of several valleys extending in to the central highland. The region is quite fertile. Although it encompasses only about one-sixth of the total area of I Corps, virtually all of the crops are grown here. Rice is by far the principal crop encompassing about 90% of the cultivated land. The remaining 10% is devoted mainly to the raising of tea, sugar cane, coffee, fruit trees, manioc, bananas and pineapples. The lowland region also contains the bulk (approximately 75%) of the I Corps population which is estimated at over 2,200,000. Control of the lowlands would give the Viet Cong guerrilla the rice needed to sustain himself as well as considerable manpower to be forced into service as replacements.

It has been said of the lowlands region that if there is a piece of land that isn't cultivated, it has a house built on it. This is not entirely true, however, its pretty close. Although there are some rain forests and open forests, most of the area has been turned into rice fields which are flooded throughout the Northeast Monsoon season (September through January). Rice fields are normally made up of a number of square paddies which, from the air look much like a checkerboard. They are constructed with dirt dikes separating each paddy so that they can be kept flooded. During the monsoon season, the paddies will usually have mud and water a foot to two feet deep making even foot movement quite difficult. Troops must avoid being canalized on the dikes. Moving across rice fields can be a particularly critical operation, especially for a small unit on patrol such as a squad or platoon. When crossing, observe the basic principles of spreading out with a covering force in support. This will reduce the chances of an entire unit being pinned down in the open.

Besides the rice fields, sugar cane fields are in this area although not in such great numbers.

When the cane is fully grown, it offers excellent concealment of which the Viet Cong have often taken advantage. From a few feet inside a cane field, one can have excellent observation to the outside but cannot be observed himself. This is made to order for snipers and should be held in mind by Marines when operating in these areas.

Highway No. 1 and a railroad traverse the length of I Corps through the lowlands area. Highway No. 1 is the major artery of Vietnam linking the North to the South and is capable of supporting military vehicles the year round. However, it has been subjected to Viet Cong interdiction in the past and may or may not be open at any given time.

The lowlands region is the strategic key to the control of the I Corps. It is not large in comparison to the highland region, but it is agriculturally productive and contains the majority of the I Corps population. The individual rifleman can look to spending much time operating in this region.

c. The Piedmont

Piedmont is a term used to indicate the hilly terrain separating the jungle highlands from the lowlands. It is the narrow belt of foothills that fronts the highlands on the East. Stream activity in the Piedmont is similar to that in the jungle. Locating drinking water (all water must be purified) is no problem. The road system is limited,

however, some dirt and rock surfaced roads do exist and are accessible to vehicles. The Piedmont is sparsely populated with the majority of the people living in the valleys between the hills. Most of the land in the hills is covered with a dense growth of trees that reach to a height of 150 to 200 feet and form a dense canopy. Ordinarily there is little undergrowth. Secondary growth which occupies abandoned fields and cutover land consists of very closely spaced small trees together with vines and dense brush. Movement through the secondary growth is difficult and slow but by no means should it be avoided because movement through these areas cannot be readily observed and reduces the possibility of being ambushed.

The villages in this region are typical of most Vietnamese villages. Virtually all parts of the valleys are devoted to rice cultivation.

d. The Jungle Highlands

This region, occupying about three-quarters of I Corps, consists of forested hills and mountains with deep, steep-sided valleys, rolling to hilly surfaces with grass and open forests, and numerous and sometimes marshy basins. Streams are plentiful and flow in all directions but eventually lead to a few large, shallow rivers which either flow into the China Sea to the East or the Mekong River in Laos to the West. All of the above streams can be forded in the dry season but during the rainy season the water level rises considerably and the current becomes quite strong making any fording attempts hazardous. A storm at the source of a normally fordable stream can turn it into a raging river in a matter of hours. In Kontum Province (II Corps Area) in 1963, an entire Vietnamese Ranger Platoon was drowned while attempting to ford a stream that they had crossed but a few hours previously.

Despite the high mountains and thick vegetation, the jungle is passable on foot with the exception of a few steep slopes. A road system for wheeled vehicles is almost non-existent with the exception of a few cart trails, however, there are many foot paths which have been made by the native highlanders over the years in their normal daily traffic.

The population in this region is sparse, composed mainly of highlander tribesmen (Montagnards) living a simple life of hunting and slash and burn farming.

The Montagnards know this rugged terrain well and move about it with ease. Montagnard villages are usually quite small with not more than 20 houses located close together. The houses are constructed of light materials and built on stilts.

In summary, due to the vastness of the highland area and the problems encountered in movement and observation, neither the Government nor the Viet Cong maintain full military or political control of this region. The Montagnards themselves can be best described as politically noncommitted and usually take sides for purposes of convenience. They have cooperated with both Viet Cong and government forces depending upon which force is in their area at that time. U.S. Special Forces personnel have worked with some Montagnard tribes for a few years and have achieved some success in developing their alignment with the RVN government. However, viewing the highlands as a region, it is still uncommitted. Although the Viet Cong lay claim to certain portions of the region, they by no means possess the hearts and minds of the people, thereby reducing their control to physical presence.

# # # # #

256-290 O-67—4

5. THE CLIMATE

The weather in Southeast Asia has a strong influence on military operations there. Of the two monsoons, the Southwest has the greater effect on overall activity since it brings heavy rains to most of the country between May and September; one exception is the strip of land East of the coastal mountain range in Central Vietnam which remains dry. This particular strip of land includes I Corps.

The Northeast monsoon, which effects I Corps, begins in September and lasts through January. The average rainfall per month is extremely heavy from September through November and then tapers off during the months of December and January. For example, Danang receives an average of 23 inches of rain each October and 15 inches each November. This period of heavy rainfall obviously affects all types of military operations, but the effect varies with the amount of mechanization of any given unit and its particular operating area. Motor transport and tracked vehicles will at times be limited to surfaced highways. There can be no mistaking that the heavy rains don't impose a handicap on movement of foot troops as well as mechanized forces, because they most certainly do. However, the foot soldier can and will continue to operate.

Much has been said about the monsoon offensive of the Viet Cong. The monsoon season is supposed to bring stepped up activity by the

Viet Cong against U.S. and ARVN Forces because of the reduced effectiveness of air and mechanized forces. Considering that observation from the air can be ruled out for a portion of the time and that vehicles are quite restricted in movement, it only seems reasonable that the Viet Cong would use the monsoon for their offensive. However, they have made one faulty assumption and that is that our forces are strictly tied to mechanization and air support. They are under the impression that Americans are fair weather fighters and that without mechanization and technology, which results in a greater degree of comfort than that experienced by the Viet Cong, the American would soon become demoralized and ineffective. They are being enlightened.

The monsoon, in that it imposes the greatest restrictions, received the majority of the attention devoted to climate and weather in Southeast Asia. However, the remainder of the year also brings to bear another difficulty: intense heat. During the dry season temperatures of 100° F. have been recorded and temperatures of 130° F. have been recorded in the sandy coastal regions. For a foot soldier to move, carry equipment and fight in an atmosphere of such intense heat requires that he be in outstanding physical condition. In such a situation no substitute exists.

The following weather charts have been simplified for quick reference. The ground trafficability charts use seven inches of rain a month as the criterion for determining the areas where military operations are difficult. Less than thought amount usually will allow an acceptable degree of traffic.

The following air operations charts are designed to show ceilings of 3,000 feet or less and visibility of 3 miles--climatic criteria selected because they impose some restrictions on most air operations.

# # # # # #

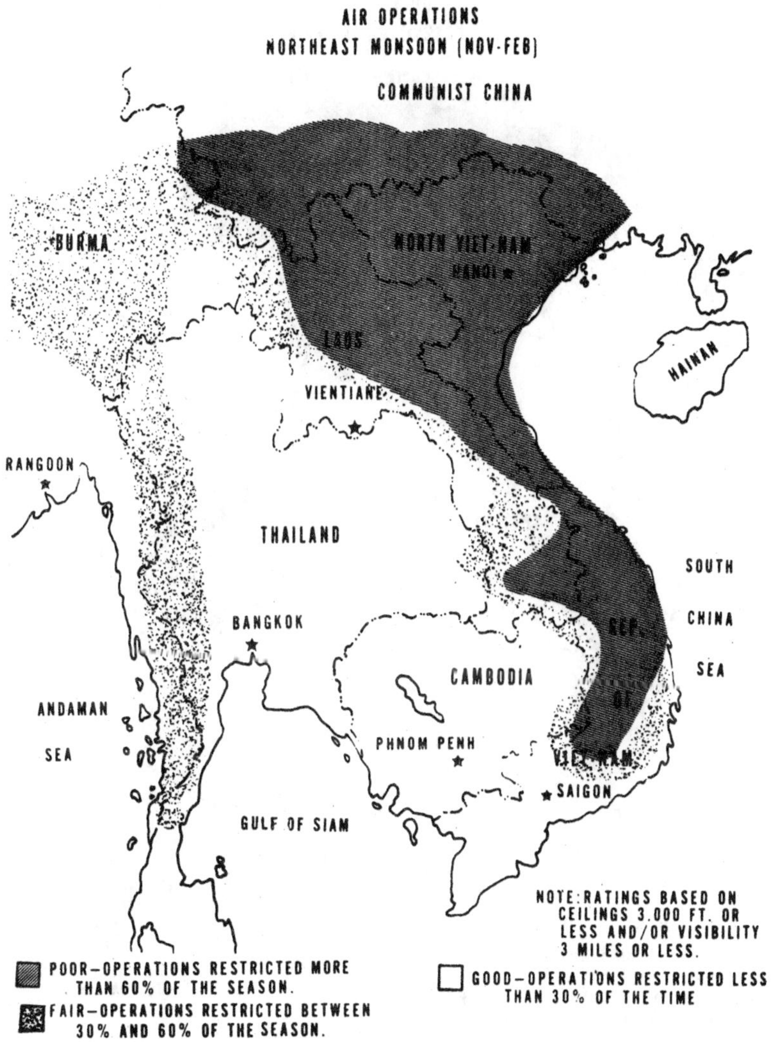
AIR OPERATIONS
NORTHEAST MONSOON (NOV-FEB)
COMMUNIST CHINA
BURMA
NORTH VIET-NAM
HANOI
LAOS
HAINAN
VIENTIANE
RANGOON
THAILAND
SOUTH
CHINA
SEA
BANGKOK
REP.
CAMBODIA
OF
ANDAMAN
SEA
PHNOM PENH
VIET-NAM
SAIGON
GULF OF SIAM
NOTE: RATINGS BASED ON CEILINGS 3,000 FT. OR LESS AND/OR VISIBILITY 3 MILES OR LESS.
POOR—OPERATIONS RESTRICTED MORE THAN 60% OF THE SEASON.
FAIR—OPERATIONS RESTRICTED BETWEEN 30% AND 60% OF THE SEASON.
GOOD—OPERATIONS RESTRICTED LESS THAN 30% OF THE TIME

AIR OPERATIONS
SPRING TRANSITION (MAR-APRIL)

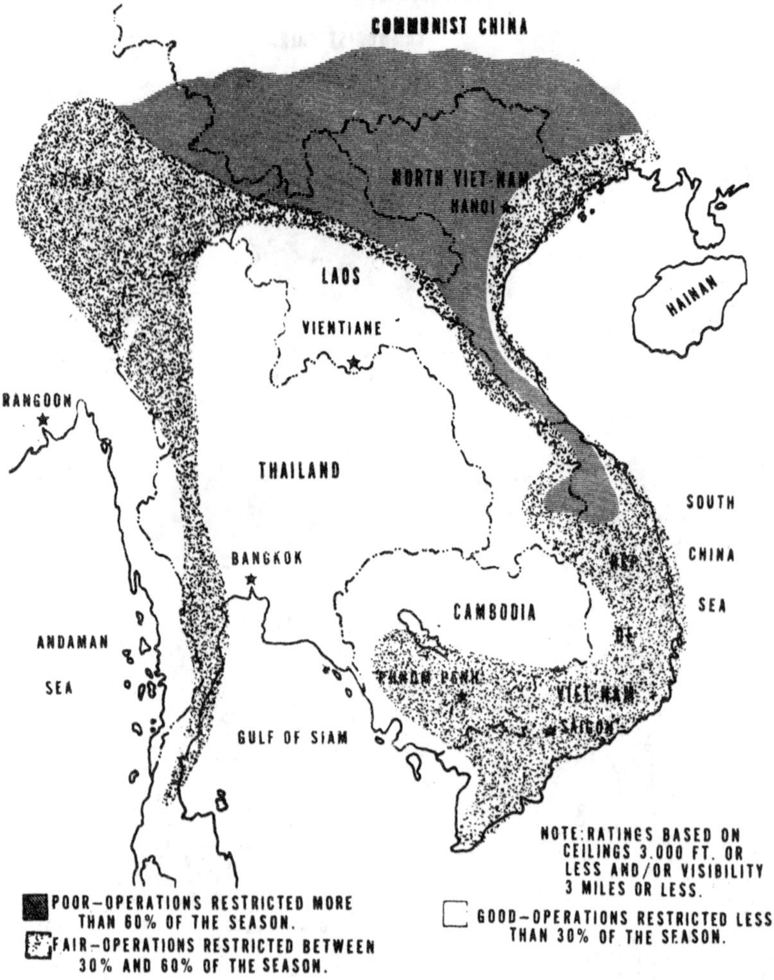

AIR OPERATIONS
SOUTHWEST MONSOON (MAY-SEPT)

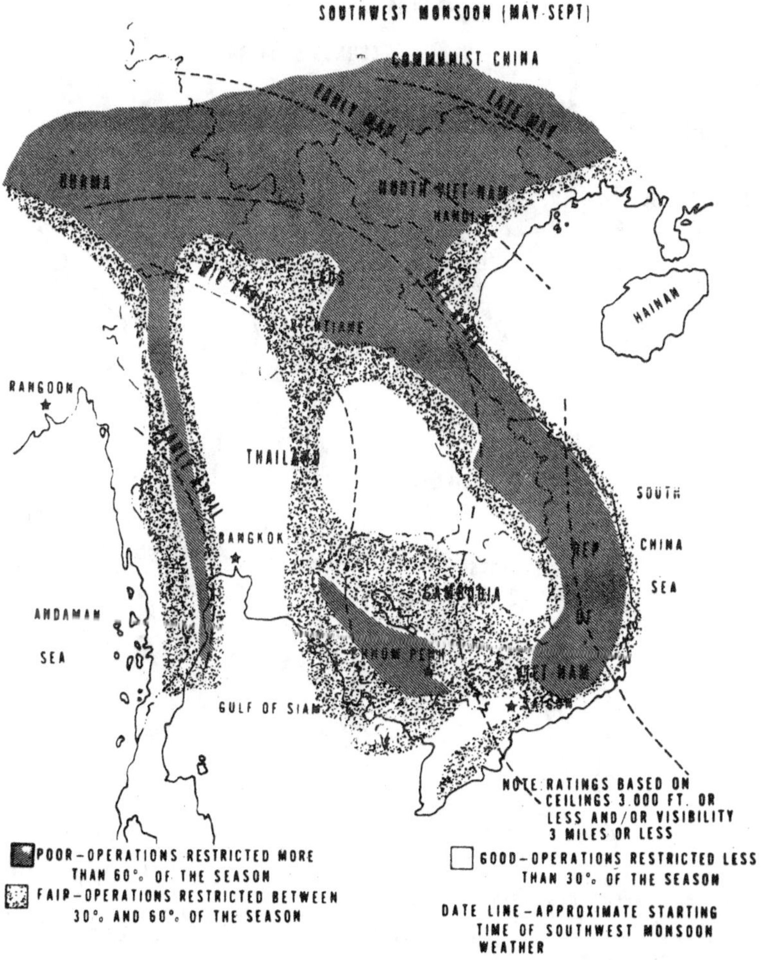

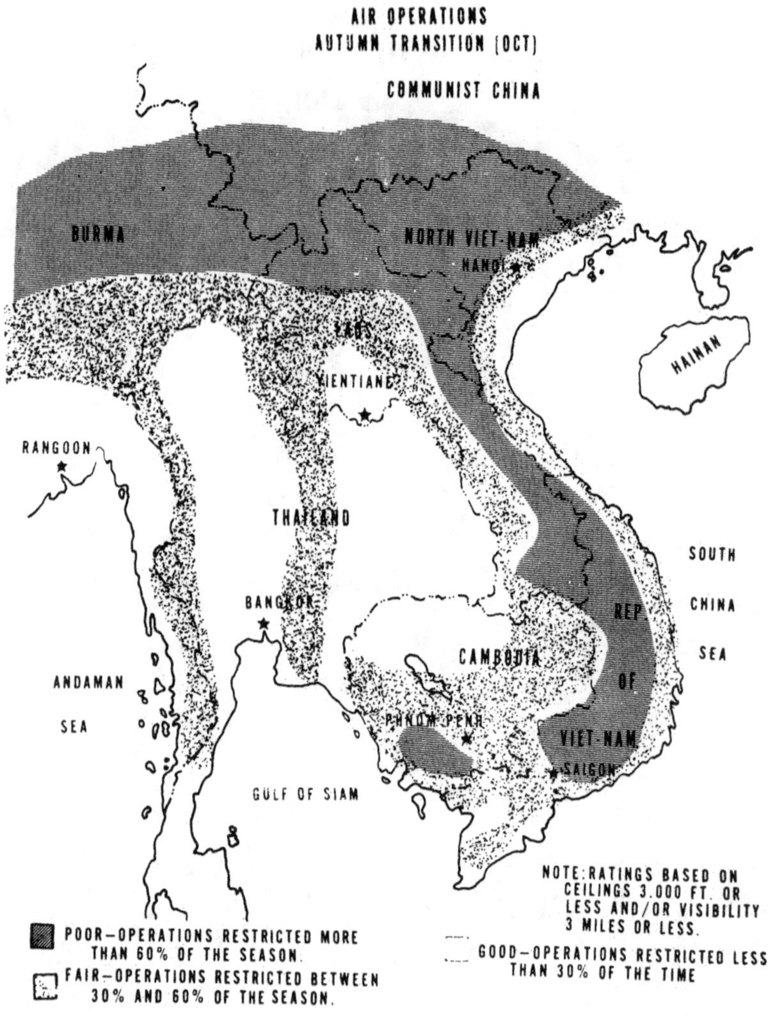
AIR OPERATIONS
AUTUMN TRANSITION (OCT)
COMMUNIST CHINA
BURMA
NORTH VIET-NAM
HANOI
LAOS
VIENTIANE
HAINAN
RANGOON
THAILAND
SOUTH
CHINA
SEA
BANGKOK
REP
OF
VIET-NAM
CAMBODIA
ANDAMAN
SEA
PHNOM PENH
SAIGON
GULF OF SIAM
NOTE: RATINGS BASED ON CEILINGS 3,000 FT. OR LESS AND/OR VISIBILITY 3 MILES OR LESS.
POOR—OPERATIONS RESTRICTED MORE THAN 60% OF THE SEASON.
FAIR—OPERATIONS RESTRICTED BETWEEN 30% AND 60% OF THE SEASON.
GOOD—OPERATIONS RESTRICTED LESS THAN 30% OF THE TIME

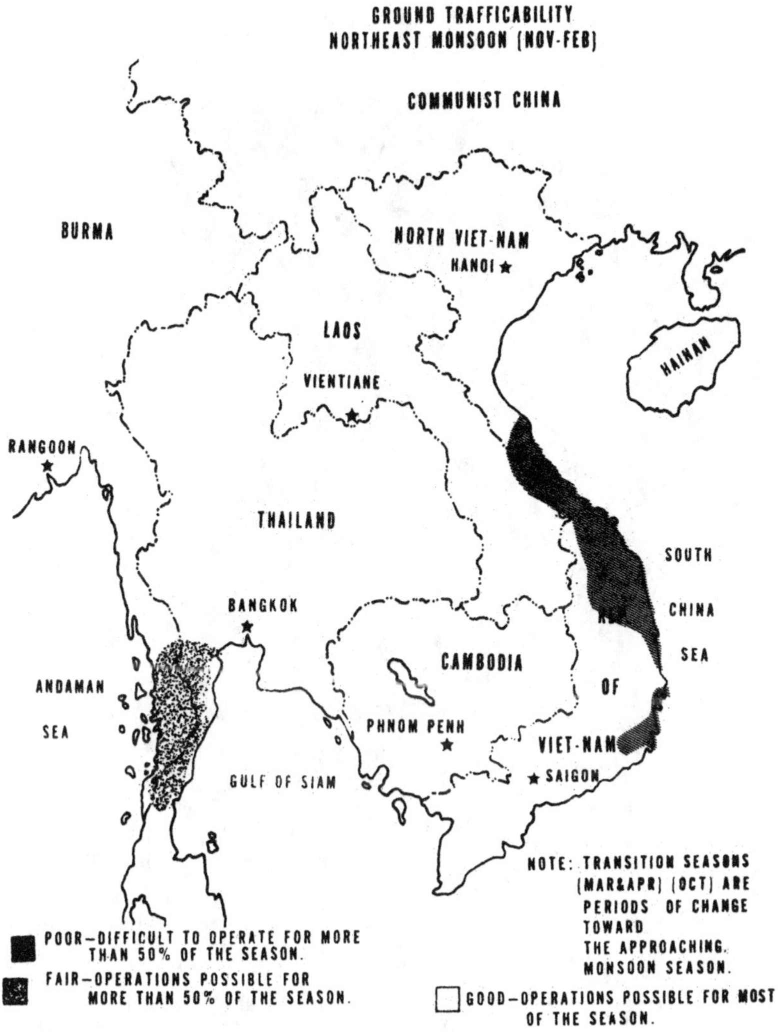

GROUND TRAFFICABILITY
NORTHEAST MONSOON (NOV-FEB)
COMMUNIST CHINA
BURMA
NORTH VIET-NAM
HANOI
LAOS
HAINAN
VIENTIANE
RANGOON
THAILAND
SOUTH
CHINA
SEA
BANGKOK
CAMBODIA
OF
VIET-NAM
ANDAMAN
SEA
PHNOM PENH
SAIGON
GULF OF SIAM
NOTE: TRANSITION SEASONS (MAR&APR) (OCT) ARE PERIODS OF CHANGE TOWARD THE APPROACHING MONSOON SEASON.
POOR—DIFFICULT TO OPERATE FOR MORE THAN 50% OF THE SEASON.
FAIR—OPERATIONS POSSIBLE FOR MORE THAN 50% OF THE SEASON.
GOOD—OPERATIONS POSSIBLE FOR MOST OF THE SEASON.

GROUND TRAFFICABILITY
SOUTHWEST MONSOON (MAY-SEPT)

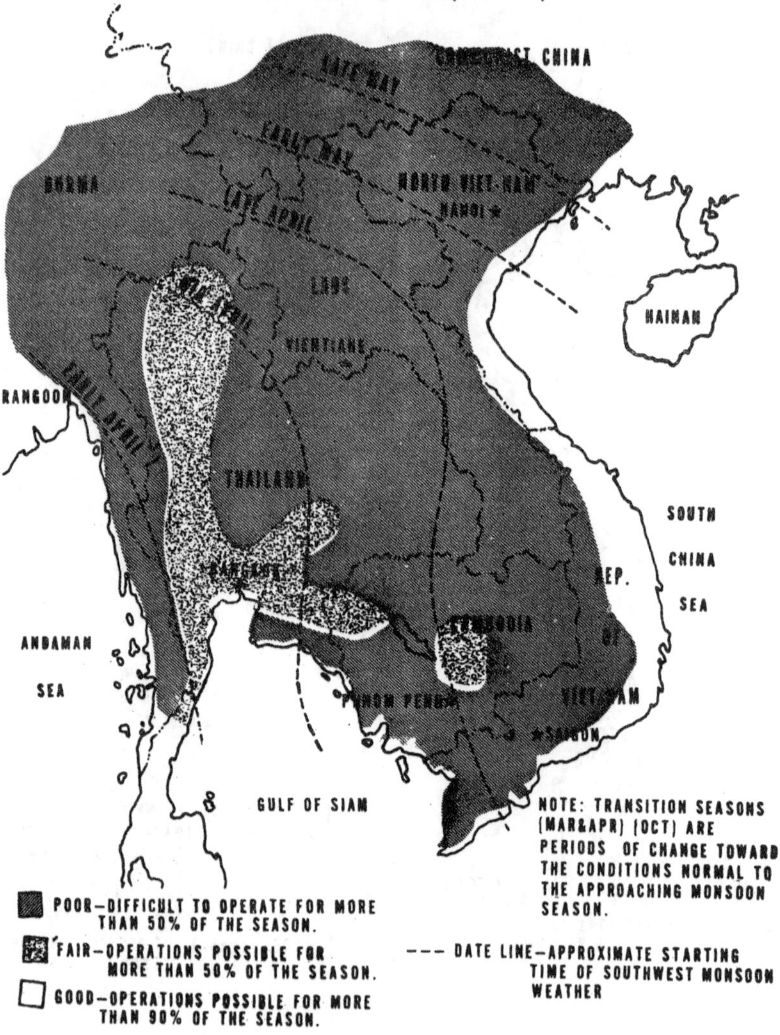

Chapter II: TACTICS

1. ONCE IS ENOUGH

Since March 1965 when Marine tactical units first landed in the Republic of Vietnam, hundreds of lessons have been learned concerning the method of operating in a counterinsurgency environment. Many of them have been learned at a high cost in Marine lives and material. Such a price is too high, particularly if it has to be paid twice. If a lesson is learned once, there should be no need to pay the price the second time.

The majority of lessons learned as a result of operations in Vietnam are published in various documents that are distributed throughout the Marine Corps. These include FMFPAC's "Tactical Trends and Training Tips" and this publication. It is the duty of all commands to make certain that this information is made available to all personnel, particularly those destined for duty with the III Marine Amphibious Force.

Let's not pay a double price for lessons learned. The price is too high already.

# # # # #

2. SAME WORDS, NEW INTERPRETATION

In analyzing an operation area in counter-guerrilla warfare, the military considerations of terrain still offer the most logical method of solving the problem. There is a difference, however, in the interpretation of military phrases such as "key terrain." For example, if a guerrilla force is known to have a shortage of medical supplies and there is a civilian hospital or dispensary located in a battalion's zone of responsibility, that hospital ought to be considered key terrain. Certainly, its seizure and control by the guerrilla force will give them a marked advantage. Even a raid or subtle pilferage of its medical supplies will offer advantage to the enemy. A province or district town should be considered key terrain for its political or psychological importance.

The guerrilla must swim in the sea of the local populace not only for camouflage but often for his food supply. This makes the rice field and the granary key terrain features in a land where rice is the staple food. During harvest seasons, the fields take on added significance. The control of the rice fields offers a distinct advantage to those who protect them. Without this protection the grain might never be harvested and much of it could find its way into Viet Cong stomachs.

One item that has become a common sight in field operations is a large burlap or cotton cloth bag in which captured rice can be collected. When a unit discovers hidden food stores, these bags are then filled, moved to a common collecting point and evacuated by helo or truck. Captured foods usually are moved to the district or provincial headquarters for storage and redistribution. Evacuation of captured food caches can serve two important purposes. First, it denies the Viet Cong a much needed staple and second, it increases the food available to the local populace. Be sure to maintain a supply of rice bags on hand in the LSA readily available to the ground units for rice evacuation.

# # # # #

3. PATROLLING

a. Attention to Detail

Sounds hardly heard or not noticed at all during the day may become extremely obvious during the still of the night. An example is that of the patrol member who departed on patrol wearing a pair of jungle boots he had not worn previously on night patrol. Within the patrol base with its normal activity or within the neighboring hamlet with its barking dogs, no detrimental

clothing or equipment noises were noticed. However, in the night silence of a jungle trail the creaking leather was clearly audible from meters away.

Prior to each night patrol, it is a good idea to have each member walk a short distance wearing the clothing and equipment he will wear while on patrol in order to detect undesired sounds. It may save your life.

b. <u>An Old Trick</u>

On one occasion a Marine night combat patrol halted to conduct a count of patrol members and discovered that there were six men too many. The patrol lost no time in separating the VC from the rest of the patrol. Two VC were killed in the process.

c. Rear Area Patrols

Rear area patrolling is an essential part of counterinsurgency operations. In addition to providing immediate security, patrols can uncover evidence of VC activity. Patrols can determine changes in the attitude of local villagers which are caused by VC terrorism and harassment. Hard evidence, such as directional arrows or mine markers may also be uncovered. The success of a patrol depends on the alertness and keenness of observation of every member of the patrol.

d. Pursue and Then Some

On several occasions when patrols have been in close pursuit of fleeing VC, Marines have been distracted by the packs dropped by the VC along the trail. While the pursuers stopped to examine the pack contents, the Viet Cong have made good their escape. You can always come back and pick up the pack, so keep your pursuit a "hot one" and don't forget security measures as you pursue.

e. Just Like Hunting Deer

While on a patrol at night or in heavily vegetated areas, STOP briefly every 10 or 15 minutes to LISTEN, SMELL the air, and take a careful LOOK AROUND. People make noise and create distinctive smells. Camp sites can be located by the smells of old camp fires or refuse. Try not

256-290 O-67—5

to smoke for at least two hours before going on patrol; smoking tobacco tends temporarily to deaden the sense of smell. When you use spiced or medicated shaving creams, hair tonics or after-shave lotion, you tend to saturate your own sense of smell, so try a little less. Remember, a little dab will do you.

f. Detailed Search

The importance of developing detailed search techniques is illustrated by the experience of one friendly waterborne patrol.

The patrol encountered an unlighted passenger junk with forty persons aboard. As the patrol craft came alongside the junk, they observed packages being dropped over the side and passengers furtively slipping vials into the bilges and under baggage.

A partial search of the junk and its occupants revealed over two hundred vials of 500,000 units of penicillin, 33,655 piasters and twenty-four new batteries. Most of the penicillin was hidden in the underclothing of two women who were feigning illness.

g. Patrol Accessory Packs

Combat patrols must be prepared for a multitude of eventualities, especially in Vietnam. Certain items of equipment should be available to each patrol leader or ambush team commander. These include demolitions for destroying enemy positions and facilities, pyrotechnics for signalling location, targets, or loss of contact, illumination grenades, flashlights and a signal mirror. A pack can be developed incorporating these and other items which can then be issued to a patrol leader.

# # # # #

4. AMBUSH

a. Ambush Insertion

Covert insertion of ambush elements can best be accomplished by moving them into the ambushed area as part of a regular patrol.

The ambush elements should be dispersed throughout the patrol formation with their radio antennas detached. Upon completion of the ambush, another patrol can be used to pick up the original ambush force and drop off another, if desired. In this manner the patrol size is kept constant making it difficult for the enemy to notice that an element has been dropped off.

Another technique is to have the pickup patrol attempt to flush the enemy toward the ambush so artillery and mortar fire can be called.

b. <u>"L" Type Ambush</u>

The following account, received from a U.S. Army unit in Vietnam, is a good example of a typical VC "L" shaped ambush action. The success attained by friendly forces can be attributed to rapid and aggressive reaction, and the use of the reserve against the enemy's weak flank.

"Company A was moving down from the high ground to the open field in a two up and one back formation, and they ran into a classic 'L' type ambush. From description, this must have included at least two different VC companies, because they had two different uniforms. The VC to the front along the base of the 'L' wore fatigues, steel helmets and packs on their backs. Along the stem of the 'L' to the left flank of A Company, they wore khakis with blue bandannas on their heads. Now actually A Company discovered the VC first. The left front platoon man crossed a small trail and noticed that the brush was bent down recently across the trail, so he got down on his hands and knees and crawled across the trail. When he got up he saw a VC in khakis moving away. The point man jumped up and shot the VC, and this triggered the VC on the base of the 'L' to fire. These VC were not dug in; they were lying on the ground. However, they had placed mines out in front of them, and grenades were put up in trees where they could be pulled to go off in the air, so the position was well protected. The right front platoon got into the fight, and deployed to conduct an assault to the front. Just as the platoon started to get ready to assault, the VC along the stem of the 'L' to the left opened up, and the platoon got caught in a crossfire. There were at least two automatic weapons across the front, and another opened up near the rear of the stem. The assault failed, as it was pinned before it got started. The commander of the rear platoon, was told to move around to the left and assault the stem of the 'L,' which he did successfully. He moved out, deployed, assaulted, and forced the VC, along with the heavy machinegun, out of their prepared positions."

c. Immediate Action

Friendly ambushes sprung along jungle trails usually do not have all of the enemy in the killing zone because of the limited fields of fire. Unless a very unusual ambush site is found, part of the enemy element will escape. Experience has shown that the VC almost always return to the area of the engagement within a relatively short time to retrieve bodies and weapons.

As soon as a patrol springs an ambush, a team, or larger unit, should move in the direction of the enemy withdrawal, approximately 200 meters, and reestablish another ambush.

Recently, this technique was employed three times by one company patrol with the second ambush making contact within thirty minutes on each occasion.

d. Comments on Ambushes

Important points to remember about ambushes are contained in these comments by a battalion commander in Vietnam.

"Ambushes are one of the most effective measures for inflicting personnel casualties on the enemy. The imaginative and skillful use of ambushes can also have a detrimental psychological impact. Aside from normal local security, ambushes should be at least 500-1000 meters distant from unit night defensive positions. The tendency to make ambushes too large should be avoided; five to eight men is a good size. Occasionally, daylight ambushes should be left in a unit position occupied during the night in order to take advantage of the tendency of local Viet Cong to search positions for materiel that might have been left behind."

# # # # #

5. SNIPERS

a. Stand To

Units serving in Vietnam report that sniper and harassing fire is often received at dusk or at dawn when Marines are either engaged in preparation for night defense or for the day's offensive

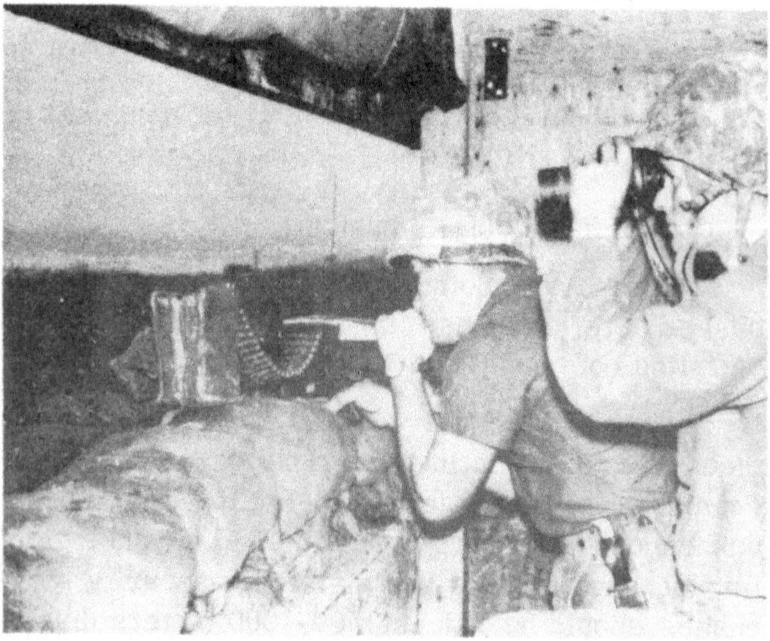

operations. Even with 25% or 50% alert, the majority of the troops are up and about with last minute preparations. In the half light, a sniper is extremely hard to see, while the friendly troops make a very good target.

There are a number of ways of countering this enemy technique. One is the British Army's "Stand To." Under this system, the period from one-half hour before to one-half hour after dawn and dusk finds all hands in their defensive positions with all weapons manned. No one is exposed to fire and any attempts to snipe or harass can be met with full force return fire.

b. Anti-Sniper Techniques

One of the most common type of contact with the VC is a sniping incident. The VC sniper force ranges in size from a single rifleman up to a squad. Usually the snipers are well concealed at a range of about 250-300 meters. Their fire is seldom effective at that range. A common tendency of individuals who are exposed to sniper fire for the first time is to reply with rifle fire alone, or to withhold fire because the target cannot be exactly located. This gives the sniper a chance to fire again. If there is no danger of involving other friendly forces or civilians, the unit should immediately deliver a heavy volume of fire into likely sniper positions in the general area from which the sniper fired. Rifle grenades, mortars, M-72s, M-79s and 3.5 inch rockets can all be used. As soon as you start returning fire, look for the

VC attempting to escape. A sniper doesn't want to fight, so look for him to move early, and when he does, you will have your best chance to get him.

# # # # #

6. RECONNAISSANCE

a. Reconnaissance Operations

Most Marine unit commanders in RVN will agree that acquiring a target, that is, finding and fixing the Viet Cong, is a difficult job. Both reconnaissance and infantry units have emphasized the need for additional training in patrolling and observing/reporting.

The large tactical areas over which ground units must maintain observation mean that infantry units must be prepared to conduct reconnaissance operations at any time. Units up to battalion size have been assigned missions of reconnoitering-in-force in areas as large as 50 square miles. Areas suspected of being used by the Viet Cong for bases and training are usually placed under observation by a series of reconnaissance posts. Both infantry and reconnaissance units contribute teams to these operations. It has been consistently demonstrated that unless a reconnaissance team is positioned in one helicopter lift, the delay resulting from multiple lifts alerts the Viet Cong. Plan these reconnaissance insertions so all patrol elements can be lifted at one time.

One particularly successful reconnaissance operation was conducted in the same general area for about three months. The method of operations included positioning an OP force at various locations overlooking a river valley known to be an

important VC supply route and line of communication. The OP itself did not remain in the same position for an extended period but occasionally shifted to another location. One team was composed of a squad from the reconnaissance battalion, a FAC, a FO team, a 106mm recoilless rifle squad, and a caliber .50 machine gun squad. These latter two elements provided added range for local security. Two BC scopes were employed and proved to be invaluable in locating targets and adjusting supporting fires. A Marine heavy artillery battery was located in a relatively secure area within range of the OP. Each fire mission was cleared through the appropriate South Vietnamese commander. As an example of one day's operations, the OP team made 166 separate sightings (1100 VC). Fifty-seven Viet Cong casualties were confirmed as a result of artillery fires directed from the OP. There has been a marked reduction in VC river traffic and freedom of movement in the valley area since this type of reconnaissance operation has been in effect.

The increased employment of this type reconnaissance operation means that each officer and NCO should learn how to call for and adjust supporting fires.

b. Reconnaissance Training

A report on reconnaissance training for operations in RVN emphasized the need for combat patrolling. Contact with the Viet Cong during reconnaissance operations is common and all patrols, even the smaller teams, must be prepared to engage the VC and not rely solely on stealth.

Training should emphasize actions to be taken when contact is first made, and counter ambush techniques. The report noted that during a period of about two months almost 60% of the reconnaissance units' patrols came in contact with the Viet Cong. In this case, the most effective tactic was an aggressive ambush or assault of the enemy. Teams should learn to break contact as a unit rather than as individuals, thus affording the VC little chance of regaining contact. The use of all organic infantry weapons was emphasized. Consideration should be given to increasing the firepower of reconnaissance teams with additional M-14, M-79 and M-60 weapons.

Since the heart of any reconnaissance operation is timely and accurate reporting, communications are a vital factor. Procedures should include a standard system for reporting - SALUTE (Strength, Activity, Location, Unit, Time, and Equipment), Spot Reports, and a fixed time schedule. For example, send a SITREP each hour or whenever a sighting is made. If no communications are made for four hours, move to a position where communication contact was last established. If there is no contact for six hours, move to the nearest friendly unit. Distances which reconnaissance teams operate from base areas may be several miles and the intervening terrain usually is rugged. This means that the time to move an attack force to a likely target can be reduced if teams REPORT RIGHT NOW. Don't sit on your report; learn to pass information as it becomes available. In order to minimize transmission time, use correct voice procedures.

Reconnaissance patrols have often been assigned a secondary mission of capturing a prisoner. This calls for careful preparation and special training.

Many patrols are from four to five days' duration with about the same period between patrols. This can be a drain on patrol effectiveness if such a routine is maintained for any length of time. A rigorous physical conditioning program and a progressive training schedule can help overcome fatigue and loss of effectiveness.

Occasionally, specialists are attached for a particular mission. These men must be alerted as soon as possible and train with their prospective patrols. Additional training in basic reconnaissance is invaluable, and specialists (corpsmen, snipers, demolitionists) must maintain a high state of physical condition for reconnaissance operations.

Force Reconnaissance Companies should not spend an excessive amount of time on specialized entry techniques. Underwater swimming, buoyant ascents and parachuting are valid reconnaissance techniques, but they should not be practiced to the detriment of the basic reconnaissance qualifications that spell the difference between success and failure in Vietnam.

Reports from reconnaissance units in Vietnam emphasize the importance of the following training:

- Scouting and patrolling (emphasis should be placed on route selection, immediate action in danger areas and reporting techniques).
- Map and aerial photograph reading.
- Use of the compass.
- Ambush and counter-ambush techniques.
- Establishment of patrol bases.
- Land navigation.
- Patrol orders and reports.
- Observation and recording.
- Personal hygiene in the jungle.
- First aid.
- River and stream crossing.
- Camouflage.
- Small arms and hand grenades.
- FO procedures.
- Communication techniques.

c. <u>Use of the Claymore Mine by Reconnaissance Elements</u>

Normally, a reconnaissance element selects a night harbor site prior to the hours of darkness, and occupies it immediately before or just after dark. The first task upon entering the harbor site is to establish security positions. Simultaneously, warning devices and booby traps are emplaced, when necessary, as additional security measures.

Rigging a booby trap during daylight hours is extremely hazardous, and during periods of reduced visibility, the inherent risk is even greater. Deactivating the device upon departure is also hazardous.

To avoid the risk in rigging and deactivating booby traps, one unit in Vietnam has gone exclusively to the use of Claymore mines as warning devices and as a means of improving defensive positions. The mine is more effective than a booby-trapped grenade and its emplacement can be more safely and rapidly accomplished without risk of improper rigging or premature tripping by a patrol member. It is important to note, that the Claymore mine can be armed and employed effectively by Marines with only a minimum of training.

# # # # #

7. SUPPORTING ARMS

a. Fire Support and Reinforcement

In any counterinsurgency operation, well developed, closely coordinated planning for both fire support and reinforcement is a necessity. If possible, the reinforcement plan should be rehearsed and timed. A primary and at least one alternate route to the attacked position should be selected. Bear in mind this is being done under the eyes of the Viet Cong.

256-290 O-67—6

b. Big Guns

In the arsenal of weapons available to you are the heavy caliber, long range naval guns on destroyers and cruisers. These are on-call for troop support directly through a naval gunfire spot team and, by request, through artillery forward observer teams. Know the ranges of the various naval weapons and the ammunition available. In one instance reported, a destroyer firing at night killed 139 VC as they tried to overrun a friendly outpost. These big guns can help you too.

c. Naval Guns - Ranges and Ammunition

Gun (Ship)	Range-Yds. (Max. Effective)	Ammunition
8"/55 (Cruiser)	26,000	HC, AAC
6"/47 (Cruiser)	21,000	HC, AAC, ILLUM
5"/54 (Destroyer)	18,000	HC, WP, ILLUM, AAC
5"/38 (Cruiser Destroyer)	15,000	HC, WP, ILLUM, AAC
5" Spin Stabilized Rocket (LSMR, IFS)	10,000; 5,000 2,500	HE

d. Tips for Cannoneers

To shift trails rapidly and accurately re-lay the 105mm howitzer, place the lid of a 20-gallon trash can under the left howitzer wheel. The can cover permits the locked left wheel to spin easily through 6400 mils while keeping constant the axis of the panoramic telescope. One circular trail pit will accommodate both trails. The right trail rests against the rear wall of the pit while the left one is blocked to fill the void between the spade and the rear wall of the trail pit.

For high angle fire, a pit is usually dug under the breech of a howitzer to permit clearance during recoil. When trails are shifted appreciably, there is a chance that one of the wheels may slip into the pit. A cover placed over the pit when not in use prevents the wheel's slipping into the pit during trail shifts.

Placing a canvas cover over the howitzer telescope mount causes condensation in the sight during periods of rain. A number 10 tin can over the mount permits the circulation of air and prevents this condensation.

Check the charges used for each artillery round by placing the excess powder increments in a mission powder pit. VT fuze boxes, sunk into the ground, have been successfully used as powder pits. They also keep the excess increments dry.

e. Right Weapon, Wrong Fuze

Recently, a VC village was bombed by aircraft and later occupied by friendly troops. Most of the structures in this village were destroyed or severely damaged, but fighting holes, trenches and tunnels were comparatively undamaged by the contact fuzed bombs. In order to collapse the tunnels and underground shelters dug by the VC, initial requests for air support should describe the target and include recommended fuzing for the bombs. Delay type fuzes probably would have collapsed those tunnels.

f. Supporting Fires

The first thing that comes to mind when someone says "fire support" is a mass of exploding artillery shells. Consider just one of the other uses that can be made of supporting fires. Artillery can be employed to assist patrols in determining their position if other means have not been effective. Start by transmitting an illumination fire mission to the supporting artillery using a grid intersection near the estimated location of the patrol. When the illuminating round detonates, shoot an azimuth from the patrol position. Adjust subsequent rounds along this azimuth line until a round detonates over or near the patrol's position. Transmit an end of mission report to the firing unit and request a replot. The shackled coordinates of the replot will then give a good approximation of the position of the patrol in question. Using these coordinates, a simple resection will pinpoint the precise position. This method can be employed in daylight or at night. Be conservative in the number of times that you use this technique. The Viet Cong can see the flares also and they can deduce from the manner and frequency in which the illumination is employed that a patrol is attempting to fix its position. The use of HE airbursts in lieu of illumination should also be considered.

g. Target Marking

Infantry sometimes takes a worm's eye view of a prospective target. What the squad leader sees as a single tree line running south, the helicopter or attack pilot sees as three tree lines all running south. A great deal of time can be spent by the ground unit attempting to describe and orient a pilot on a target. Even more time is spent by the pilot trying to translate the ground unit's message into recognizable terrain features. Extended time over target areas and risk of ground fire both can be reduced if ground patrols will mark their targets. The M-79 grenade launcher, the 3.5 rocket launcher, the 60mm mortar, and even pyrotechnic grenades provide effective means of marking a target with precision and definition. Use them as a common practice in target marking.

# # # # #

8. VIETNAMESE

a. Use of Regional and Popular Forces

A great deal of value can be obtained from combining Marine and Vietnamese forces during certain operations. The RFs and PFs know the

terrain, are familiar with the habits of the Viet Cong, and make the presence of Marines in hamlets more acceptable to the inhabitants. In addition, the morale and effectiveness of the RF and PF forces improve considerably when operating with Marines.

b. Combined Operations

The frequency with which U.S. and the Republic of Vietnam Armed Forces are participating in combined operations is on the increase. Such operations often prove more than their apparent value. The tactical and morale benefits derived

can be considerable for both forces. During a recent Marine operation, a Vietnamese infantry battalion provided troops for area security, fire support, guides and intelligence. A local Regional Force platoon was lifted on a tactical mission with U.S. Marines. This was the first time these local soldiers had participated in helicopter operations and they handled themselves like professionals. Not only did they gain valuable experience, but considerable prestige and pride of achievement. That RF platoon is a better one now thanks to the cooperation of the Vietnamese and U.S. commanders involved.

c. Establish a Working Relationship with Vietnamese Army Units

The following extract was taken from a report submitted to the Commandant by the Senior Marine Advisor to the Vietnamese Marine Brigade. It contains a wealth of information and although it is designed for the Marine serving as an advisor, it contains information of outstanding value for all Marines who will be taking part in combined operations with Vietnamese units.

(1) General

The relationship between the advisor and counterpart must be based on the solid ground of competent professional knowledge, a mutual respect of services, and if possible, friendly personal contacts. The amalgamation of these will give best results. The advisor should at all times be himself, and not adopt a "new face" for dealings with his counterpart. The manner of extending advice or offering suggestions depends upon personalities, moods, and the situation. It has been found that using the same methods one would use to recommend a change of action to an American commander produces excellent results with the Vietnamese commander. Quick changes are not to be expected and every effort should be made to continue the programs of the previous advisor, so that a continuity of programs and aims is apparent. The advisor should work from the "soft sell," with a gradual but persistent approach, featuring repetition of ideas and proposals. It is common, however, that the counterpart will not consider the new arrival as "his advisor" until the two have been exposed to combat together. The new advisor must have patience; the opportunity usually arrives within weeks after arrival in country.

(2) "Rapport"

The word "rapport" which describes the harmony, accord, or affinity of the advisor with his counterpart is as nebulous to attain as it is to describe accurately. And it is perhaps an overworked word, since everyone seeks "rapport" without knowing what it is. To be sure, there must be developed between the advisor and his counterpart a workable, recognizable basis from which common goals can be achieved. Mutual respect between the two seems to be the first step. The advisor must learn all there is to know about his counterpart and the unit he commands, the problems of his command, and the strong points and weak points--both personal and professional--of the counterpart. To understand the commander will be to understand the command. Such knowledge will permit an honest interest in assisting the commander and his command without the inference of interference in the command.

The advisor must also earnestly strive to learn the customs, history, taboos, and superstitions of the Vietnamese people. He must learn to eat their food and attend their social functions.

To know the commander/counterpart and to understand his problems, the advisor must be with the counterpart almost continually--without, however, "crowding" the counterpart. He likes his privacy as well as the next fellow. But he must be made to know that the advisor's personal loyalty is to the counterpart, and that the advisor will not participate in any personality clashes within the unit.

The advisor's goal: To develop a genuine friendship and personal loyalty to his counterpart which will not interfere with the advisor's professional relationship with the counterpart or his objectivity to his job.

(3) Assistance to the Unit

Since advisory duties involve all aspects of the battalion with which the advisor will work, the advisor will find that he must extend his influence through all levels of the command including the senior staff noncommissioned officers. It will often be necessary to give recommendations to, tutor, and encourage the staff officers as well as the company and platoon commanders. This must be done openly with no inference of usurping the Battalion Commander's authority. Generally, the commander will welcome such assistance.

The advisor must show interest in all facets of battalion operations and training, not solely the activities in which the Battalion

Commander is directly concerned. The advisor must get out and look around, being alert to new practices or new procedures. He must talk to company commanders, platoon commanders, staff officers, and noncommissioned officers, learning their names and their interests. Only in this way will the advisor obtain a feel for the entire battalion. It will also help him know what is going on at all levels of command within the unit.

The advisor should take an interest in the dependents. Vietnamese are proud family men. They love their children, especially boys; and any genuine interest shown will have a great effect in cementing relationships. There is one caution in this respect. The advisor must not by word or expression express surprise or dismay at the primitive living and unsanitary conditions. Regardless of what the advisor may think, dependents are usually far better off than most civilians. Any improvement which the advisor can accomplish in this area should be low-keyed, except when the counterpart acknowledges unsatisfactory or below standard conditions.

As mentioned previously, in regards to social functions, the advisor is expected to and should attend parties, ceremonies, and other functions to which he is invited. He should also be prepared to reciprocate social dinner engagements he may receive from the battalion officers. And he should make it a point to attend, and participate wholeheartedly, in battalion athletic events.

The advisor, then, must spread his efforts far and wide to make his presence felt in the battalion. This is done with the primary purpose of assisting the battalion in every way possible and not necessarily with the aim to display the American way of doing things.

(4) Approaches, Attitudes, Techniques

There will be no attempt here to describe precisely how an advisor gives advice and counsel to his counterpart because this is influenced by many factors. The advisor will have to find this out for himself, through cautious application, with the hope that his intuition and innate good judgment will prevail. However, the following are considered basic methods of approach:

→ Retain a sense of humor. There are many occasions during the advisor's tour where a sense of humor will be a necessity--and an advantage. The Vietnamese are happy people and like to laugh, sometimes in situations which might be considered under strange and morbid circumstances. It is not proposed that the advisor join a crowd in appreciation of the particular effect artillery has on the human body, but neither can he afford to be appalled if the Vietnamese show such an interest. But the advisor can expect to have some embarrassing moments--losing his footing in a tidal stream, reacting too quickly and violently to an incoming mortar round--and the Vietnamese will think that this is hilarious. At a time like this, the only thing the advisor can do is laugh at himself with them.

→ Always remember that the counterpart is the commanding officer. It is more practical for an advisor to proffer a suggestion prior to a commander's decision than it is to try to change a decision once it has been made. If there is any one point to be considered absolute doctrine, this is the one. And it behooves the advisor to be alert to anticipate decisions through circumstances and make his suggestions accordingly. The commander can then gracefully accept the advice by appearing as though it was his idea in the first place.

→ Do not outwardly display displeasure or disagreement with decisions which have ignored the advice of the advisor. The advisor must make a decision on his own as to whether to fight for his principles, or to save his ammunition for another time, another place, a more important battle. Usually, the advisor finds it advantageous to wait. There have been many instances where the commander, realizing that the advice was good, has reversed himself on his own volition. Further prodding by the advisor would have had the reverse effect of setting the commander's decision irrevocably. The advisor will find that demonstrations and examples will show the relative effectiveness of advisor ideas as compared with existing methods, and changes will eventually result.

→ Never boast or attempt to take credit for practices or procedures which are implemented. The fact that the counterpart knows that the original idea was the advisor's is enough credit. This, too, is a vitally important point.

→ Set a personal example of dress, bearing, industry, and initiative. The advisor must strive to be professionally correct and military in appearance at all times. The Vietnamese expect a U.S. Marine to be the epitome of strength, endurance, appearance, courage, and military skill. Though the advisor will seldom be aware of this, the Vietnamese will often compare their "Co Van" with those of other Americans serving with the ARVN. The Marine advisor must not let them down.

→ Try to visit with U.S. Marine Units. The counterpart and his battalion are proud of the fact that they are Marines. When possible, the advisor should make an attempt to take his counterpart to visit a U.S. organization. With a little assistance and briefing by the advisor, the USMC Commander can give the full VIP treatment to the counterpart, thus increasing his prestige. The visit also provides live training aids for programs in sanitation, staff functioning, unit training, etc., which the advisor may be suggesting. The advisor will be surprised at the many practices which a Vietnamese battalion staff will adapt after they have watched a USMC battalion staff go through its paces.

→ Understand the Vietnamese view. Usually, it is drastically different. But the advisor must realize that a valid suggestion cannot be accepted unless he understands the Vietnamese reason for doing something the way they have been doing it for years. The suggested changes have to be made with a view towards customs and circumstances.

→ Give the counterpart time to think over a suggestion. The advisor must learn to offer new ideas or suggest new procedures sufficiently in advance of the need. He will sometimes find that a recommendation given yesterday is being put into practice tomorrow.

→ Never lose your temper. This is a sign of weakness and must be avoided. It is permitted to be angry, but the advisor must retain control of his temper. This is not to suggest that occasionally a display of irritation is not appropriate. The advisor will often be irritated, but he must retain his composure most of the time. If a discussion becomes heated and the basic idea is being lost, the best idea is to forget it.

→ Trivialities must not become unbearable. The advisor will find that many inconveniences are an inherent part of the advisor tasks; just grin and bear it.

→ When deployed, a USMC advisor will spend about all of his time with the Battalion. Advice offered during normal conversation, such as mealtime or during a break, allows the pros and cons of the suggestion to be discussed without the pressure of an immediate decision. The question and answer game also works. By asking questions, you can discover what the counterpart is thinking. Remind him of items which he may have forgotten. He can answer questions and give orders as though he were going to do it that way all along. And the job can be done before the break is over and the advisor can check.

→ The advisor must be patient, persistent, and considerate. If the counterpart has demonstrated himself to be a competent leader, it then becomes the advisor's task to build the counterpart's confidence, to help him attain the respect and confidence of his subordinates. By being selective in the problems to tackle, the advisor can help the counterpart achieve results which will encourage him to go on to bigger problems.

(5) Approaches to Avoid

→ Don't attempt the "hard sell" as a matter of habit. It may produce results occasionally, but as the counterpart becomes accustomed to this approach, it will be more difficult to employ. Be selective on the areas where the "hard sell" is to be used.

→ Don't assume that some action will be accomplished as indicated in conversation with the counterpart. The advisor may be assured by his counterpart that orders have been issued.

However, the advisor should follow up and do some discreet checking. Supervision will also be required.

➔ The Vietnamese have their internal and external politics, a different financial accounting system, personal differences--many areas not involving the advisor. Advisors should keep abreast of such areas, but should not get involved except in matters which effect the battalion's ability to perform its basic functions.

➔ Don't attempt to win over the counterpart by ingratiating favors. When the advisor runs out of favors to do for the counterpart, he also runs out of influence.

➔ Don't be a combination supply officer and magician, pulling "goodies" from an inexhaustible supply hat. The advisor will invariably be asked to procure material for the counterpart through U.S. sources. This should be avoided by stubborn insistence that the Vietnamese supply system be made to work. Once the advisor embarks upon the role of supply officer, there will be no stop to it and he will end up merely an errand boy.

➔ Requests will be received by advisors for purchases from the U.S. Exchange services. If the advisor honors one request, it will engender countless other requests. The best way out of the situation is to quote the Exchange regulations. A bonafide gift under special circumstances may be warranted, but that should be the extent of the involvement.

→ The "buddy system" or mutual admiration society in lieu of a sound professional basis and sincere personal respect is highly undesirable and offers no advantages.

→ The Vietnamese system of officer-enlisted relationship and methods of inflicting commanding officer's punishment is very much different from what the advisor will be accustomed to. The advisor is cautioned not to intercede in any way. He should just try to understand the system--not change it.

(6) Conclusion

The success of the advisor's efforts to win the respect and the cooperation of his Vietnamese conterpart is the direct equation of professional competence and knowledge multiplied by the amount of time that the advisor and counterpart spend together. In other words, the platform for a lasting and firm relationship is built slowly upon solid blocks of good advice. The officers of the Vietnamese Marine Corps are trained, experienced, and proud. The advisor, accordingly, should not expect his counterpart to come to him seeking advice. The advisor should be there, when he is needed, with an encouraging word, a possible recommendation, and enthusiastic support of the commander's eventual order. The patient but persistent advisor who hears his counterpart ask, "What do you think?" has just been informed that he is a success.

d. County Fair Operations

The war in South Vietnam is a unique war in many respects because victory, unlike wars in the past, will not be won on the field of battle alone. USMC strategy is predicated upon gaining the confidence of the people as the primary objective which must be won. Historically, no military force has ever existed successfully for any protracted period of time in the face of a hostile population. In terms of counterinsurgency, this means that the insurgent infrastructure must be destroyed. In Vietnam, we must exterminate the Viet Cong political and military structure and destroy their supplies, arms and fortifications. Without accomplishing this, purely military success becomes empty even if we are victorious in every engagement.

From the outset, Marine operations in Vietnam were oriented to the reality that killing Viet Cong would contribute to their defeat, but that victory in the end must derive from freeing the people from VC domination and bringing them tranquility.

To assist in the accomplishment of this mission, the III MAF has developed a technique which is designed to weed out guerrillas, destroy his infrastructure and tip the balance among the people of South Vietnam from the endemic oppression and fear they now suffer, to true freedom and loyal support of the government of South Vietnam. This technique is termed COUNTY FAIR and was first employed by the 9th Marines in the heavily populated area around Danang.

Just what is COUNTY FAIR? Essentially it is a tactical search and clear operation combining and coordinating governmental, civic and psychological warfare activities to reestablish Vietnamese government control over the populace of a given area. It is designed to flush the Viet Cong from the community of which he is a member or a parasite, while at the same time attempting to establish the confidence of the people in their government. Military actions are accompanied by a vigorous civic action and psychological warfare program, the purpose of which is to convince the people that their government is an effective one, that it is interested in the welfare of the people and that a government victory against the insurgents is inevitable.

USMC participation in County Fair Operations is effected by establishing a cordon around a target area (village or hamlet), to isolate it for the duration of an operation, and to provide limited medical and logistical assistance. To the largest extent possible, Vietnamese military, police and civil authorities perform the task of searching the target area and handling the populace. This is considered an essential element of County Fair Operations since one of its primary purposes is to restore the populace's confidence in the governmental structure and to instill a sense of trust and loyalty toward duly appointed officials.

The County Fair process begins when a cordon force of U.S. Marines encircles a selected village or hamlet in the early morning hours, prior to the lifting of curfew, to prevent the escape of guerrillas. Shortly after first light, Vietnamese police and Army units enter the area and move the villagers into an assembly area. Here government administrators take a census, fingerprint and photograph the villagers, identify families with dwellings, issue identity cards and determine the whereabouts of absent family members. Viet Cong suspects are segregated for additional interrogation, as are their families.

While they are waiting to be processed, the villagers are given clothing, soap, medical and dental treatment by combined Vietnamese/Marine/Navy teams. Also, since the villagers are temporarily separated from their homes, families are given meals prepared in Marine field kitchens. Psychological warfare films, movies and band concerts provide a measure of education and entertainment during the operation.

Concurrent with the processing of the villagers, Vietnamese Army units make a detailed search of the area, attempting to discover caves, tunnels, VC supplies, and secret escape routes, as well as any guerrillas who might be in hiding.

The County Fair Operation itself is short, ranging from one to three days in length. However, after it is completed, and the Marines and Vietnamese Army units that have conducted the operation move elsewhere, continuing security must be provided for the village or hamlet. Only by maintaining this security in the area until the VC infrastructure is completely eradicated, can village or hamlet be protected from reinfection. Usually, a Popular Forces squad or platoon will be lodged in the vicinity. If the area is particularly troublesome, a Combined Action Company of a Vietnamese or a U.S. Marine Force may be positioned nearby.

The basic logistic support for each County Fair can be reduced to a standard package which can be maintained for required operations. Such a package could include:

- 5 Fly tents
- 2 Lister bags
- 4 Battery powered hand speakers
- 2 Mallets
- 12 Metal stakes
- 1 Pair wire cutters
- 5 Wooden collapsible tables
- 10 Folding stools
- 1 Plywood bulletin board
- 1 Immersion burner
- 1 Trash can (24 gal.)
- 1 Water Trailer
- 16 Water cans
- Sufficient Rope or Engineer's Tape for delineating restricted areas

As a result of the search operations, a portion of the villagers will be dislocated temporarily and will not have access to their homes. Those unable to provide or prepare their own meals will have to be fed. Remember that village economy is marginal, and if a villager is denied access to his crop land for even a day it means his family goes without food. The U.S. force assigned to support a County Fair can greatly assist in providing and preparing meals for these villagers. Frequently, it will be necessary to provide and prepare up to 1200 meals per day. Based on that figure, foods can be obtained through USAID and civil affairs channels. The following amounts will support an average of one County Fair operation per week (1200 meals per day):

600 lbs. - Milled rice
100 cans - Assorted foods (vegetables, meat, etc.)
8 cans - Soup base (100 rations)

There is much detailed planning and preparation involved in successful County Fair operations. It is important to emphasize this detailed planning and close coordination at all levels to both U.S. and GVN participants. The measure of success of each operation lies in this coordination and cooperation.

e. County Fair Search

COUNTY FAIR operations call for the encirclement of a village, clearing village inhabitants to a collection area, and the subsequent search of homes by PF and Marine personnel. The procedures of searching the villager's home in his absence could result in allegations by the homeowner that property belonging to him has been damaged or stolen by the search team. During a recent COUNTY FAIR operation, one person from each household was escorted from the collection point to his home and was present during the search. This enabled the search team to question the villager about suspicious findings and the villager was satisfied that his property rights had not be violated. Additionally, such a procedure

allowed the team to observe the homeowner for suspicious or nervous actions, while the search was being conducted.

f. Minimizing Noncombat Casualties

The government of Vietnam (GVN) is engaged in a fight for its survival against the Communist Viet Cong (VC) supported and reinforced by the forces of North Vietnam. It is the objective of the VC to seize control of the hamlets, villages and towns by a combination of military action, terrorism, political action and subversion. It is the objective of the GVN to resist this process and where it has occurred, to reverse it. This means that the

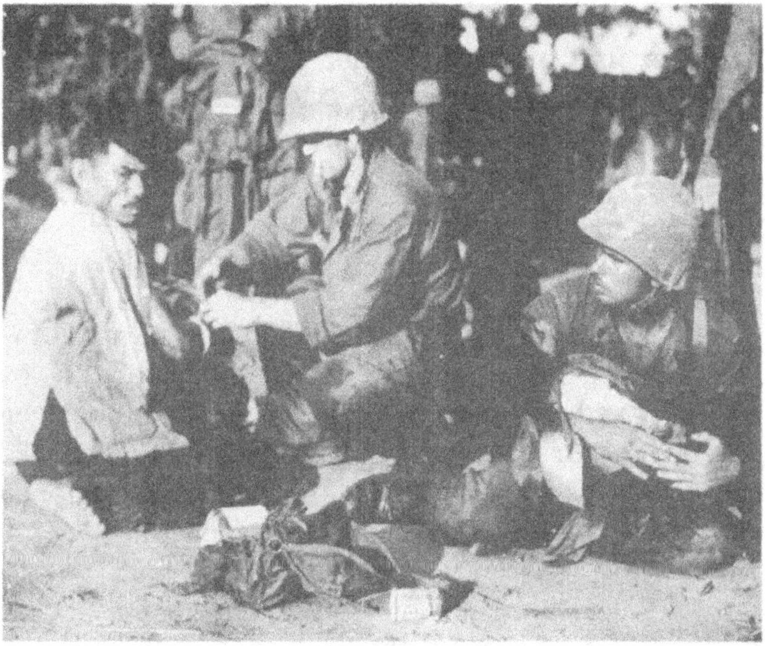

battle for Vietnam flows backward and forward across the homes and fields of the helpless rice farmer and the small town inhabitant. Whether, at any time, he lives in a VC or a GVN controlled hamlet depends to a large extent upon factors and forces beyond his control. Eventually, of course, the GVN plans to regain control over all of the hamlets and all of the people.

The use of unnecessary force leading to noncombatant battle casualties in areas temporarily controlled by the VC will embitter the population, drive them into the arms of the VC, and make the long range goal of pacification more difficult and more costly.

The circumstances described above call for the exercise of restraint not normally required of Marines on the battlefield. Commanders at each echelon must strike a balance between the force necessary to accomplish their mission and the high importance of reducing to a minimum the casualities inflicted on the noncombatant populace.

The VC exploit fully incidents of noncombatant casualties and destruction of property by RVNAF and US combat forces. Their objectives are to foster resentment against GVN and the United States, and to effect the permanent alienation of the people from the Government.

To minimize noncombat casualties, commanders should take the following actions when considered appropriate:

→ Commanders should consider both the military and psychological objective of each operation. Strikes in populated areas, reconnaissance by fire into hamlets, and poorly selected harassing and interdiction fires are examples of military measures which will be counterproductive in the long run.

→ Troop indoctrination briefings should be held before each operation to emphasize both the short and long range importance of minimizing noncombatant casualties.

→ The proper selection of landing zones, the careful planning and execution of airstrikes and the proper employment of artillery and armed helicopters will avoid unnecessary damage to lives and property of noncombatants.

→ With due regard to security and success of the mission, whenever possible the people should be warned of impending airstrikes or operations by leaflets and broadcasts. Blame for military action in the area should be shifted to the VC.

→ A civic action plan should be developed to support each large operation even if the area has been controlled by the VC.

→ Free strike zones should be configured to eliminate populated areas except those in accepted VC bases.

→ Operations should be planned in coordination with Province and District chiefs with due regard to security of plans. Liaison should be established with appropriate civilian authorities.

→ Use of assigned RVNAF Liaison Officers is essential and should be arranged for each significant operation. These Liaison Officers through their knowledge of the area of operation and the population can assist in identification of friend from foe and can help to ensure close coordination with all Vietnamese Forces. In this connection, the participation of Vietnamese Forces in operations should be encouraged so that the war does not appear to be a U.S. action against the Vietnamese people. Regional and Popular Force participation should be sought at battalion or even company level so that they may assist in the search of private dwellings, obtain information, and contribute to the desired effect of the cooperative war effort.

→ Established rules of good military conduct and discipline must be enforced.

→ It is absolutely essential that U.S. Forces establish the reputation of being able to move at will throughout SVN and to defeat any VC Force encountered. This reputation for invincibility will produce innumerable psychological benefits and hasten the end of the war. On the other hand, these same forces must constantly demonstrate their concern for the safety of noncombatants--their compassion for the injured--their willingness to aid and assist the sick, the hungry and the dispossessed.

g. Ancestor Worship and Removal of the Dead

Most Vietnamese practice a form of ancestor worship which incorporates the belief that if a dead body is not buried near the bodies of its ancestors, the spirit belonging to the body will wander for all eternity and cannot return for family festivals.

This belief accounts in great measure for the fanaticism displayed in battlefield recovery of bodies, as does the desire to keep total numbers of casualties suffered from friendly forces.

To prevent the VC from removing their dead, units must continue to harass the battlefield and likely routes of withdrawal with fire.

Remember--the Viet Cong often break off attacks and stop firing abruptly. If friendly forces also cease firing and relax their guard, the enemy will use the lull to recover his dead and wounded.

h. Viet Cong Farmers

The Viet Cong are using Montagnard agricultural methods to grow food for their sustenance and resupply. The jungles are replete with numerous areas where the undergrowth has been cleared by burning or cutting to allow space for planting or areas for grazing water buffalo. After planting, the fields are cultivated intermittently, but during harvest time, a large number of personnel might be present.

A continuing effort should be made to locate these agricultural plots, and periodic monitoring made of their development. The information obtained could be used to establish ambushes.

# # # # #

9. SECURITY

a. Local Security

One area of operations closely associated with military operations is local security. It is fair to say that the unit which neglects it is bound to suffer. A Marine recently returned from duty with an infantry battalion in Vietnam puts it this way: "The VC are just like a bad smell; they're everywhere." While this is an over simplification, it does infer that VC sympathizers and agents can be in and around base areas and tactical units. Any position offers a target to the VC whether it is a major airfield or a small outpost.

One principal indicator that the VC look for when judging a prospective target is the degree of local security exercised in and around the target. Consider that you, as the leader of a raiding party, are examining an enemy target for a future raid. What are the items you want to know about the enemy position and force? The following list contains a few sample items of information that you would need to know:

➞ Layout of the position; location of individuals and crew served weapons.

➞ Routes and frequency of close-in patrols; location of static security posts.

➞ Degree of training and security consciousness of enemy personnel.

➞ Fire support available in the target area and lapse of time between request and delivery.

➞ Reinforcements within a given distance and the probable route they would travel.

→ Communication facilities and their location within the target, particularly land line communications.

Now turn your hat around and examine this sample list from the standpoint of the commander responsible for providing local security for any position.

The location of fortifications, individual and crew served weapons, and vital areas within the position will be governed by the mission of the unit and the application of fundamental tactical principles (mutual support, fields of fire, number of weapons available). Probable avenues of approach, dead spaces, terrain and vegetation all will affect weapons positions. The guiding theme in patrol routes and frequencies, and the routes of walking security posts is to avoid patterns. The key word is RANDOM. Try not to cover the same route at the same time night after night. By varying routes, times, and sizes of local patrols you can cover a larger area, gain just as much information, and avoid ambushes. Fixed security positions may be needed; however, make every effort not to restrict their hearing or fields of observation.

Aggressive training and unit leadership are the prime motivators in the unit attitude toward local security. A system of positive identification of indigenous and friendly personnel is a basic ingredient of this training program. Rarely is the attitude toward security a poor one if the value and techniques of good security have been demonstrated and closely supervised. Security is everybody's business every minute of each day. It is just too late to acquire a change of heart when the VC are in the gunpits.

Equally important is the vital communications system. Only a complete operational system is of value. This should include both radio and wire with alternates for each. Constant checking of these systems particularly during the hours of darkness and at dusk and dawn is a good means of insurance. Know the locations of land line junctions, the relatively inaccessible portions of the system and those sections which are accessible to nearby trails, hamlets, and roads. This knowledge can point to the areas to be checked initially in case of land line failure.

This sounds like a primer in local security procedures, and not at all peculiar to operations in South Vietnam. The peculiarity lies in tactical situations in which the Viet Cong can be anywhere and everywhere with little or no warning. The burden of responsibility for local security lies squarely on the unit commander. Through his imagination, energy, and constant supervision comes the umbrella of security so eagerly sought after and appreciated by the Marines of his command. Fight to overcome a tendency toward taking security for granted. Remember the saying--

"Laziness explains more failures than ignorance, but the combination is catastrophic."

b. Wire Team Security

Recently a wire team sustained a number of casualties from a booby trap while servicing a land line in a pacified area. Wire team security had not been requested because the area was considered to be pacified.

Wiremen cannot detect all booby traps while tracing wire breaks. Remember that the booby-trapping of wire lines by the VC is very effective since they know that most wire line breaks will be repaired. It is well to provide wire teams with security, even in pacified areas when they depart

the perimeter. Remember, pacification does not mean that the area is completely free of the VC.

c. Security Training

One of the favorite tactics of the Viet Cong continues to be the ambush. Attention to security by Marine forces is a necessity if casualties from this source are to be avoided. Security is just as important in defense situations as it is during patrols. Training should include automatic drills by units at all levels in measures to counter surprise actions by the enemy. Immediate action drills must be perfected and all Marines must be imbued with the necessity of never relaxing their guard and being alert and suspicious at all times.

d. Shifting Positions

Unit commanders should consider shifting defensive positions after dark to avoid giving the local populace the opportunity of pinpointing their positions for the Viet Cong.

Recently, a platoon established a harboring site during daylight hours which was under observation of local indigenous personnel. Shortly after dark the platoon commander shifted his platoon approximately 150 meters from the original position. At 2030 the original position was brought under intense small arms and mortar fire by the enemy.

e. Defense Against Mortar/Recoilless Rifle Attacks

The Viet Cong successes in launching mortar and recoilless rifle attacks, though limited in total effect, have been sufficient to encourage similar efforts in the future. U.S. and ARVN airfields provide the VC with a means of inflicting heavy equipment losses and, in some cases, high personnel casualties. Experience has shown that the Viet Cong will continue to exploit a proven tactic or technique until it is forcefully, effectively, and repeatedly countered. The ability of friendly elements to counter enemy attacks lies in the application of lessons learned from previous attacks.

Friendly elements must realize that the enemy is very methodical and plans his attacks with precision. The enemy normally employs mortars and recoilless rifles at night from positions that enable him to fire for effect on the long axis of an airfield at preselected targets.

To prevent an attack, a good internal passive defense and an external plan which includes aggressive patrol action beyond the range limits of the enemy weapons are essential. The implementation of a sound intelligence reporting system which will provide indications of an attack will enhance the overall effort to reduce the chances of an attack.

Enemy attacks seldom last more than 20 minutes. Therefore, time is of the essence in its detection. Constant surveillance by aerial and ground observation and use of electronic devices will enable defensive elements to detect enemy fires immediately. Once the firing is detected immediate deployment of armed aircraft, artillery, and flareships will force the enemy to cease fire and withdraw. Immediate reaction by a ground force to preselected ambush positions along the route of withdrawal may result in elimination of the enemy. Each successful counteraction will reduce the frequency of enemy mortar and recoilless rifle attacks.

Some techniques that should be employed along with aggressive patrolling are as follows:

→ Establishment of a ground reaction force that is well rehearsed and capable of instant reaction.

→ Variation in placement of sentries, ambushes, listening posts and patrol routes, and their employment on random schedules will reduce the enemy's ability to conduct surveillance by denying him freedom of entry into the area.

→ The surveillance of prime target areas is apparently accomplished by personnel having access to the installation. Exacting and detailed screening of the local laborers to ensure proper identity and loyalty will reduce the enemy's surveillance capability and his knowledge of the key installations and their locations within the defensive area. Daily entry and exit screening must not be relaxed.

→ Once an enemy attack is launched, return fire must be delivered immediately if the destructive effect of the attack is to be minimized. This can be accomplished by preselecting concentrations on likely mortar positions. These concentrations are assigned to friendly mortar and artillery units and are fired automatically. When not engaged in other missions the artillery and mortars are laid on these concentrations to facilitate rapid response.

→ The enemy normally establishes several positions so that maximum fire can be placed on the target. To reduce the time that the enemy can place effective fire on a target, ground alert must be responsive immediately.

→ Aircraft should be repositioned frequently to prevent enemy registration on one area. Repositioning should be done at random and in response to local intelligence.

→ Establishment of alternate and multiple means of communications, particularly with units having the capability to fire on enemy mortars and recoilless rifles.

f. Rapid Illumination

When illumination is required to locate infiltrators, the delay between the request and the bursting round can be reduced by using the following technique. Preset four 81mm mortar illuminating rounds for detonation about 800 meters from the perimeter position. The rounds are then positioned in the gunpit at 3, 6, 9 and 12 o'clock (North). The illumination is requested by specifying clock direction from their position. When an outpost or listening post requests illumination at 9 o'clock, the mortar crew quickly moves the tube and bipod to the 9 o'clock position and fires. Illumination is then a matter of seconds rather than a delay of several minutes.

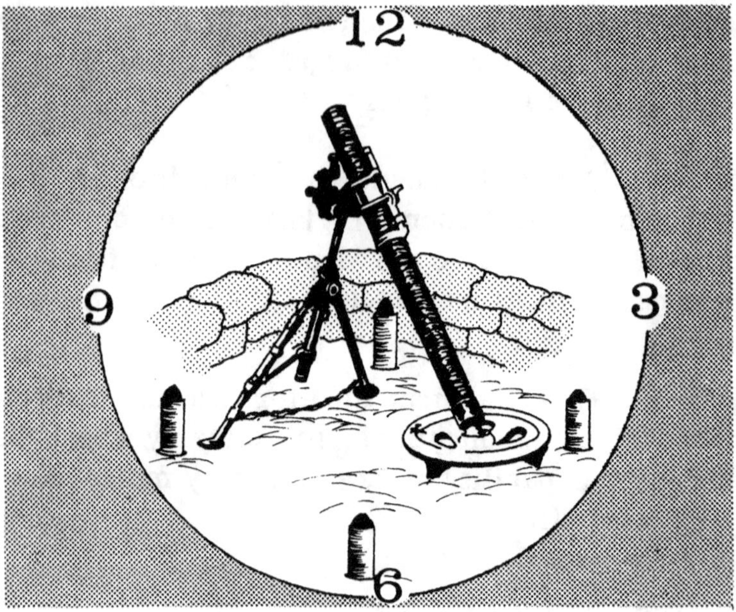

g. Perimeter Floodlights and Trip System

One unit in Vietnam has developed a unique way of illuminating the perimeter with material that is readily available. Sketches II-1 and II-2 depict an illumination system which utilizes standard 28 volt vehicle headlamps which are normally discarded when one of the filaments burns out.

The voltage source for the system is standard 110 VAC power which is normally available at most command posts. The voltage is dropped across four headlamps which are wired in series. Several switches are integrated into the system to enable a sentry to control the illumination. In addition, trip switches are incorporated which are designed to turn on the illumination when the enemy attempts to infiltrate or attack the position.

Switch S-1, Sketch II-1, is the main power switch while switch S-2 is a sentry by-pass switch which is designed to by-pass the trip switches. The latter switch would be used whenever illumination is desired and normally would be in the off position. This allows trip switches S-3 through S-6 to function if an intrusion of the perimeter is attempted by the enemy.

Sketch II-2 demonstrates how an ordinary household clothes pin can be modified to act as a contact switch. The screw type contacts are kept insulated by inserting nonconductive material between the two prongs. By attaching the nonconductive material to the trip wires, the switch is activated whenever the nonconductive material is withdrawn.

The arrangement of lamps and trip switches can be adapted to suit the installing units situation and is limited only by the ingenuity of the user. Further, if the noise of the engine generator is prohibitive, batteries could be used as the power source if the vehicle headlamps are connected in parallel.

PERIMETER FLOODLIGHT SYSTEM

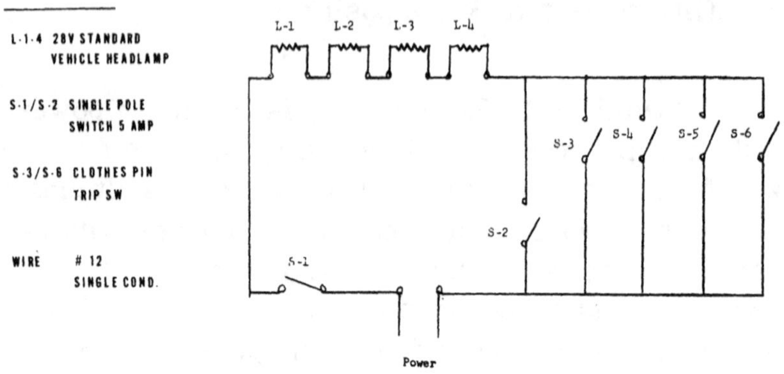

Sketch II-1

CLOTHES PIN TRIP SWITCH

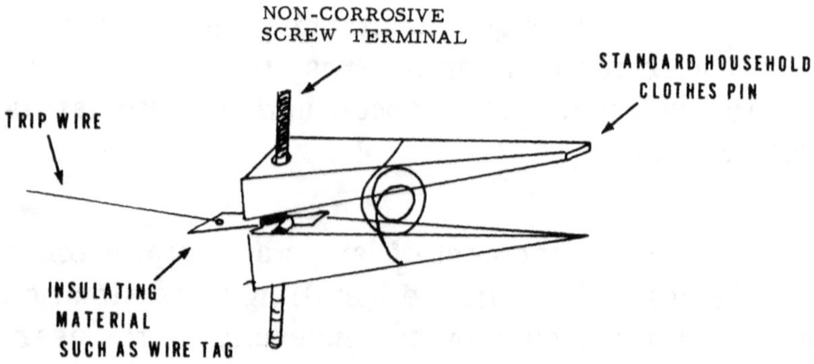

Sketch II-2

# # # # #

10. TUNNEL CLEARING TECHNIQUES

a. Tunnel Clearing

Each day of operations in Vietnam produces more evidence that the Viet Cong are actually going underground. The reasons for this are apparent. The VC leaders, particularly those who fought in Vietnam with the Viet Minh, are experienced in constructing fortifications and tunnels. Guerrillas need to have some type of base facility from which to operate, be it a cave, a dense jungle forest or a tunnel complex. Tunnels discovered and destroyed by Marines in Vietnam have ranged in size from those which were 6 feet long with a small entrance (2 x 2 feet) to larger ones with individual sections over 400 meters long and with entrances 6 feet square.

In areas where the Viet Cong have been operating, tunnel construction is continually improved and interconnecting systems are developed. False doors and water locks are two features which play an important part in limiting access to certain sections of a tunnel complex. Trapdoors are used both at entrances and exits and inside the tunnel itself, concealing side tunnels and intermediate sections.

One characteristic of all tunnel complexes is their camouflage. Entrances and exits are concealed and within the tunnel itself sidewalls may conceal arms caches. Hidden trapdoors are prevalent and dead-end tunnels are used to confuse the searchers. Trapdoors of different types have been used at entrances and exits and inside the tunnel. The most common types include one of concrete covered by dirt, hard packed earth reinforced with wire or lengths of light metal or a basin type consisting of a frame filled with dirt.

This last type is difficult to locate by probing unless the probe happens to strike the outer frame. Mines have been discovered attached to the entrances and exits of both tunnels and caves. Grenades are frequently attached to a wire on the trapdoor with the grenades placed in an adjacent bush or tree outside the tunnel.

Not all tunnels are dug completely underground. In sandy areas or where the water table is comparatively high, long narrow trenches are dug then shored and covered with bamboo matting. The spoil is thrown on the top of the mat covering, and the excess spread over a wide area or thrown into a nearby stream.

Tunnel clearing and destruction is an operation calling for attention to detail and careful coordination. Preparations should include a checkoff list of equipment and supplies to be used. Specialist personnel such as demolitionists and interpreters are useful. When a tunnel is discovered, an interpreter should be used to urge any occupants to leave. Every possible inducement should be used to get people out of a cave or tunnel before proceeding with its destruction. If the occupants refuse, a small token charge can be exploded near the tunnel entrance as an encouragement to come out.

If the decision is made to search a tunnel complex before destroying it, the following is a suggested technique:

→ The immediate area surrounding the tunnel should be secured by a 360-degree perimeter to protect the search party and prevent the escape of any persons flushed from the tunnel.

BEWARE OF MINED ENTRANCES

EXAMPLES OF TUNNEL COVERS

→ The tunnel entrance is carefully examined for mines and other traps. Then designated searchers enter the tunnel with ropes attached to their waists and with wire communications to the surface.

→ The search team works its way through the tunnel probing for mines, false walls, hidden entrances and caches of arms and supplies. Air vents should be noted and plotted. Compass headings and distances are reported to the surface where they are recorded. A second team maps the tunnel from the surface while another small group follows the search team from the surface by moving along above their search party's location.

→ As other entrances are discovered and plotted, they may be marked in such a way to show whether the VC use them after discovery but before destruction. Tunnels which are too extensive to be searched and destroyed in one day may be reentered during the night by the Viet Cong who can place mines and traps on the approaches and tunnel entrances.

→ After search and exploitation, destruction can begin. The amount of explosive and its location is a matter of judgment and experience. C-4 plastic charges are normally used. The larger individual cratering charges are effective on large complexes, if it is logistically feasible to use them.

b. <u>CS Grenades</u>

M-25A2

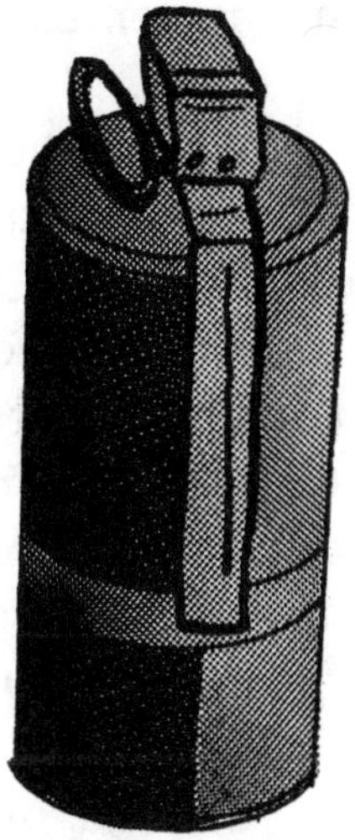

M-7A2

One method employed by U.S. forces to destroy extensive complexes is to place 40-pound cratering charges about fifteen to twenty meters apart inside all the known tunnel entrances and 10-pound bags of CS-1 Riot Control Agent at intervals down the tunnel at sharp turns and intersections. The CS-1 bags are then tied into the main charges. Where sufficient detonating cord is not on hand to tie all CS-1 bags to the main charge, bags of the agent can be dispersed in the tunnel by the detonation of a defuzed M-26 grenade fuzed with a non-electric cap and a length of time fuze. Sharp turns in the tunnel protect the demolitionist from the grenade blast. Denial by the use of CS-1 is temporary in nature. A word of caution at this point;

the explosion of charges in a closed tunnel produces a deadly gas and partially uses up the oxygen. Ensure that the tunnel has been vented before personnel re-enter.

When the tactical situation does not permit a detailed tunnel search, hasty methods include throwing a CS grenade (M-25) followed by a fragmentation grenade into the entrances, or the use of the Mity Mite portable blower to disperse burning CS Riot Control Agent grenades (M7A2) throughout the tunnel. After flushing with CS grenades, powdered CS-1 can be blown into the entrances to deny the system to the VC for a limited time.

Ground operations in areas where tunnels and extensive underground complexes have been previously discovered require repeated thorough searches for additional structures. Because there is less work involved in restoring a cave or tunnel that has been destroyed by explosives than in digging a new one, the Viet Cong choose the easier task. Infantry and engineering units must be prepared for repeated tunnel search and destruction operations. Experience has shown that once tunneling in any area has been thoroughly destroyed, repeated searches of a few days duration can deny the enemy access to the area.

A representative list of equipment for tunnel search teams is shown below:

M7A2 CS grenades
Powdered CS-1

Colored smoke grenades to mark additional entrances
Intrenching tools
Compasses
Bayonets
Probes - in lengths of 12 and 36 inches
Pistol, cal. .45 - used by the searching team
M3A1 sub-machine gun
Mity Mite Portable Blower
TA/1-PT telephone
Communication wire - one half mile length
Protective masks and/or self contained breathing devices
Sealed beam flashlights
Insect repellent

Tunnels are frequently excellent sources of intelligence and should be exploited to the maximum.

c. Operational Employment of the Mity Mite Portable Blower

The Mity Mite portable blower is now in the hands of Marine forces operating in South Vietnam. When properly used in conjunction with various chemical agents, it will force smoke throughout a tunnel system and normally reveal all entrances and vents.

The machine is an agricultural backpack spray-duster (Sketch II-3). It is powered by a 2-cycle gasoline engine, weighs 25 pounds, without fuel or agent, and displaces 450 cubic feet of air per minute. The fuel tank holds approximately 1 quart of gasoline-oil mixture which permits operation in excess of 30 minutes. It is equipped with a 2-foot-long flexible tube that has a metal nozzle on the end. The agent tank can be filled with either 10 pounds of powder agent or 3 gallons of liquid agent.

The following account reveals one technique of employing the Mity Mite blower as practiced by an infantry unit in Vietnam:

→ Training for a newly organized tunnel tracing and flushing team included operation and maintenance of the portable blower, and practical exercises in operation of the blower with smoke. The total time devoted to training was 2 hours. The team also prepared for the operation by cutting a 5-gallon can in half. A hole the size of the blower nozzle was cut in the upper half to facilitate blowing smoke into vertical entrances of tunnels. It was planned to use the lower half to block tunnel entrances (Sketch II-4).

The team was placed in direct support of one of the attacking battalions and engineer personnel attached so that tunnel complexes might be destroyed after they had been cleared and searched.

On the first day of the operation a large tunnel was discovered and the Mity Mite blower was immediately put to use by placing it near the tunnel entrance and spreading a poncho over the horizontal aperture. The hose nozzle was placed through the head opening of the poncho and the hood strings fastened securely. Earth was placed around the edges of the poncho to form a seal (Sketch II-5).

The lower half of the 5-gallon can was inserted in another tunnel entrance located a few feet away from the original entrance to prevent the smoke from dissipating before penetrating all portions of the tunnel system.

A smoke grenade was placed in the tunnel and the Mity Mite blower started while infantry units deployed in all directions.

The infantry units detected smoke escaping from a number of tunnel vents and entrances and promptly marked and closed them.

When it was determined that all entrances and vents of the tunnel system had been detected and the tunnel trace was apparent, the introduction of smoke was stopped. However, some vents were opened and the blower continued to operate until all smoke had been cleared from the tunnel system and it was safe for search teams to enter.

The foregoing account explains a very basic method of using the portable Mity Mite blower.

There are other, more sophisticated methods, which include the use of different chemical agents, gas masks and other types of equipment.

We have the equipment that can do the job. It is only as good as the imagination of the commanders employing it.

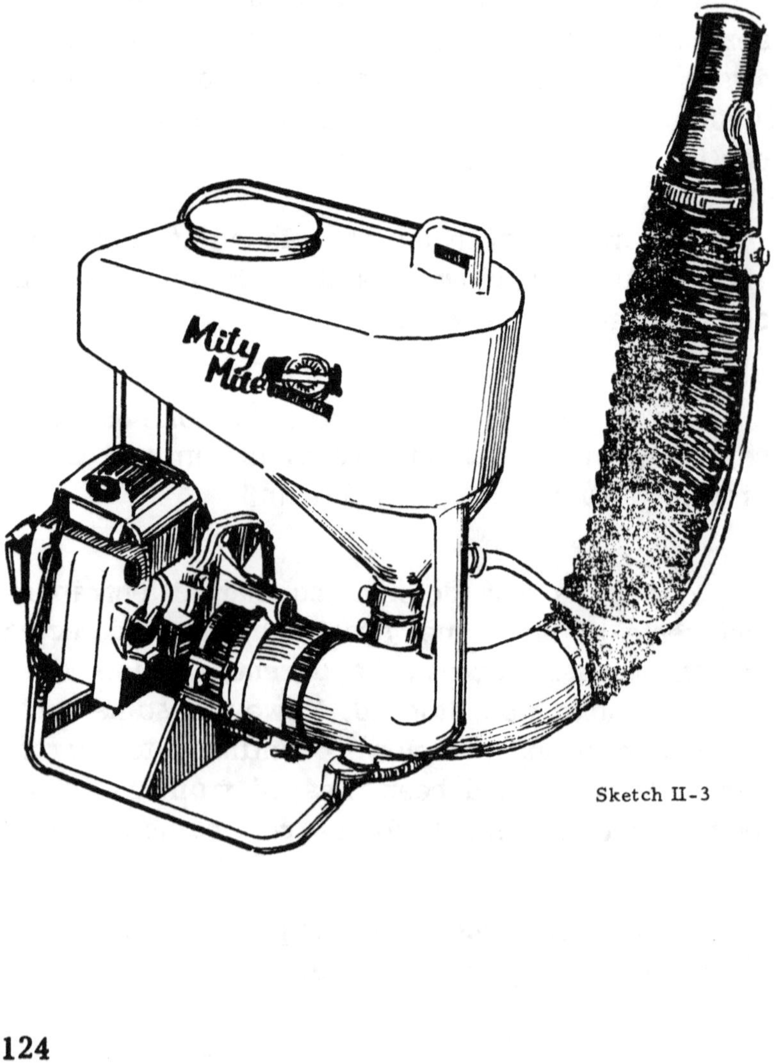

Sketch II-3

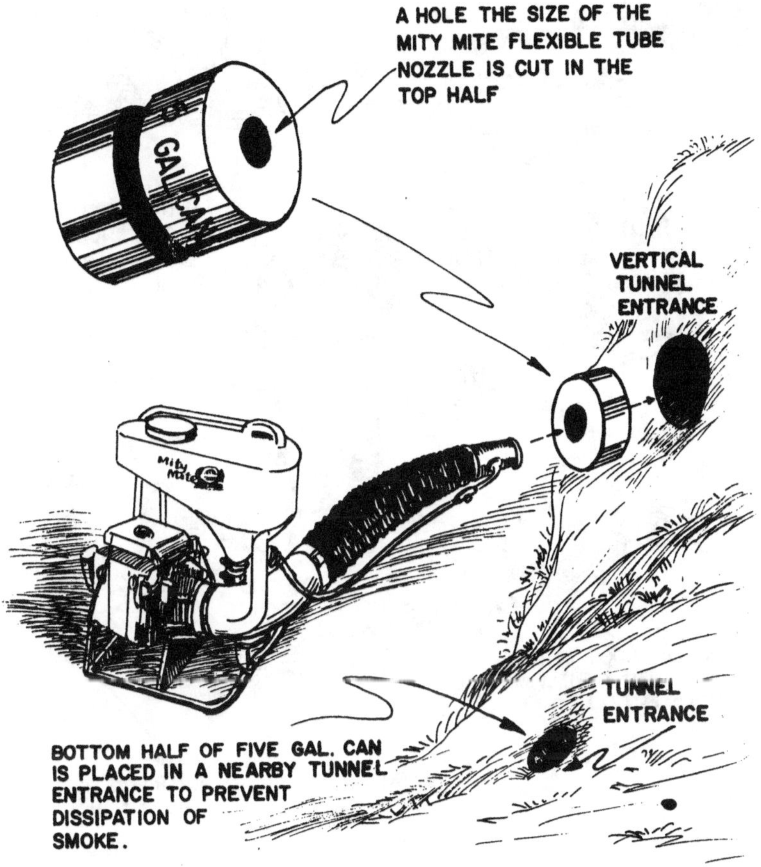

FIELD EXPEDIENT METHOD USING
5 GALLON CAN

Sketch II-4

USE OF PONCHO WITH MITY MITE BLOWER

Sketch II-5

d. The Use of CS

A report received recently from an Army Division in Vietnam contains a great deal of information on the use of CS. The unit claims that the use of CS in a combat support role has many unique advantages in fighting a counterinsurgency type war.

Some of the situations for which they have employed CS to advantage are as follows:

→ Reconnaissance by CS fire: CS has proven to be extremely effective when delivered by helicopter into a suspected enemy area where observation can be conducted. Experience has shown that the Viet Cong move out quickly, even from well camouflaged positions.

→ Assisting in the attack of villages and in clearing operations: The use of CS from a helicopter permits the rapid clearance of villages. Little time is available to the VC for hiding or caching of weapons because of the haste with which they must leave the buildings to avoid the effects of the CS. Single munitions, especially the M25 grenade, can save lives when reconnoitering caves, tunnels and houses within a village.

→ Curbing fire at helicopters: CS has been successfully used to discourage villagers from firing at helicopters. This method works particularly well when psychological warfare leaflets and loud speakers explain beforehand that CS will be used if they persist in sniping at helicopters. In one instance, not only did the sniping cease from the village but it also ceased throughout the entire area.

→ Proving our desire to safeguard noncombatants: In heavily populated areas, noncombatants frequently hide in caves and tunnels along with the VC in order to avoid artillery and airstrikes. If CS is used, the noncombatants are not injured and there is a good possibility the VC will be captured and provide information of an intelligence value. In one case, forty-three armed VC were captured after exiting a cave to avoid the effects of CS.

→ Tunnel attacks: CS used with a Mity Mite blower has been found to be extremely effective in quickly clearing large tunnel complexes and in locating exits.

→ Denial of tunnels: Powdered CS may be used to deny tunnel complexes to the enemy until supporting troops can destroy them. This method has proven effective for periods up to two weeks. Normally, the unit uses smoke to reconnoiter the tunnel, followed by airing, and inspection of the tunnel for intelligence information. Upon completion of the intelligence search, powdered CS is used for denial purposes until supporting units can destroy it.

→ Use in patrolling: On occasion, patrols have used CS to prevent the VC from following. On one occasion, when the enemy attempted to pursue a small, long range patrol along a jungle trail, the patrol ignited a CS grenade which allowed them enough time to move farther down the trail and establish an ambush.

e. Electrical Storms and Claymore Mines

The 1st LAAM Battalion reports that during a recent electrical storm, three Claymore mines were simultaneously detonated by lightning. All shorting plugs were in place at the time of the detonation.

All personnel should be aware that the shorting plug doesn't necessarily make a Claymore safe. Appropriate precautions should be taken by all hands when working near these devices during electrical storms.

# # # # #

11. TRAINING

a. H&S Company on the Perimeter

An increasing amount of correspondence is being received from personnel in Vietnam which stress the importance of General Military Subjects Training. In one letter, a Staff Sergeant assigned to the Communications Platoon of Headquarters and Service Company of one of the infantry battalions recounts his experiences while manning the battalion perimeter. A portion of his letter reads as follows:

'Make no mistake, and you can spread this to the troops as gospel--if they have time enough to be sent over here, they better pay attention to their general military subjects. No MOS is exempt from a certain amount of perimeter duty. Here, the H&S people also conduct night patrols and ambushes in front of our sector of the perimeter. And there are VC out there, even in what is supposed to be a pacified area. We get probes and harassing small arms and grenades nearly every night. I never thought it would come to pass, but I have had occasion to call in 81 illumination, and have to be prepared to use HE and if necessary, artillery. Of course this starts with being damn sure you are reading the map correctly. I would hate to be the SNCO who didn't know what to do out here. The CO doesn't accept excuses. Admittedly, I had to do a bit of boning up, but am used to it now. This participation of H&S, etc., in the activities of the 'grunts' is, of course, what THEY always said would happen one of these days, but I don't think many of us took it seriously. This extends, so far as I know, all the way up to division level - there, H&S and supporting/attached units furnish men to a platoon for a week or a month at a time, similar to mess duty. This for perimeter duty and patrols. Doubtless there are exceptions, but I wouldn't count on it. All of this H&S type participation is apparently so that the line companies can release troops for more activities outside of the perimeter."

What the Sergeant says is gospel and happens every day in Vietnam. The information contained in the letter is not new, but there is a tendency for some Marines to overlook it. General Military

Subjects Training is still the best conditioner for combat. Proper attention to training while in the States, will save your life in Vietnam.

b. Night Operations Training

Effective operations during the hours of darkness are essential in all warfare, but in particular, in counterguerrilla warfare. The basic ingredient of successful night operations, offensive or defensive, is the confidence of the individual Marine in his ability and that of his unit to operate in the night environment. This confidence comes only from detailed planning and painstaking, successful training.

A well organized training program that devotes considerable time to night operations can provide Marines with the necessary knowledge, confidence and skill they need for night combat. The key is to schedule training which includes transition of operations from day to night and, if possible, the training should be scheduled as an uninterrupted tactical exercise. The scope of such training should not be limited, but should include all aspects of tactical operations. Offensive actions involving night movement should be stressed.

Areas in which emphasis should be placed are as follows:

→ Techniques of fire during periods of darkness.

→ Individual weapons firing under all conditions of natural and artificial illumination.

→ Night relief procedures at small unit level.

→ Night reconnaissance patrols.

→ Individual proficiency in land navigation at night.

→ Individual and unit night discipline.

→ Use of detection devices in offensive and defensive night operations.

→ Night live firing exercises for squads and platoons.

In conjunction with night operations, it becomes apparent that to cope with the rigors of the Vietnamese environment and sustained day and night operations, personnel must be in the best possible physical condition. To do this will require much more than the average physical training program. A high and continuing demand must be placed on the physical capacity of the individual in order to build confidence in his ability to function properly under conditions of prolonged physical exertion.

c. <u>Call for Fire Support</u>

An increasing number of operations are being conducted by units of platoon size or smaller. Since there are not sufficient numbers of Forward Air Controllers, Forward Observers and Naval Gunfire Spotters available for assignment to the smaller units, it is of extreme importance that all NCOs be capable of calling for and adjusting supporting arms of all calibers.

d. Cross-Country Movement in Mountainous Terrain

The following excerpt from a report furnished by the 3rd Marine Division provides a lucid account of the difficulties inherent in operating in the mountainous terrain of ICTZ:

"The terrain was the greatest single limiting factor in a recent operation. Ninety percent of the area consisted of dense jungle undergrowth with a 60 to 100 foot canopy and the other ten percent was elephant grass up to fifteen feet high.

"Marine assault units were directed to move parallel to trails and stream beds to a location above the suspected enemy position and to launch their attack downhill to the rear of the enemy force. Although this type movement took hours to accomplish, friendly units always had the advantage of attacking downhill into the weakest part of the enemy's defense."

e. Field Expedient for the 106mm Recoilless Rifle

When contact with the enemy is imminent, the 106mm gun covers and breech covers must be removed. This, of course, causes excessive dust and sand to collect in the barrel and firing mechanism of the gun, creating the possibility of misfire.

One unit in the III MAF has solved this problem by placing a plastic polyethlene bag around the breech and gun muzzle of the weapon. When the gun is fired, the bags melt and do not affect firing in any way. The bags are inexpensive, easily stored, and available in abundance in Vietnam.

f. Helicopter Medical Evacuation in Jungle Areas

During a recent operation in an area of dense jungle canopy, operating units found it extremely difficult to evacuate their wounded by helicopters. Adequate landing zones were extremely scarce. Once they had moved into the terrain covered with dense canopy, they had two alternatives. One was to keep an element in the elephant grass to secure an adequate landing zone where a medevac helicopter could land and then carry the evacuees back to that position over extremely difficult terrain. This proved unsatisfactory since it took up to five hours to traverse only 500 to 600 meters of this terrain with litters. The other alternative was to cut a landing zone through the dense canopy and undergrowth suitable for evacuation by hoist from a hovering helicopter. The latter method was used with much success on numerous occasions although the inability to secure

more than 200 meters around the zone resulted in a number of helicopters taking hits from enemy snipers outside the perimeter.

Although both the UH-34 and the UH-1E could pick up evacuees while hovering above terrain that averaged 2400 MSL, the CH-46 proved to be the most suitable for this type mission because of its power and load capability.

The attachment of a Helicopter Support Team to units operating in this type of terrain is recommended. The team should be equipped with long handle axes, hand saws and demolitions with which they can cut and clear an adequate zone to safely accommodate a hovering helicopter. The zone should provide as much cover from enemy snipers outside the perimeter as possible. Additionally, all CH-46 helicopters used for medical evacuation should be equipped with a litter so that men with serious wounds will not have to be lifted by the horse collar device.

It is interesting to note that a Helicopter Support Team during one operation in mountainous jungle terrain, carried a large heavy power saw for thousands of meters only to find the equipment inoperable on reaching the proposed landing site.

g. <u>Calling Medevac Helicopters</u>

Medical evacuation of casualties by helicopters can be hazardous and difficult, particularly when a unit is deployed in a hostile or densely vegetated area. In many cases, small unit leaders coordinate the evacuation. If the leader becomes a casualty, some individual in the unit must be qualified to control and coordinate the operation. The unit must be provided with a minimum amount of equipment and training which will enable it to communicate with the aircraft and use the approved procedures and techniques for medical evacuation by helicopter.

Equipment should include smoke signals, pop-up flares, hand illumination grenades, at least two flashlights, and radio equipment capable of entering the medevac nets.

The following is a checklist of helicopter evacuation information that the pilot should have before attempting a landing:

→ MEDEVAC Helo this is (call sign).
→ (Type of Signal) will be popped at your command.
→ Recommend you make approach from (compass direction) due to (enemy position or obstacles) at (compass direction) from zone.
→ Zone is secure, or (probable/possible) enemy fire at (compass direction) from zone.
→ Friendly troops are (compass direction) from zone.
→ Terrain in LZ is (description).
→ Number of casualties and type of wounds.

h. Helo Evacuations

Operations in mountainous and otherwise inaccessible areas can require evacuation of casualties by hovering helicopters. This means hoisting the casualties from a small cleared area to the aircraft. Corpsmen operating with infantry units should train in the use of the sling and basket litters. All Marines should receive indoctrination training in these specialized evacuation procedures.

i. Small Unit Tactics

During a recent operation in Quang Ham Province, the Viet Cong used their standard tactic of sniping and then breaking contact as friendly units closed their positions. To counter this, the Marine battalion used an OE on station to report when the enemy broke contact. This proved to be of inestimable value in placing timely air and artillery fire on the fleeing enemy.

Also, prep fires and reconnaissance by fire on anticipated trouble spots or routes of advance were used by the battalion to facilitate movement and reduce casualties.

Another tactic used by friendly troops and which has a great deal of potential was the leaving behind of Marines when the unit left its nighttime position. In almost all cases, the VC will move into a vacated CP area, and if friendly troops are present, a lucrative ambush can be established.

# # # # #

12. INTELLIGENCE

a. Exploit Intelligence

The importance of exploiting intelligence of immediate tactical value obtained from captured enemy documents is illustrated by the series of combat actions described below. Major success was achieved by utilizing information initially gained from the capture of one document and following up subsequent intelligence gathered during engagements with the Viet Cong.

Recently an ambush patrol killed a Viet Cong Company Commander and captured a number of documents he was carrying, including one that directed four VC companies to establish a training base at a given location. The following day, a two company size force moved by foot toward the suspected enemy concentration. An assault on the objective, preceded by an intensive artillery and aerial bombardment, was launched and immediately encountered heavy opposition. The Viet Cong occupying fortified positions on high ground, employed a high volume of automatic weapons and small arms fire causing friendly forces to withdraw to more favorable positions and await reinforcements. Contact with the enemy was continued and numerous airstrikes were conducted. Four hours later the friendly units were reinforced by an additional company and VC defenses began to crumble. By nightfall, the enemy had been driven from their positions and forced to flee the area. Total VC casualties were 130 killed by ground and air action, with an undetermined number of VC wounded. No weapons or captives were taken, indicating that this VC unit possessed a high degree of military discipline and training.

A search of the battlefield uncovered documents that revealed the presence of a VC battalion command post to the south in a land development center. To exploit this information, two companies were ordered to attack the location. On the same day, following intensive airstrikes, the companies were landed by helicopter on the objective. Heavy contact with an estimated company of VC was immediately established. As the VC resisted stubbornly for more than two hours before they retreated, it was apparent that they possessed the same high degree of discipline as those engaged in the previous day's action. A total of 33 VC were KIA and 9 were captured.

Evaluation of all intelligence acquired during these two operations and interrogation of the captives revealed the most likely infiltration routes used by the VC in their movement through this area. A few nights later, a company established an ambush on one of these routes. Just after dark, an estimated VC battalion entered the killing zone from the south and, at the same time, a local VC platoon moved in from the north. Both VC units were immediately taken under intense fire by automatic weapons, small arms and three Claymore mines. Enemy casualties from the initial burst of fire were apparently heavy but, recovering quickly, the VC returned fire and counterattacked the friendly positions, both frontally and on one flank. These attacks were thrown back. Contact with the VC continued until 0100. 155mm artillery support and flare ships aided the outnumbered friendly force in holding back the VC. Again, the discipline of the VC was demonstrated by their evacuation of most of their dead, wounded and equipment from the battlefield. By 0115, all firing ceased as the VC broke contact and withdrew. First light revealed only 4 VC bodies and 1 wounded VC remaining on the scene. However, numerous blood trails and other evidence of high VC losses were found. A number of rucksacks, 1 LMG mount, 1 mortar base plate and miscellaneous ammunition were captured. Friendly losses in these three actions were light.

b. Sources of Information

Counterguerrilla operations offer most of the usual sources of information for combat intelligence with one considerable difference. Rather than the enemy being the most abundant source of information, as in conventional operations, the operating area itself provides the bulk of information. And within the operating area, the civilian populace is probably the best source. The effective exploitation of civilian sources may require more sophisticated procedures than usually practiced at battalion/regimental level. Reliability of source information is the principal consideration. Usually a battalion level S-2 does not have the readily available knowledge to determine source reliability. A source file is therefore suggested as a means of collecting data on local sources. This file should include as a minimum the following information:

→ Name and description of source

→ Particular area in which source is capable of obtaining information.

→ Reason for source's cooperation

→ Method of contacting source

→ Record of remuneration

→ Past reliability

Three considerations must be kept in mind when a civilian source is interrogated. First, the attitude of the source - is he openly hostile or merely passive? Second, his knowledge of the area of operations will normally be limited to his immediate hamlet or village depending on the nature of his employment. A bus driver can be expected to have different observations from a farmer. Thirdly, the source's ability as a military observer will be inferior to that of an average Marine. It is up to the interrogator to translate the source's information into military language.

With these considerations in mind, a civilian might be able to provide information on:

→ The political attitudes and sympathies of local villagers.

→ Terrain and how weather can affect it.

→ Logistical support available to guerrillas operating in the resident area of the source.

→ Identification of guerrillas, either cadre or part-time members or both.

→ Guerrilla techniques for sabotage, espionage and terrorism.

→ Vulnerabilities and weaknesses of the guerrilla force.

→ Location of fixed guerrilla installations such as tunnel systems, caves, and supply caches.

Exploiting civilian sources can be done either openly through direct contacts or through an agency not recognizably associated with the friendly forces. This latter technique of covert exploitation can involve transmitting information through several persons without the transmitting party learning the identity of the receiver. Delay and misunderstanding are probable when using this method. The direct contact system provides for immediate collection of information; however, it presents two disadvantages. It singles out the contact to any unknown enemies, making him susceptible to reprisals, and it makes the intelligence requirements of the friendly forces known to all. The second disadvantage lies in the fact that usually the friendly intelligence officer is an occidental and his source is oriental. Language and cultural differences can distort the information gained or make it incomplete.

Military agencies can be particularly valuable as primary and corroborating sources of information. Patrols of all types are extensively employed and missions range from local security to long range reconnaissance. Patrols should have the capability of interrogating local residents within their area of operations. This requires the extensive use of linguists and other personnel with language training. Judicious use must be made of these men up to the limit of those available. Aerial surveillance and photography can be one of the most rapid means of obtaining information when employed properly. Certainly nobody can argue with the reliability of a photograph.

Visual reconnaissance by a well trained observer in an aircraft which can penetrate deep into enemy controlled territory is another reliable means of long range reconnaissance.

Interrogation teams contain personnel who qualify both linguistically and in interrogation techniques. Full use of their services should be considered in counterguerrilla operations. The use of qualified indigenous personnel or ex-guerrillas to assist in interrogations may be limited because of security restrictions. Sole reliance should not be placed on the use of indigenous personnel.

Cooperation and liaison with the agencies below will provide the intelligence officer with additional sources of information:

→ Intelligence collection and counterintelligence specialists.
→ U.S. civil affairs teams.

→ Representatives of non-military U.S. or allied agencies (USAID).

→ Civilian agencies of the government or allied countries.

The sources available to the unit S-2 officer are varied and numerous. The S-2 must learn to evaluate both the reliability of his collection agencies and their sources. Small unit leaders must appreciate and understand the need for timely reporting and learn to develop their own intelligence sources. The importance of the intelligence officer in counterguerrilla operations is skyrocketing. Many units are finding that while little attention may have been paid to the importance of intelligence training in years past, the demand for high quality intelligence is needed right now--TODAY.

c. Provisional G-2 Section

Several methods have been used in Vietnam to form a G-2 Section when provisional headquarters have been formed for field duty. In one instance the entire section was formed from personnel from the Division G-2 Section augmented with personnel from the intelligence sections of subordinate units. This procedure had its drawbacks primarily in that it threw together strangers who had to function as a team.

Another procedure utilized was to augment the S-2 Section of the Regiment conducting the operation with selected skills from the Division G-2

Section, and designated the S-2 Section as the Task Force G-2 Section. This procedure was used on Operation Hastings with good results. The specific skills that should be provided the regimental S-2 are an Order of Battle Officer and one assistant, a Combat Intelligence Officer, and clerical assistance consisting of one man. Operation Hastings proved that a G-2 Section so constituted can provide good area familiarity from the Regimental S-2 personnel, and good order of battle, combat intelligence and intelligence reporting procedures from the augmentation personnel from the Division G-2.

d. Captured Documents

Captured documents are an important part of the intelligence collection effort. In many cases the circumstances surrounding the capture of a document have proven to be as important as the document itself. As an example, a document containing enemy unit designations is more valuable in Order of Battle work if the precise location and time of capture are known.

e. The Counterintelligence Team at Company Level

Within the 3rd Marine Division areas of responsibility, CI personnel maintain constant contact and liaison with all District Headquarters and other agencies. Through this liaison, they obtain Black Lists and other information on possible targets.

During a recent operation, two CI team members, ten district intelligence personnel and a company scout formed an "Intelligence Platoon." This unit operated immediately behind the assault platoons, and on occasion, representatives from the "platoon" operated with a rifle platoon during search and destroy operations.

This method of operation resulted in the identification and apprehension of many VC hamlet leaders, and the location of mines and booby traps, caves and tunnels.

# # # # #

13. TRACKED VEHICLES

a. Retrieving Tracked Vehicles

Tracked vehicles are usually forced to traverse rice fields when operating cross-country. What appears to be a well drained field may not support the heavy ground pressure of a tracked vehicle, as the soil under the surface has absorbed all the water. If a tracked vehicle becomes mired, the LVTR M-51 retriever can be used to recover it employing cables and pulleys rigged in a 3 to 1 or 4 to 1 advantage.

The recovery vehicle should be placed on firm ground with the cable spanning the distance to the mired vehicle. Tank units must assist in vehicle recovery when an LVTR is not available.

This can be accomplished by use of a 50-100 foot length of 1 1/2 inch cable. Each tank can carry on its rear tank deck a 25-30 foot length of cable eye-spliced at each end. Tank sections can then combine their cables for mutual support in recovery operations.

b. Use of Tank Communications and Armament in Calling Airstrikes

During a recent tank-infantry operation in Vietnam the tank RT-70 radio and 90mm gun proved to be an effective combination for calling airstrikes. The frequency range of the RT-70 included those frequencies used by FAC teams. Knowing this, a Forward Air Controller whose radio became inoperable, requested that the tanks call for the air support. When the air arrived, the tanks clearly marked the target for the aircraft by firing 90mm WP rounds.

c. Adjusting Artillery Fire with the Tank Rangefinder

The M17B1C rangefinder, a component of the tank fire control system, is a highly accurate instrument for determinating ranges from 500 meters to 4400 meters. When terrain conditions make range estimation difficult or when trained artillery observers are not available, the rangefinder can be used as an aid in adjusting artillery fire.

An intersection obtained from two widely spaced tanks reduces human and instrument error to a minimum. If successive targets are anticipated, the tank azimuth indicator should be oriented by a compass or aiming circle. Thereafter, the azimuth indicator will provide an accurate and continuous observer - target azimuth reading as the tank turret is traversed from target to target.

d. Assembly of Tank Units

Many times armored units are moved forward to infantry CPs hours or even days prior to an operation. This is a sure indication to the Viet Cong that an operation is pending. Also, armored and infantry units often move to the jump-off positions during the hours of darkness which serves to alert the enemy and permit him to vacate the area under the cover of darkness.

Arrangements should be made for tanks and other armored units to join the infantry at the jump-off point at "H" hour or be staged at a distance, on call, in order not to telegraph the operation. This, of course, requires precise coordination and control, but is possible with the versatile communications system available within the tank unit.

e. Tank-Infantry Coordination

Planning at the infantry regimental/battalion S-3 level sometimes does not include the attendance of the appropriate tank unit leader. This reduces the overall effectiveness of the tank-infantry team in regard to minimizing tank limitations and maximizing the tank capabilities. When tank unit leaders are present, terrain is picked which increases the effectiveness of the tank-infantry teams. When terrain in the operational area restricts tank mobility, tanks can be placed on the flanks of the advancing infantry axis. Support by fire is then effectively placed on targets marked by smoke. This also permits tanks to establish a "kill zone"

for the enemy flushed out by the advancing infantry. When the operation area has rice paddies in the route of advance, a thorough and careful reconnaissance must be conducted prior to the commencement of the operation. Rice fields with as much as two feet of water can be crossed if the bottom is firm.

Presence of the tank unit leader at the planning conference will increase the effectiveness of the tank-infantry teams.

f. Employment of Tracked Vehicles with Engineer Sweep Teams

The employment of tanks to accompany engineer road sweep teams can serve a number of valuable purposes. Tanks can detonate any pressure type explosive device, and have the ability to provide added security for the sweep team. On occasion, the enemy has employed devices so constructed and emplaced that mine detection equipment has been unable to pick them up. The weight of an accompanying tracked vehicle is sufficient to detonate the device, and the armor protection of the vehicle can shield the crew. Mine sweep teams are frequently the target of enemy ambushes. The presence of a tank with its fire power and shock action will, in many cases, be enough to discourage any enemy action. Tanks so employed should be positioned no closer than 100 meters to members of the sweep team.

This will decrease the possibility of engineer personnel being hit by fragments, should the vehicle detonate an explosive device.

g. ONTOS Employment

The primary mission of the antitank battalion is to provide antimechanized support to the division for the destruction of hostile tanks and other gun or personnel carrying, armored or tracked vehicles. The battalion's secondary mission is to provide direct fire support to infantry units and to motorized reconnaissance patrols when enemy mechanized attack is not probable.

The 1st Antitank Battalion has gained a great deal of experience in executing their secondary mission since arrival in Vietnam. They have employed Ontos sections at infantry company combat bases in support of company platoon, and squad size operations.

This method of employment, while having certain drawbacks, has many significant advantages. It provides the Company Commander with a weapon that is characterized by massive firepower and shock action, while at the same time educating him in the capabilities of a weapon which in the past has not been used to its fullest capability.

The Antitank Company, on the other hand, has become proficient in supporting small unit operations from remote locations. This is a large size order when logistic problems are taken into consideration.

h. Security of the M-76 Otter

Like all vehicles in Vietnam, the M-76 Otter is subject to enemy mining and ambush. In a guerrilla environment, it is quite vulnerable. Experience of the 3d Marine Division has demonstrated that when the Otter is carrying supplies and is accompanied by security personnel, sandbags should be placed on top of the cargo compartment to afford protection from sniper fire and blast effects. Sandbagging of the floor boards, under and around the driver is highly recommended. A sandbag on the seat not only provides

additional protection, but also allows the driver to operate the vehicle in a semistanding position. By standing, the driver has better visibility of the terrain and is less hampered in his operations by engine noise. The current special allowance for Otters provides for one caliber .50 machine gun per two vehicles. They should be dispatched in pairs for security.

i. Stream Crossing with the ONTOS

Numerous difficulties have been encountered by the Ontos in traversing steep banks while crossing streams and rivers. The proper use of demolitions, however, will alleviate many of these problems. Seemingly impassable river banks can

be altered by detonating small demolition charges to create better routes of access and egress.

j. Tank-Infantry Cooperation

Infantry units have sustained numerous casualties from booby trapped munitions and grenades. Tree lines, bamboo thickets and hedgerows are favorite hiding places for these devices.

When it becomes necessary for infantry units to move through such areas, routes can be cleared by using tanks and LVTs to crush the foliage. Such tactics clear the area of anti-personnel boobytraps and provide the infantry units with a more casualty free approach to the objective.

k. Direct Fire Support

On occasion, the LVTH-6 has been utilized in a direct fire role in support of infantry units. During Operation Georgia, the 3d Marine Division achieved notable success by placing an LVTH on one or both flanks of advancing infantry units. In this manner, the vehicle provided a continuous direct fire capability across the entire front and to both flanks of the attacking unit. Target acquisition and point destruction were excellent out to about 2000 meters.

This is just one example that demonstrates the flexibility of the LVTH-6. There are others. Use your imagination!

1. Trafficability in Rice Fields

Following the spring harvest in ICTZ, some of the areas shown on maps as rice fields are drained until the next planting cycle begins. The period of dry rice fields lasts from approximately March through May, depending upon rainfall and local planting customs. Tracked vehicles have experienced excellent trafficability in rice fields during these periods.

Don't automatically exclude the use of tracked vehicles when a map reconnaissance indicates rice fields on your route of approach. Check the weather and harvest cycle before making your decision.

m. River Operations

River operations are normally timed in order to take advantage of optimum tidal conditions. Predictions of 2.5 foot tides have been found to usually provide sufficient flotation for the LVT to permit successful movement. However, experience has shown that the LVTP-5 family of vehicles can negotiate rivers and waterways when considerably less than optimum conditions prevail.

When less than optimum conditions prevail the following suggested actions can be taken:

→ When low water level precludes continuous vehicle flotation the vehicle should be

operated in the land steer mode with the driver selection lever in low range.

→ No more power should be applied than is absolutely necessary to maintain momentum and steerage.

n. Trafficability

The rivers, waterways, and lowland areas near the coast are subject to quick flooding and overflow following a tropical storm. The trafficability for tracked, as well as wheeled vehicles can completely change in less than 24 hours. When tracked vehicles have not operated continuously in an area, a thorough route reconnaissance is a good practice prior to entry in that area. Selection of alternate routes is advisable.

o. ONTOS Afloat

In a recent amphibious operation, the ONTOS was employed effectively from the deck of an LST. Wood planking was placed under the tracks to prevent slipping and to protect the ship's deck. Care must be taken to shield the backblast of the recoilless weapons.

p. Use of the Tank Mounted Xenon Searchlight

Enemy mining of portions of the MSR has been prevented in some forward areas of the TAOR by use of the tank mounted Xenon searchlight to maintain surveillance of the MSR throughout the night. When a suitable vantage point is available, a road can be periodically illuminated with the white phase of the Xenon searchlight to a distance of approximately 3000 meters. When the tactical situation prohibits visual illumination or, when secrecy of observation is desired, the infrared phase of the Xenon light may be used, permitting observation to a distance of 800 meters.

The Xenon searchlight has also been successfully used in the interdiction of enemy river traffic. Initially, the otherwise undetectable passage of an enemy sampan at night can be discovered during the periodic use of the infrared mode of the light. The target can then be fired upon immediately as the searchlight is boresighted with the tank's main gun. The Xenon white light may be used later to determine target effect or to search for other possible targets.

The powerful beam of the Xenon light has also proved of great value in night search and clear operations. A tank equipped with the light and located on favorable terrain can detect any enemy attempts to escape from the area of operations.

q. Dozer Tank Support

Operations in ICTZ have demonstrated that the M48A3 dozer tank is an invaluable asset for normal tank operations and tank operations in support of infantry units. It has been used by tank units to prepare fording sites, reduce otherwise impassable dikes and to prepare tank slots for night defensive positions in forward areas.

In support of infantry operations, the dozer tank has been used to destroy enemy trench lines, fighting holes, bunkers, reinforced fence lines and to clear fields of fire for defensive positions.

# # # # #

Chapter III: NATURE OF THE ENEMY

1. VIET CONG TACTICS - NOTHING NEW

The Viet Cong are not employing tactics that are new or peculiar to South Vietnam. They are employing the tactics of General Giap of North Vietnam who in 1959 published a book titled "People's War, People's Army." The volume includes accounts of the Viet Minh war against French forces, and how it developed from small attacks and ambushes by guerrilla bands to operations by regular mobile battalions, culminating in the Army-size attack at Dien Bien Phu. The development of a Campaign of Operations, as practiced by Giap during the Viet Minh war, has taken place in South Vietnam as evidenced by the battalion and regimental operations of the Viet Cong and North Vietnamese.

It is important to know how the tactics recommended by Giap are practiced by VC/NVA today. They embody two principal features. First, grind down the enemy by a series of harassing actions and small scale attacks, and then entrap him in a situation not of his own choosing. The grinding down process is practiced daily around our combat bases in the form of snipers, mine warfare, attempted ambushes, and small scale attacks. They are guided by the "Four Quicks and One Slow." That is, quick advance, quick assault, quick battlefield clearing, quick withdrawal, and slow preparation. Emphasis is placed on detailed planning (sand table models are often used), thorough reconnaissance, and rehearsals. Rarely do they deliberately risk their resources, except when they believe the probability of success is high.

The Viet Cong lack the firepower of the free world forces in South Vietnam; therefore, it is usually not to their advantage to hold terrain. Instead, they concentrate on inflicting casualties, and "wear down the enemy forces." This is characterized by their technique of attacking a small Vietnamese outpost with the intention of ambushing and annihilating the friendly relief column.

Baiting an ambush is another technique practiced and recently used against a Marine patrol. A platoon engaged in a day combat patrol was investigating intelligence reports of a VC weapons and ammunition cache. While moving to the suspected position, two VC riflemen were observed moving away from the patrol. The leading fire team took them under fire and the platoon pursued. When the platoon reached the position where the VC were first observed, they came under the sniper and machine gun fire of an enemy platoon. Fire was returned and reinforcements were requested as the VC began withdrawing toward a hamlet in their rear. Once in the hamlet the VC fire on the exposed Marines increased. Soon an orderly withdrawal by the VC was underway, covered by sniper and mortar fire. A second Marine platoon reinforced the original platoon and an advance on the hamlet was commenced. Sniper and mortar fire continued to harass the advance to such an extent that six members of one platoon were killed by sniper fire alone. Additional reinforcements established blocking positions to prevent an escape, but, although their movement was rapidly executed, they were too late.

Techniques such as this comply with the VC military doctrine of "force the enemy to fight at a preselected location." To a Marine in combat this means he must maneuver his forces rapidly to envelop the enemy units seeking to execute an entrapment. Bear in mind Giap's guidelines:

"Is the enemy strong? Avoid him. Is the enemy weak? Attack him."

# # # # #

256-290 O-67—12

2. KEYS TO VIET CONG TACTICS

A knowledge of Viet Cong tactics and techniques by unit commanders and individual riflemen will save Marine lives and contribute to success of each mission. The following discussion emphasizes the major principles of enemy tactics and techniques.

a. Viet Cong Operational Planning and Preparation

Viet Cong tactical success is a result of many factors, most of which are widely recognized as being advantages inherent in the hit-and-run tactics characteristic of the guerrilla. Less widely known is the importance which the Viet Cong place upon long range planning and preparations to extend these other advantages and minimize the risks involved in every overt action they initiate. Meticulous and thorough compilation of information concerning the objective characterizes Viet Cong operational planning. Particular emphasis is placed on knowledge of the enemy at and near the objective, of the terrain in the vicinity of the objective, and of the local populace residing in the area of the objective.

Close, undetected observation of the objective and the enemy is accomplished over a period of days or weeks by special reconnaissance units, or specially selected personnel. A detailed sketch of the area is prepared with particular attention

to the size, location and nature of natural or man-made obstacles. Intelligence collectors move as close as possible to feel out, measure, sketch and record. Locations of guard posts, sentry schedules and weapons are noted. Collection of detailed data on enemy movement into and out of the area discloses the interval between movements of personnel and equipment, the weapons and firepower available. A telling example of the length to which the Viet Cong go to obtain information on the enemy was discovered in September 1965 in the Cam Ranh Bay area. U.S. forces apprehended several children attempting to indicate the U.S. defensive positions. Sticks, approximately one foot long and pointed on one end, were being propped up on racks, or on other sticks, and pointed toward the main positions. These sticks also have been found in bushes with pointed ends aimed at a main gun position.

Knowledge of terrain is a key to Viet Cong strength. It is largely the result of living off the land. However, it is enhanced by the limited scope of Viet Cong operations, which facilitates detailed terrain analysis. In studying terrain, the Viet Cong seek to capitalize on favorable terrain. The VC gather extensive data on roads, villages, rivers, streams, lakes, ponds and canals. Also, if there is even a slight possibility of their affecting the operation, dimensions and locations of bridges, bushes, walls and fences are recorded and sketched. Attention is given to likely enemy defensive positions and observation posts.

b. Viet Cong Movement

The Viet Cong are as thorough in planning their movement to the objective as they are in reconnoitering the objective. They practice rigid movement discipline plus tactically sound assembly and dispersion procedures. Their doctrine in this regard varies little, if any, from that of the United States or other Western countries. What does differ, however, is the manner and discipline with which such doctrine is practiced. Viet Cong leaders have fought for years and have learned the benefits to be gained from careful movement, assembly, and dispersion.

Most movement by VC units is at night, but occasionally they travel by daylight. Using local guides, much of this movement is cross-country. Upon halting, the VC immediately prepare for defense against air or ground attack. Sentries are usually posted in pairs at a distance of several hundred meters from bivouac areas; this distance is reduced during darkness. Sometimes VC caution the nearby villagers to leave prepared positions undisturbed so that they can be used again at a later date. Then in later withdrawals back to base areas, the VC often travel portions of previously used routes. A pursuing force does not normally anticipate that the VC have prepared elaborate defense positions at points along their withdrawal route.

On an operational mission, a Viet Cong Battalion moves over trails, roads, canals or any terrain which will conceal its movement to battle positions. Terrain is the determining factor in march formations, but in any case the leading elements are liaison agents or scouts who precede the main body by a considerable distance. They are followed by a reconnaissance intelligence unit which provides forward and flank security. A rifle company with at least one machinegun or automatic rifle is next, followed by the available weapons or combat support unit. The battalion headquarters and a protective rifle company are the next elements, while the third rifle company is the last march unit and provides the element, usually a squad, which serves as the rear guard. Units smaller than battalion try to follow the same principle no matter how meager their force or how limited their weapons. Such a formation provides for local security in all directions and places combat elements and supporting weapons well forward for immediate employment if necessary. The command element is centrally positioned to coordinate and rapidly control any actions necessary, including the deployment of the ready reserve.

River, canal, and road crossings are conducted in a conventional manner. Initial security and scouting patrols are sent forward and to the rear. Crossing is swift and units are dispersed. Security elements are recalled after the main body has control of the area to which it crossed. When water crossings are hampered by lack of watercraft, field expedients are used; e.g., rafts for weapons and equipment are made from sheets of plastic that are a part of the individual equipment of each man.

c. Disposition of Forces

Relative to the enemy - practically all Viet Cong attacks feature assaults from an encirclement or some variation of an encirclement. Doctrine almost flatly refuses to tolerate attacks using a purely frontal disposition; however, the Viet Cong may resort to this when natural or manmade obstacles on flanks or to the enemy's rear can be integrated into attack plans.

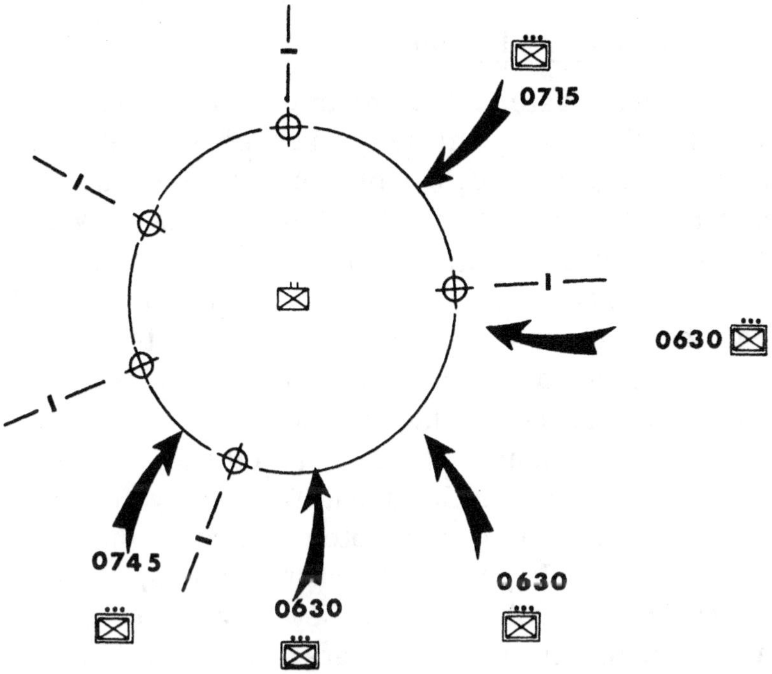

Encirclement permits the VC to exploit their mobility and adaptability and also facilitates interdiction of enemy withdrawal routes through establishment of ambushes or obstacles on routes over which the enemy might reinforce.

The Viet Cong do not normally attempt to hold terrain. Rather, they seek to close with and destroy the opposing force, provided the circumstances overwhelmingly favor success. They strive for a disposition of forces that will limit the enemy's maneuver room and hinder his development of firepower. Maximum use is made of terrain for concealment and camouflage, observation and fields of fire.

d. Offensive Tactics

Deliberate, effective offensive action is the key to Viet Cong military successes. Viet Cong attacks are thoroughly planned and then quickly and ruthlessly executed. Maximum fire is delivered at the onset of the attack, at a predetermined time or upon order of the commander. After the attack has been completed, the VC immediately move from the area leaving only a small element to evacuate the dead and wounded and to remove weapons, ammunition, brass and other useful supplies from the battle area. When they feel that time does not allow complete clearing of the area, the residual elements hide what they can, planning to return and salvage what they leave. If no enemy reinforcements are anticipated and if the area is populated, the Viet Cong are almost certain to remain in the area and engage in propaganda activities. Viet Cong offensive actions are not designed to allow them to occupy, hold and deny strategic terrain. Rather, even major military actions are designed to inflict casualties on friendly forces and to erode the peoples' confidence in the government's ability to protect them. Viet Cong offensive actions are commonly characterized by surprise, speed, conditioning of the enemy and withdrawal--all of which facilitate Viet Cong goals.

→ SURPRISE. Viet Cong attacks endeavor to achieve surprise, hitting the enemy at a time, place and in a manner which is not anticipated. Surprise is not necessarily dependent on misleading the enemy. The enemy may know from the attendant situation that he will be attacked, but, if the Viet Cong efforts are effective, he will not know how, when, where, or with what strength the attack will be conducted.

➞ SPEED. Related to surprise is the element of speed. Viet Cong forces attack swiftly, withdraw quickly, disengage rapidly, and counter-attack without hesitation. Normally Viet Cong attacks last from 10 or 15 minutes to several hours, at most.

➞ CONDITIONING OF THE ENEMY. The Viet Cong, on occasions, will attempt to "condition" enemy installations into a state of vulnerability to attack. They try to generate conditions whereby the enemy underestimates Viet Cong potential. Ruses are created and false information is planted to create suspicion, doubt, hesitation, and confusion in the mind of the enemy. To further psychologically condition the enemy, the Viet Cong sometimes have the local population evacuate the area.

➞ WITHDRAWAL. Costly mistakes during the Viet Minh struggle taught the Vietnamese Communist leaders that planning the withdrawal was of equal importance to planning for other phases of an operation. This lesson has been well learned, with the result that the planning of the routes, timing and method of withdrawal is normally

treated in great detail. (See page 188 for detailed information on Viet Cong withdrawal tactics.)

e. Ambush

The ambush is the most common and probably the most effective form of combat employed by low level (guerrilla and local) Viet Cong units.

A most successful ambush technique employed by the Viet Cong features entrapment. (This tactic was exploited time and again by the Viet Minh against the French.) The trap is baited by a Viet Cong attack upon a fixed objective, for example, a stronghold. This prompts the dispatch of reaction forces in sufficient strength to provide worthwhile ambush targets. In the

Viet Cong planning of such operations, the type of terrain apparently plays a subordinate role. Instead, the main determining factors appear to be:

➞ The availability of superior VC forces in the area to cope with extended enemy reaction.

➞ The assured cooperation of the local populace to prevent betrayal of VC preparations.

➞ A suitable fixed objective for the initial VC attack, which could be expected to draw significant enemy reaction.

➞ The nearness of RVN forces which would be compelled to react using a predictable, canalized approach.

The climate and terrain of the Republic of Vietnam lend themselves to the successful execution of ambushes. The not-too-severe climate permits ambushing units to remain in place for extended periods of time without undue discomfort. These periods may exceed 48 hours. The terrain and jungle vegetation offer excellent hiding places at the ambush sites, and provide concealed routes to and from the selected location. They hope that the variety of terrain and vegetation will produce an element of uncertainty in the minds of U.S. or Vietnamese troops. "Where might the ambush take place? In the higher country, where the thick foliage and hilly contour provide hiding places, or along an open stretch of road sandwiched by wide, flat rice paddies?"

Viet Cong ambush sites are unpredictable. Sites are carefully selected to avoid establishment of a pattern which would enable friendly forces to predict ambushes. Obvious sites, such as ravines, stream beds, defiles, etc., are often avoided in favor of open rice fields, villages or other unlikely sites. Some attacks have been made in villages in the hope that friendly forces, reluctant to harm innocent civilians, would not respond in full force.

Movement to the ambush site is over covered routes which avoid villages and roads as much as possible. Training and preplanning allow individuals to move directly to their positions upon entering the ambush site. On occasions when terrain does not offer the desired concealment, the Viet Cong choose not to occupy positions until the last possible moment. In the interim, they remain close by with only scouts in position. When the enemy is near, the scouts sound the alarm for rapid occupation of the site. Once in position, the ambush party imposes movement and noise discipline. Prior and subsequent to occupation, the Viet Cong have been known to prohibit the populace from occupying any part of the anticipated battleground.

Troop dispositions depend on Viet Cong strength, enemy strength, and terrain. Regardless of disposition, the force is divided into sections, each being assigned and enemy target. Usually two-thirds of the force attack the enemy. Up to one-third of the force, using mines, barricades or other obstacles, is employed to prevent the enemy's escape. Any reserve is deployed to fill areas of potential weakness. Security teams are usually placed on the flanks and to the rear. Their mission is to warn of, or ambush, enemy reinforcements. Viet Cong disengagement is called for when there is some possibility of successful enemy reinforcement.

Ambush targets include dismounted troops, vehicles and watercraft.

→ DISMOUNTED TROOPS. Many successful ambushes are conducted against small or poorly trained units. Such units are lulled by what apparently is an unlikely site. In this type of an ambush the VC are extremely vulnerable to organized

counteraction, especially flanking movements which threaten their escape routes. If escape routes are being threatened or if the VC are being outfought by a superior unit, they will immediately attempt to break contact.

→ VEHICLES AND CONVOYS. This is one of the most difficult ambushes to counter. The technique makes the vehicles' speed a liability rather than an asset. Flank and point security is difficult to provide, and often when provided it has not proved effective. Strict convoy discipline is essential, for once a convoy is stopped, it is easily destroyed. Troops are easily surprised and grouped into easy targets for automatic weapons. The machine gunners on armed vehicles are especially good targets in their exposed positions; other troops must dismount before they can engage the VC. When firing at vehicles, the VC most frequently adjust firepower at a 90-degree angle to the road, and direct it toward either end of the formation. When direct fire on the end vehicle is impossible, mortars are used. Viet Cong techniques have achieved a high degree of sophistication. For example, the VC often place mines on the inside of a curve. When a vehicle detonates the mine, the force of the explosion, coupled with the centrifugal force acting on the vehicle as it turns, causes it to overturn. Passengers are spilled out in front of the VC on an almost exactly predictable spot. The body of the vehicle shelters the VC from the force of the blast and allows them to be close to their target, ready to pounce.

→ WATERCRAFT. This type of ambush is used most effectively by the VC in the delta region where inland waterways constitute the principal means of transport for the rice farmer and all others engaged in economic activity. The ambush is conducted near a curve or gulf where craft move at lower speeds. Defensive preparations are further complicated by the fact that prior to counteraction, craft must make their way to shore. During this movement point and flank security are limited. VC troops cleverly deploy around probable landing sites to surprise reaction forces attempting to break up the ambush.

Ambush sites are kept in strict security until the ambush is sprung. The site is maintained in a constant state of readiness. Often after preparing the site, the ambush party moves off into a safe area to await the moment of attack. Guards

left in the area apprehend and detain local inhabitants who may have strayed into the ambush site. Thus, there are no suspicious persons reported in the area, and none to be found by Vietnamese reconnaissance patrols. The safe area might be a wooded section, a tunnel network, or a river, in which VC, using reeds for breathing, have reportedly hidden underwater for moderate periods of time. These techniques keep the area secure, prevent compromise, and heighten the surprise effect. Experience has demonstrated that the Viet Cong are using the same ambush sites more than once. In many cases it has been noted that these frequently used sites have permanent and elaborate firing positions. The fields of fire are carefully prepared, including holes in treetop areas through which mortar shell trajectories are plotted.

During withdrawals or disengagement, the Viet Cong occasionally organize impromptu ambushes, conducted by small elements attempting to delay, disrupt, and disorganize the pursuing enemy. No attempt is made to close with or destroy the opposing troops because the VC in this instance are usually at a disadvantage. The purpose is simply to enable major elements to break contact.

f. The Raid

Another successful Viet Cong offensive tactic is the raid. Careful selection and reconnaissance of the target is important. Since the conservation of VC forces is a paramount consideration, the most vulnerable targets are usually sought; e.g., isolated villages, security posts, paramilitary organizations or government offices. A raid is often coordinated with an ambush of the relieving force.

The VC raid force consists of the following:

→ Specialized elements (bangalore torpedo teams, demolition teams, grenade teams, and ladder teams).

→ Firepower units (automatic rifles, light and heavy machineguns, and mortars).

256-290 O-67—13

→ Assault troops (one or two infantry assault units).

→ Liaison, communications, reconnaissance and command.

Captured VC documents and information gained from prisoners and defectors seem to bear out the fact that two types of raids exist. In one document they are called "overt and cover" raids. In another, they are known as "superior strength" raids and "secret and surprise data" raids. A third document uses the nomenclature "power tactics and limited tactics." Whatever names are chosen to describe them, these two tactics are defined as follows:

→ Power Tactics: The Viet Cong employ forces and firepower more than ten times greater than that of the adversary in order to overpower enemy positions.

→ Limited (or surprise) Tactics: The VC approach the target secretly and attempt to breach enemy fortifications and security without being discovered. This has been a favorite tactic of the VC.

The power raid makes the maximum use of firepower and shock action to demoralize and paralyze the enemy from the very beginning. With support from the firepower units, the specialized elements move in first. They clear lanes for the assault troops by blasting fences and wire, exploding mines, uncovering traps and underground defense systems, and bridging ditches or moats. As one member of the specialized element falls, another immediately replaces him in a human wave type breaching operation. Once the lanes are cleared, the two assault units begin advancing toward the target, one behind the other, with the rear unit providing a base of fire. If the lead unit falters, it is replaced by the second unit. When the assault units overrun the target, the results of the battle are determined and quick withdrawal is effected. During the withdrawal phase, all dead and wounded VC, valuable equipment, and prisoners of war are carried away. The firepower element withdraws first under the cover of a rear-guard team, which withdraws last. Because it is usually necessary to begin fighting at a distance, more VC casualties are incurred in power raids than in surprise raids.

The surprise raid depends primarily upon stealth, not power. First, the firepower units quietly advance close to the target. The specialized elements go about their work quietly, cutting fences and wires rather than blasting them, removing mines rather than exploding them and discovering traps by hand rather than by inspection. The involved nature of the task accounts for the specialized element being larger than is required by the power raid unit. Once the raid is discovered, remaining obstacles are blasted and "power" tactics are resorted to. Because the surprise raid attacks an unsuspecting and unprepared enemy, it usually results in fewer Viet Cong casualties than does the power raid. However, since the surprise raid requires a relatively great amount of time to breach fortifications, an alert defense poses a serious obstacle.

g. The Meeting Engagement

Refusal to engage on any but their own terms is a principle to which the VC have attempted to adhere; however, their forces are trained to cope with unexpected meetings with the enemy. A meeting engagement is defined in VC doctrine as "an unexpected and sudden confrontation of two opposing forces, neither of which is aware of the other's strength, weapons, composition, or mission." Since no offensive plan will have been devised for the particular situation, the VC realize they will be at a disadvantage. Doctrine calls for avoiding this situation; however, being aware that there will be instances where this cannot be done, they have formulated three objectives to accomplish when the meeting occurs:

- ➔ Be the first to deploy troops to critical terrain.
- ➔ Be the first to open fire.
- ➔ Be the first to assault.

They teach that the first unit to deploy to key terrain will gain important tactical advantages. By so doing, they attempt to force the enemy into an unfavorable and perhaps untenable position. In seeking to be the first to fire, the VC hope to create sudden and extreme confusion by forcing the enemy to hastily deploy under fire. Application of this theory requires Viet Cong troop movements to be preceded by "look-out teams" or scouts. In addition, rear security and flank security are provided. The distances to which security elements reconnoiter are dependent on the terrain. When the enemy's presence is detected, rapid and silent notification is passed to the commander and the scouts immediately take positions which offer them observation and fields of fire. Concurrently, the commander performs a hasty estimate of the situation and deploys the main force. If these actions allow advantageous terrain to be occupied, fire is commenced as a prelude to the assault. When good terrain cannot be quickly occupied, the scouts open fire to pin down the enemy. The commander, in the meantime, maneuvers his other troops to positions from which sufficient fire superiority can be gained to permit assault. When a favorable situation cannot be obtained due to enemy strength or terrain, the commander is taught to continue the fire fight with a few elements and hastily disengage. Once the main body has broken contact, the forward elements execute a retrograde movement.

A captured document sums up the Viet Cong approach to meeting engagements as follows:

"Therefore, the side which ... practices good scouting procedures, has well-trained personnel thoroughly acquainted with their jobs, and cool-headed, active and determined leadership--will have the initiative and will occupy good terrain features first, open fire first, and assault first. This side will be the winner."

# # # # #

3. ENEMY WITHDRAWAL TACTICS

The withdrawal phase is as much a part of VC planning as the approach march and the attack. Rally points for the platoon, company and battalion are established as are routes to and between these points. Instructions are provided in detail concerning the method of withdrawal, usually in the order: security elements, wounded, dead, captured materiel and rear guard elements (Sketch III-1).

Viet Cong withdrawal is begun only on a prearranged signal. The route of advance may be used as the route of withdrawal, particularly when the the operation is successful and there is little fear of enemy reinforcements, aircraft or artillery fire. In some instances, antipursuit defenses (mines, booby traps, etc.) are prepared during the approach march and armed during the withdrawal. VC support units, such as antiaircraft and artillery, not in close contact with the enemy, frequently use same routes for advance and withdrawal.

It should be noted that the VC have a negligible ability to support a withdrawal with indirect fire weapons. His chief defenses against pursuit are the use of rapid movement, ambushes, booby traps and snipers along his routes of withdrawal.

Recognition of the VC doctrine of emergency dispersal is of vital importance to successful pursuit. The VC commander may exercise one of two options, both of which are based on prior planning. He may elect to withdraw his force as a unit(s) or order dispersal into small groups. If emergency dispersal should be required due to

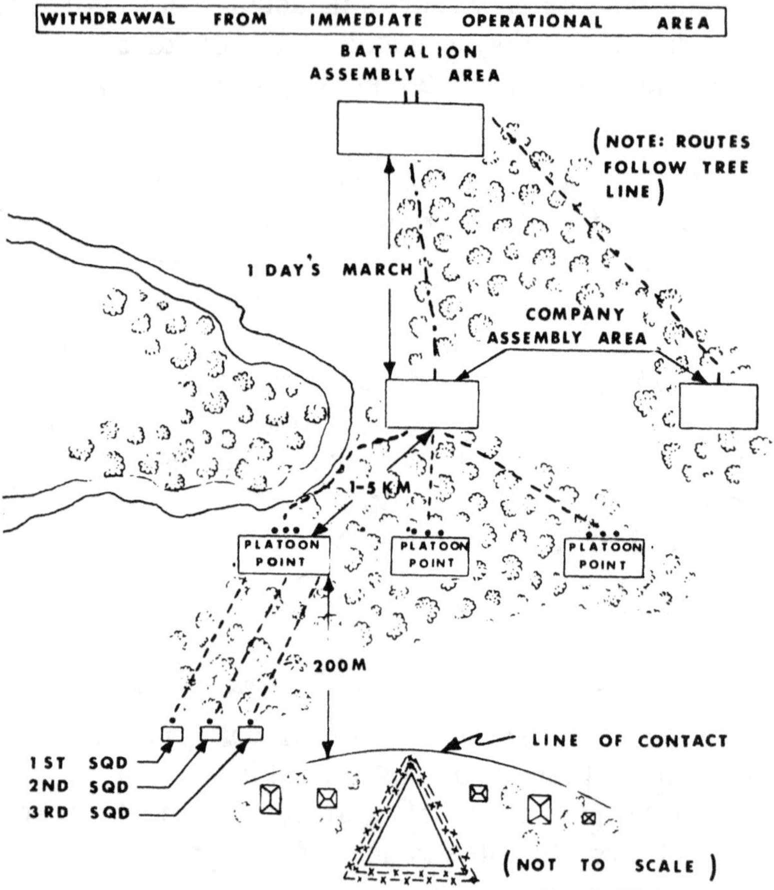

Sketch III-1

pursuit, blocking of the withdrawal route or intensive air effort, small unit leaders take over again, possibly ordering total dispersal on a man for man basis. If the unit commander sends a few men off in different directions to draw fire and mislead the aircraft, when dispersing as individuals and being pursued by ground forces,

VC will seek concealment in the local area in preference to panic and purposeless flight. The individual's knowledge of fieldcraft, evasion techniques, and familiarity with the local area are decisive factors. If pursued to a settlement, he is taught to hide his weapon and other equipment and demand concealment from the villagers whose fear of possible reprisal from the VC may provide him temporary protection. His personal safety is the VC's only responsibility. If VC personnel have to hide out for weeks before returning to their unit, this is acceptable as they have no requirement to be back by reveille, and in their absence, they leave no vital installations unguarded or in danger of attack.

# # # # #

4. VIET CONG AMBUSH

A number of lessons can be learned from a large scale Viet Cong ambush of a Vietnamese Marine battalion while it was moving from Hue to Dong Ha by motorized convoy. The action was a classical example of an ambush and resulted in 137 Vietnamese Marine casualties.

However, prompt reaction to the ambush by the battalion, coupled with the speedy arrival of a reaction force prevented a serious defeat from becoming catastrophic.

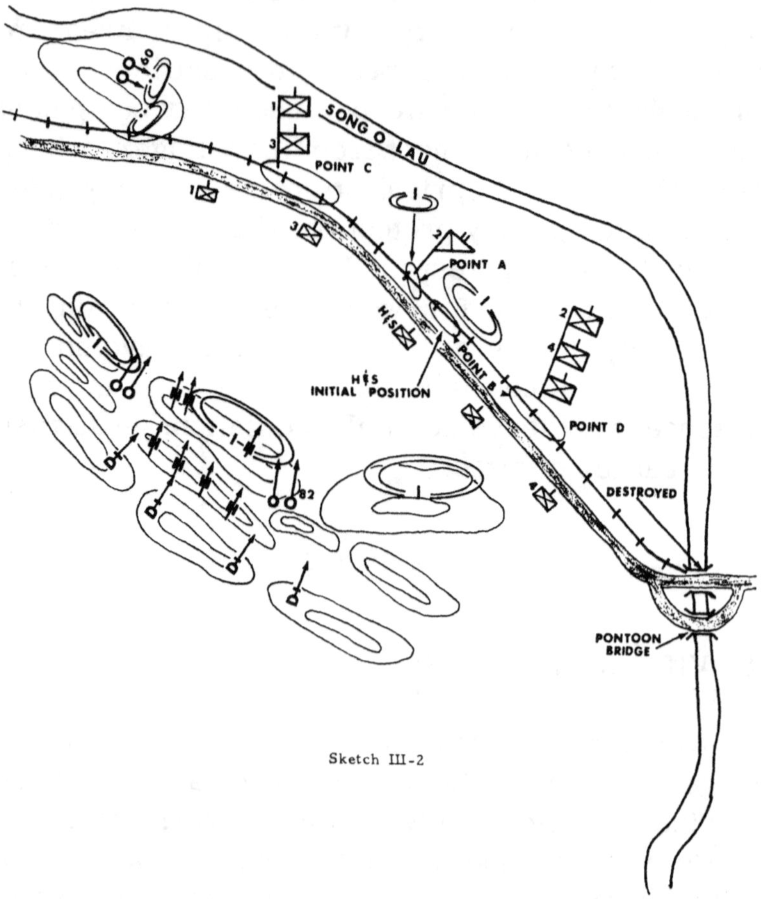

Sketch III-2

A narration of this action and the lessons to be learned therefrom are as follows:

a. Mission of Battalion: Move by motorized convoy from Hue via Quang Tri City to Dong Ha in preparation for future operations.

b. Intelligence: Available intelligence indicated that no major contact or ambush had occurred along the route of march in the past ten months.

c. Weather: The weather was hot with temperatures ranging from 85 to 90 degrees during the day. Skies were clear and visibility was excellent.

d. Terrain: The terrain was generally open with rolling hills interspersed with short shrub lines and thin stands of trees. Vegetation was heavier northeast of the road, with a dense tree line at a distance of 300 meters.

e. Observation and Fields of Fire: Southwest of the road, observation ranged up to 500 meters with excellent fields of fire. Ranges greater than 500 meters were in defilade from the road. To the northeast, observation from the road extended approximately 75 meters to the top of a slight rise which masked the terrain farther east. Excellent fields of fire were available for all weapons emplaced on this rise.

f. Support Available: One battery of 105mm Howitzers and one battery of 155mm Howitzers of the 12th ARVN Field Artillery Battalion were to support the move during the initial stages. Initially it was planned to have a U.S. L-19 aircraft on station for visual reconnaissance and communication assistance, but just prior to execution of the movement, this support was canceled and replaced by a VNAF L-19 which joined the column approximately five kilometers north of Hue.

g. Narration of Action:

Troops were tactically loaded on vehicles by company. The order of march was 1st Company, 3rd Company, H&S Company and the CP Group, 2nd Company, and 4th Company. Personnel were required to face outboard and have weapons at the ready. Artillery fires were planned along the route of march and an artillery FO team was attached to the battalion. The battalion commander's anti-ambush instructions to the battalion were to dismount, form up by units, and stand and fight as he directed.

The battalion crossed the I.P. at 0730 and moved toward Quang Tri City. At approximately 0830 it entered the ambush site and was taken under fire by an estimated Viet Cong battalion. (Location of all units at various times throughout the action is graphically depicted in Sketch III-2.) The VNAF L-19 aircraft had failed to discover the enemy ambush force and no warning was received.

Initially, a heavy volume of accurate mortar and recoilless rifle fire was received as well as heavy small arms fire. The convoy came to a halt immediately as three trucks were hit and deployed along the side of the road. Positions along the road afforded little cover and concealment and as enemy fire improved in accuracy, casualties began to mount.

From the battalion's position, backblast from recoilless weapons was easily observed along the crest of the low, rolling hills to the southwest. Also small groups of enemy troops could be seen maneuvering toward the road.

At this point, the Battalion Commander ordered the rifle companies and the CP group to move to the relative sanctuary of a railroad cut, 60-75 meters northeast of their present position along the road. No fire had yet been received from this area.

The movement to the railroad cut was conducted simultaneously by all companies. However, as the units closed on the position, H&S Company, the CP Group, 2nd Company, and 4th Company were met with a withering volume of small arms fire and hand grenades from an estimated two companies of Viet Cong in well camouflaged positions along the northeastern side of the railroad cut. In the initial fusillade, the Battalion Commander was seriously wounded and virtually the entire CP group was killed outright or incapacitated by wounds (Point A).

In the vicinity of the decimated CP group, 15 to 20 Marines had managed to gain the railroad cut and were establishing a perimeter, when they were struck by machinegun fire directed down the railroad tracks into their left flank. The machine gun fire was followed by a vicious enemy infantry attack of company size from the northeast. All the Marines holding in the cut were either killed or wounded. The successful completion of this phase of the enemy plan left the CP totally decimated and inoperable.

Approximately 75 meters southeast, down the railroad cut, the remainder of H&S Company had formed into a defensive perimeter (Point B). This group was engaged in close combat with an estimated VC company which was positioned 20-25 yards to the northeast. After the successful VC assault on Point A, this position became untenable and H&S Company pivoted south and fought its way to the 2nd and 4th Companies which were located at Point D. Several casualties were sustained during this move from mines laid along the railroad cut.

While the preceding actions were taking place, 1st and 3rd Companies had formed a joint perimeter at Point C and were establishing a heavy base of fire in a 360 degree arc.

At this point in the action (5-6 minutes had elapsed since initial contact) the enemy had succeeded in dividing the battalion into two separate forces 500 meters apart. The perimeters were not mutually supporting and in view of the heavy casualties already sustained, it was decided to stand fast and await reinforcements.

Approximately five minutes after the engagement began, a U.S. L-19 arrived on station with a Vietnamese artillery observer aboard. Artillery fire on enemy concentrations began about ten minutes later. Shortly thereafter, a U.S. Air Force forward air controller arrived and commenced calling in airstrikes. During the entire engagement, aircraft were subjected to heavy anti-aircraft fire from weapons emplaced along the high ground to the southwest.

Approximately 20-25 minutes after initiation of the ambush, the Viet Cong began breaking contact. Enemy units northeast of the road began withdrawing toward the river and those to the southwest were observed moving rapidly to the west. Devastating air attacks coupled with an intense volume of small arms fire from the two friendly positions inflicted considerable casualties on the Viet Cong during this phase.

The excellent air support alleviated some of the pressure on the battalion and steps were taken to link up the two separated forces.

Forty-five minutes after the initial contact, a U.S. Marine rifle company arrived at the ambush site and immediately and aggressively pursued the Viet Cong. The Company moved as far as the high grounds on which the enemy had emplaced the majority of his force during the ambush, and continued to pursue by fire.

By 1200, a three battalion ARVN force, assisted by two U.S. Marine Companies, were in the area and had succeeded in trapping the Viet

Cong. The reaction part of the engagement lasted three days and resulted in 223 enemy KIA in addition to the 52 that had been killed by the Marine battalion caught in the ambush.

h. Lessons Learned:

The Viet Cong have for many years demonstrated an ability to execute ambushes of this nature without premature disclosure of their positions. However, this particular ambush was conducted in broad daylight, by a large Viet Cong force which was encumbered by heavy crew served weapons and within three kilometers of bivouacked major friendly units. Effective patrolling and well placed listening posts would have surely provided some indication of the presence of an enemy force of this size.

The enemy commander, who must be given credit for establishing the classic ambush, made two glaring errors which caused him to incur heavy casualties during the withdrawal phase. First, he miscalculated the time required to introduce a reaction force. Second, he failed to provide for an adequate covered and concealed withdrawal route for his southwestern elements. Units withdrawing to the southwest had to move through wide open terrain for 3000 meters and presented friendly artillery and air with superb targets. On the other hand, units withdrawing to the northeast were afforded a heavy forest canopy and escaped unharmed.

The initial decimation of the CP group, and the subsequent death of the Battalion Commander, left the battalion in crucial straits for approximately fifteen minutes. The battle quickly evolved into two separate and distinct actions with loose overall control. The southern element, Point D, under the command of the Battalion Executive Officer, fought a rugged, face-to-face encounter with a dug-in and determined enemy and managed to hold its own. The northern element, Point C, while out of the primary killing zone, and not having to contend with enemy units close-in to their positions, took the brunt of recoilless rifle and mortar fire in good order. They were able to return a heavy volume of effective fire. The key factors in avoiding the disaster that was so imminent in the first fifteen minutes of the engagement was the maintenance of the unit integrity of the rifle companies, the skillful maneuvering of these companies by their commanders, and the outright doggedness, determination and raw courage of individual Marines.

The U.S. Marine Advisor was moving with the CP group when it came under fire. In the ensuing action he was able to observe enemy troops at close range. They were expertly camouflaged and all wore the standard fiber VC helmet covered with freshly gathered vegetation. All of the Viet Cong observed wore a cape type garment made of camouflage material. At the introduction of U.S. FAC aircraft, a platoon of Viet Cong were observed to "hit the deck," arrange the camouflage cape over their backs and remain motionless. Aircraft flew over them as low as 500 feet and never noticed their presence.

# # # # #

5. VIET CONG TUNNEL CHARACTERISTICS

Tunnel complexes are used extensively by the Viet Cong as hiding places, caches for food and weapons, headquarters complexes and for protection against air attack and artillery fire. Many tunnel complexes are the result of many years of labor, some in all probability having been initiated as early as World War II, with extensions and improvements added throughout the campaigns against the French, and up until the present time.

The first characteristic of a tunnel complex is the superb use of camouflage. Entrances and exits are concealed, bunkers are camouflaged and within the tunnel complex itself, concealed side tunnels, hidden trap doors and dead end tunnels are employed to confuse the attacker. Spoil from the tunnel system is normally distributed over a very wide area, but on occasion it has been left in piles close to an entrance where natural growth is luxuriant.

In many cases, a trap door will lead to a short change of direction or a change of level, followed by a second trap door, a second change of direction and a third trap door opening again into the main tunnel. Trap doors are of several types; they may be concrete covered by dirt, hard packed dirt reinforced by wire, or a "basin" type consisting of a frame filled with dirt. The latter type is particularly difficult to locate.

Booby traps are used extensively both inside and outside entrances and exit trap doors. Grenades are frequently placed in trees adjacent to the exit, with an activation wire which may be pulled by a person underneath the trap door or by movement of the trap door itself.

In some cases tunnel complexes are multilevel with the storage and hiding rooms generally found on the lower levels. Entrance to the lower level is usually through concealed trap doors which are boobytrapped with explosives or punji sticks. Air or water locks which act as "fire walls," preventing blast, fragments, gas or smoke from passing from one section of a tunnel to another have been encountered on numerous occasions.

The following photographs and sketches depict in detail the extensive and skillfully constructed underground tunnel networks and hiding places of the Viet Cong:

Arrangement of material in the house appeared suspicious.

A board is found under the arrangement of bottles, baskets and jugs.

Several Viet Cong were discovered hiding in this hole.

CONCEALED TUNNEL ENTRANCES

Sketch III-3

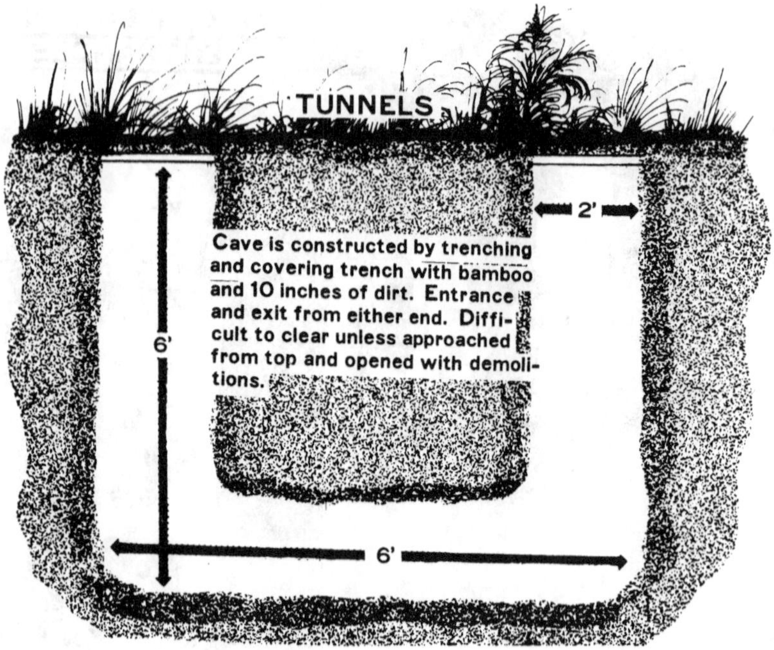
TUNNELS
2'
Cave is constructed by trenching and covering trench with bamboo and 10 inches of dirt. Entrance and exit from either end. Difficult to clear unless approached from top and opened with demolitions.
6'
6'

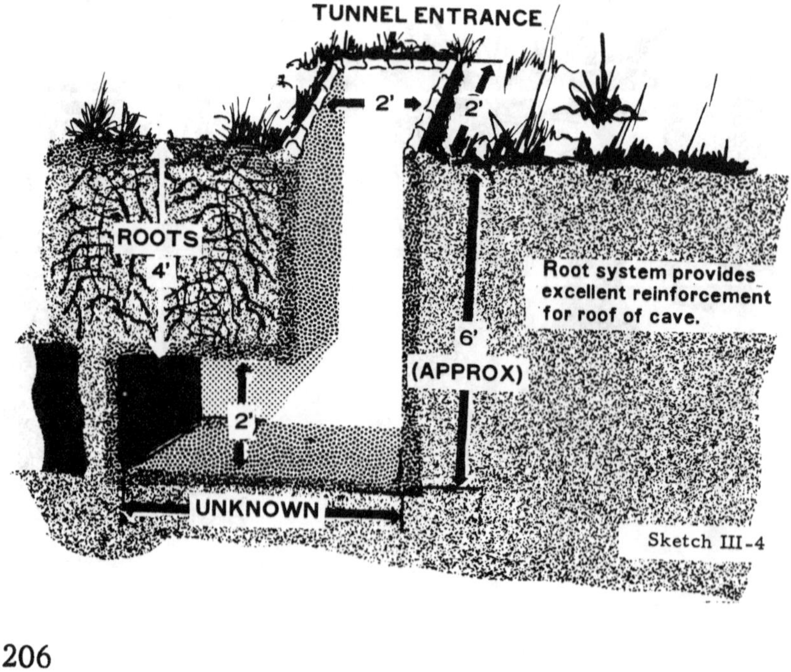
TUNNEL ENTRANCE
2'
2'
ROOTS
4'
Root system provides excellent reinforcement for roof of cave.
6'
(APPROX)
2'
UNKNOWN

Sketch III-4

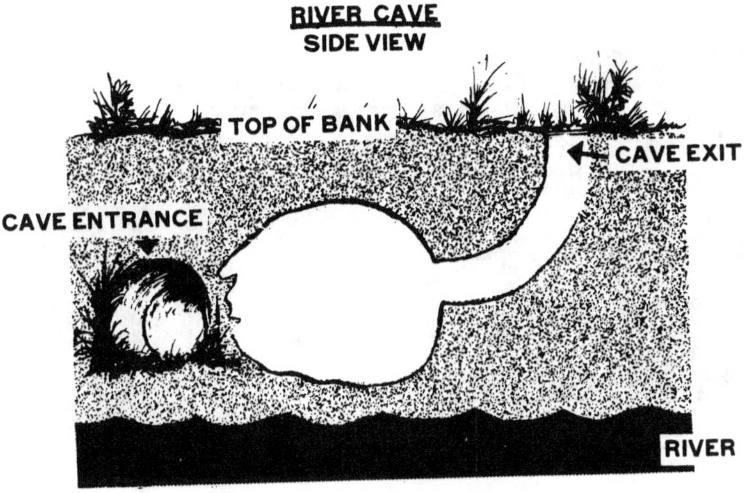
RIVER CAVE
SIDE VIEW
TOP OF BANK
CAVE EXIT
CAVE ENTRANCE
RIVER

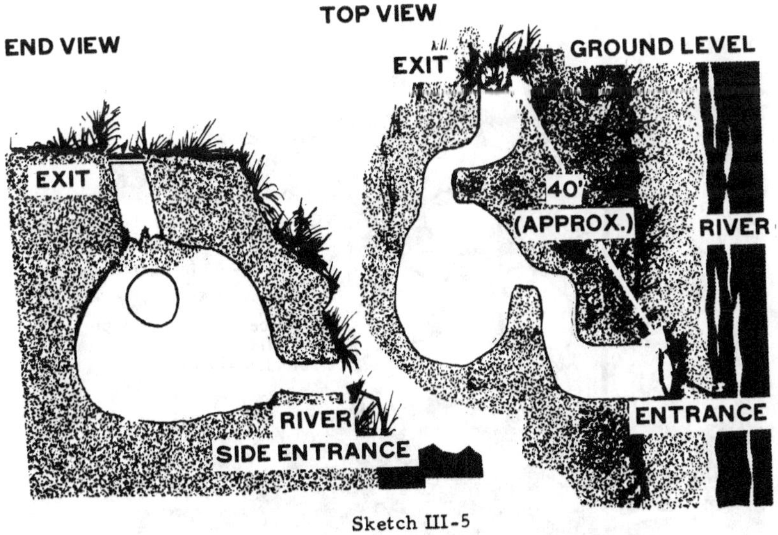
TOP VIEW
END VIEW
EXIT
GROUND LEVEL
EXIT
40'
(APPROX.)
RIVER
RIVER
SIDE ENTRANCE
ENTRANCE

Sketch III-5

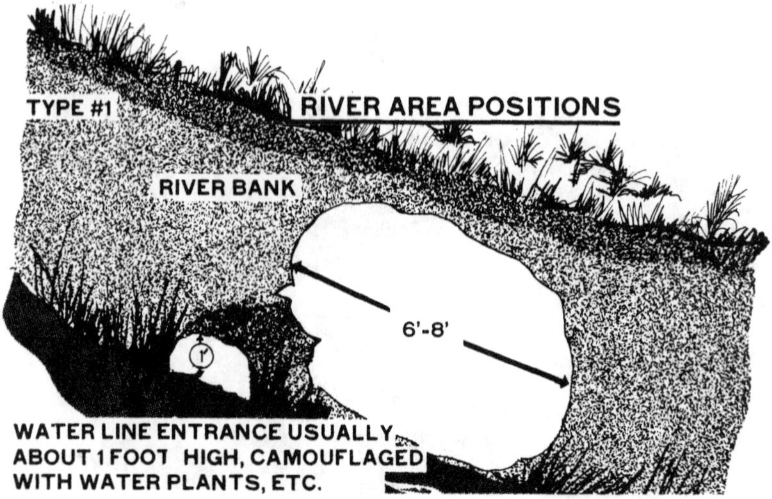

This type of cave usually has entrance from below water line to about 1 foot above. There is about a 2 foot approach leading to the main room which is circular and about 6 to 8 feet across. Can only be entered from the water.

Sketch III-6

HIDING PLACES
UNDER LOCAL HOMES
CONCEALED ENTRANCE
UNDER A COOKING POT
VENT
UPPER TRENCH
LOWER TUNNEL AND HIDING PLACE
Sketch III-7

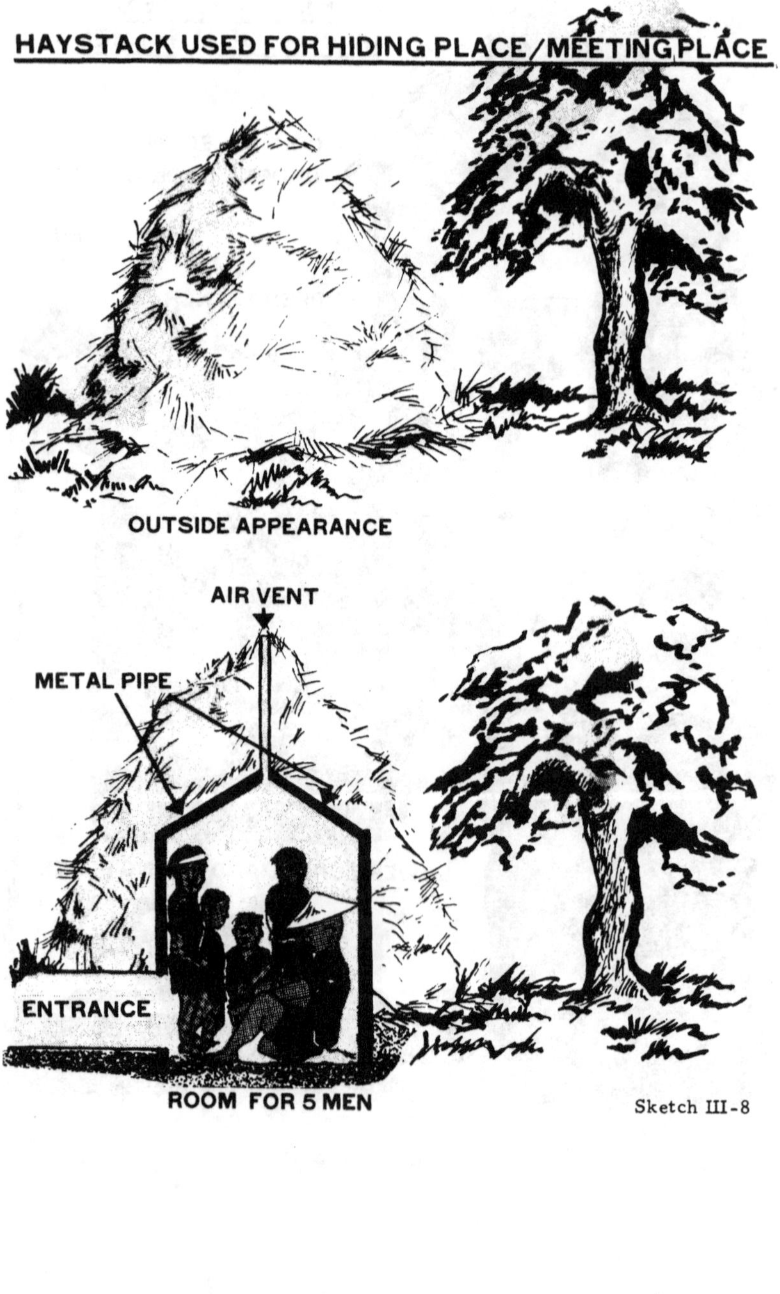
HAYSTACK USED FOR HIDING PLACE/MEETING PLACE
OUTSIDE APPEARANCE
AIR VENT
METAL PIPE
ENTRANCE
ROOM FOR 5 MEN
Sketch III-8

WELL-TUNNEL COMPLEX

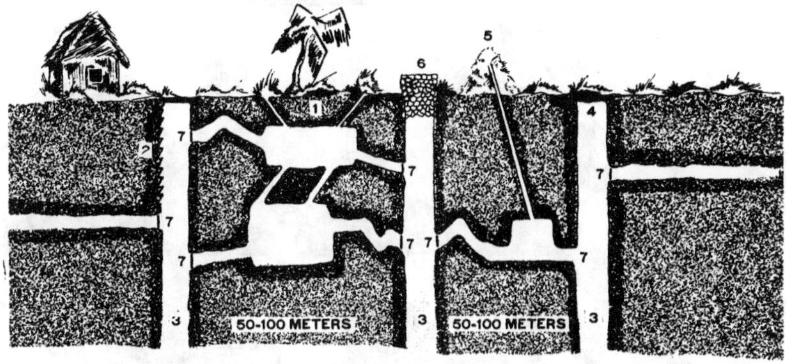

1. AIR VENTS
2. NOTCHED DIRT STEPS
3. WATER
4. CAMOUFLAGED COVER
5. CAMOUFLAGED VENT HOLE
6. NORMAL WELL TOP
7. CAMOUFLAGED ENTRANCE COVERS

Well-Tunnel Complex above was discovered near Ben Cat in September 1965. It is a series of multi-bunker tunnels with angled connecting tunnels. Each bunker has space available for 15 to 20 men. The entrance to and exits from the VC bunkers are built into the walls of actual or simulated wells which are 20 to 30 meters deep. Access to these skillfully camouflaged entrances and exits is by way of notched dirt steps or by the use of notched bamboo pole ladders.

Sketch III-9

VC UNDERGROUND BUNKER

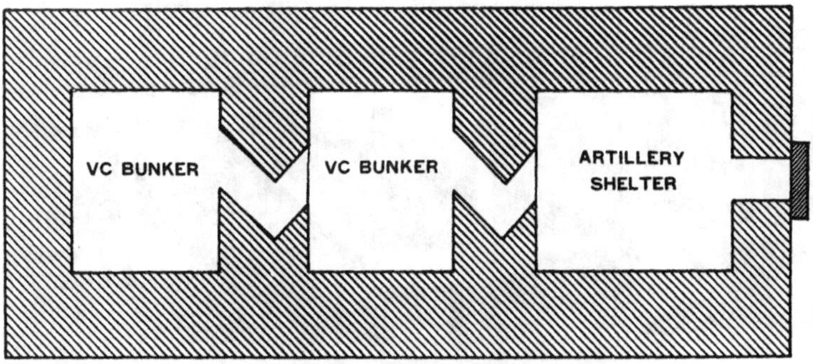

VC ENTRANCE SKILLFULLY CAMOUFLAGED

Bunker shown above was discovered in the vicinity of Da Nang during June/July 1965 by ARVN units.

It is a multi-bunker tunnel with angled connecting tunnels. Each bunker has space available for 3 or 4 men. The entrance to the VC bunker is built into the wall of the artillery shelter and skillfully camouflaged. A second bunker is concealed behind the first; each entrance in turn is camouflaged on the outside by local inhabitants.

Sketch III-10

GUERRILLA BASE

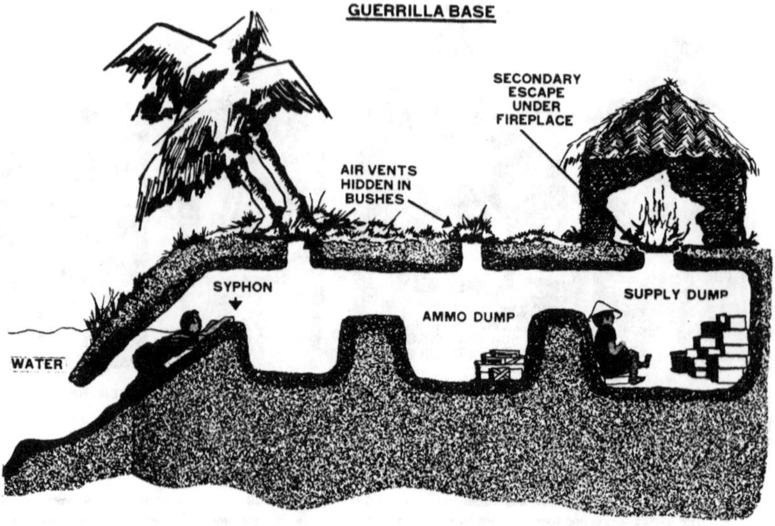

Sketch III-11

A TYPICAL VC FORTIFIED VILLAGE

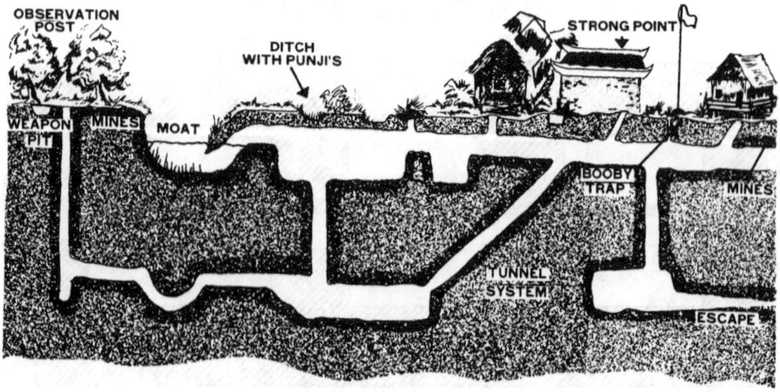

Sketch III-12

6. VIET CONG REACTION

The following quote from a captured Viet Cong document points up the reaction of the enemy to a well planned, aggressively executed friendly operation supported by modern firepower.

"The enemy sweep was different this time. Their firepower, was more violent, and they used new tactics. For this reason, our forces moved forward discouraged and afraid. The health of our forces was poor, because they were continuously active. Confidence was not high (especially among the guerrillas). Combat hamlets, hampered by the floods and bombings, were not reinforced. We did not have experience fighting Americans and Koreans, and did not grasp their weak points in strategy and tactics. Because we could not determine enemy strong points and weak points, our forces were demoralized and afraid. These were our difficulties: The enemy was very destructive. Our demoralized masses, cadre, and guerrillas left the villages, and we lost support. The forceful enemy attacks split us up, and we lost contact with some villages and districts. During the early stages we lost contact from district to province. While the enemy conducted a big sweep and was destroying violently, the masses were further demoralized by the lack of cadre confidence, and the nonchalant soldiers who ran far away (this is our principal difficulty)."

# # # # #

7. TIPS ON ENEMY TACTICS

→ The Viet Cong sometimes use an advanced patrol point to gather information and reconnoiter a proposed patrol route. The advanced point might consist of only one man and it may precede the actual patrol by many hours. By interrogating villagers and by observing friendly patrols the advanced point is able to determine areas most likely to be used by friendly patrols and locations of friendly ambushes. Various signals, including seemingly innocent activities by local civilians, are employed to warn the patrol.

→ The enemy has used specially organized and equipped units against Marine artillery positions on at least two occasions. In both cases, the land communication lines were cut just prior to the VC assault. Aiming stakes were used to point toward Marine automatic weapons and points along the protective barbed wire where entry could be made.

→ The enemy uses low level agents to acquire detailed information about U.S. personnel, positions and installations. The agents are usually laborers, barbers, farmers, soft drink vendors, bar girls and the like.

→ The Viet Cong have the capability to monitor radio transmissions and tap wire lines. Marine units have discovered considerable evidence of this.

→ The most common VC hiding place is underground. The means of hiding personnel and equipment underground range from simple "spider trap" holes to elaborate tunnel systems. From the surface, VC underground installations are extremely difficult to detect. Entrances are located under fireplaces, food storage bins and water containers, and in real or dummy heads--any place where a hole can be easily concealed.

→ The enemy has attempted to gain a tactical advantage on many occasions by using English phrases. This is an old trick and was employed by the Chinese during the Korean War and by the Japanese during World War II. Two such instances encountered in Vietnam are as follows: Elements of a U.S. division had a number of Viet Cong in a crossfire when the VC called out in English, "Hold your fire; we're friendly; don't shoot." On another occasion, when mortar fire was adjusted on a VC unit, the battalion mortar platoon heard the following radio transmission on their frequency, "Cease fire, cease fire; you are hitting friendly troops."

→ Engagements with the Viet Cong forces indicate that they are fairly well trained, organized and adequately equipped for their mission. Marksmanship has generally been excellent. Viet Cong probing and harassing actions against friendly CPs and perimeter security forces have been conducted between sunset and 2400 or from 0500 until BMNT. Contact with the Viet Cong at other hours has usually been a result of U.S. initiated action or from isolated snipers.

256-290 O-67—15

→ Viet Cong camps are generally close to major trail networks and water.

→ Viet Cong firing positions are often characterized by excellent camouflage; good cover to include small caves in foxholes as protection against overhead fire; small firing ports; ideal site selection such as strategically located trees for snipers. Often the VC dig into the middle of bamboo clusters or into the rear of giant ant hills. Spider holes along rice field dikes are often used by the enemy. Stream banks in contested areas are sometimes lined with trenches and fighting holes and provide a concealed escape route for harassing and delaying forces.

→ The Viet Cong are very skillful in sniping from well camouflaged tree and ground positions. They normally get off a quick series of well aimed shots and then either cease fire or move to a new location. Experience has shown that the Viet Cong frequently employ snipers in three man teams, using mutually supporting positions in a triangular configuration with about 50 meters on a side.

→ The VC take advantage of the kill emphasis, employing deception techniques such as deliberate exposure at far distances, prolonged sniper fire from a position, or open smoke fire to bait patrols into ambushes, crossfires and boobytrapped areas, or to steer them away from established base camps or other guerrilla facilities.

→ The enemy normally exercises his jamming capability during critical phases of an operation such as airstrikes, preparations or medical evacuations. Units must be alert to switch to the alternate frequency without order.

→ The Viet Cong often fire their mortars at friendly positions when these units are firing their indirect fire weapons. This makes counter-mortar radar detection difficult and causes confusion, sometimes leading to a cease fire by friendly elements in order to investigate the possibility of short rounds having been fired by friendly weapons. This practice should be carefully explained to all personnel so as to maintain confidence in our indirect fire weapons. It also underlines the importance of shell reporting.

→ The guerrilla is concerned about his wounded; he can less afford losses than his opponent. Wounded and dead are an important source of intelligence and the Viet Cong make every effort to retrieve their casualties. In some areas they attack with one leg wrapped in a length of vine or with a length of crude rope tied around their waist. This permits the soldier to be dragged hastily from the field should he become a casualty. During lulls in the attacks, Viet Cong will remove their dead and wounded from wire entanglements. In some cases VC casualties, particularly those with serious body-cavity wounds, are summarily killed on the battlefield or removed from the immediate battle area and then left unattended to die.

→ Following an engagement, friendly forces often find an area used by the Viet Cong as a forward aid station. Discarded items discovered there point to the limited treatment of applying dressings, and administering antibiotics and life-saving procedures to those selected for care. The local population may be forced to carry wounded from the forward areas back along the evacuation trails to base areas for further treatment. These villagers can be a source of information.

→ VC forces are alerted to Marine patrols approaching and exiting villages by the beating of drums and cans. Variations in cadence signal the approach to the village or exit therefrom.

→ There has been sufficient correlation between casualties received under varying conditions to conclude that the VC are attempting to be selective in their targets. Key personnel easily identified by distinctive equipment or actions have been selected by the VC as their initial targets in a fire fight. Officers, NCOs, radiomen and AR men are typical examples.

→ The Viet Cong normally establish harboring sites close to fresh water. Draws at the base of hills with fresh water available are favorite locations.

→ Angled holes dug into the ground have served as simple well camouflaged mortar firing positions. Mortar tubes with rocks, wooden blocks, or other simple field expedient base plates, are inserted into the pre-prepared angled holes, rapidly fired without adjustment, then the tubes are quickly camouflaged and left under bushes. Units searching for firing positions must be aware of these unconventional techniques in order to conduct a thorough search of the area.

→ VC may be using narcotics before going into battle. A U.S. officer who participated in a large operation in II Corps area reported that his men found two one-pound cans of opium in a communist position. He believed it to have been used as a narcotic rather than as a legitimate medicine. Fire fights in this operation were conducted frequently at a range of four to five feet. Some of the guerrillas appeared totally unaware of danger.

→ The VC are experts in the art of camouflage. One method of individual camouflage practiced by them is a bamboo lattice interlaced with three or four foot strips of green vegetation which is placed over the back and tied around the waist.

→ The VC place Claymore type mines around the edges of jungle clearings where helicopters might land in order to inflict personnel and material casualties on friendly forces. For use in aiming at helicopters, they plant a stake about 2.5 meters high and about 100 meters from the mine. The mine is remotely detonated when a helicopter is at an altitute of 2.5 to 5 meters.

→ In areas where only a few natural helicopter landing zones exist due to terrain obstacles such as dense vegetation, the VC anticipate probable landing areas for heliborne operations and prepare their defense by "spiking" the area. Sharp bamboo spikes, six to fifteen feet high and two to four inches in diameter, are planted close enough together to make landing or disembarking troops from a hover hazardous.

→To counter American helicopter tactics, the VC have developed a number of devices. One particularly lethal device consists of a number of grenades laid on a board which covers a hole containing a remotely controlled explosive charge. The explosive charge will launch the grenades 400 to 800 feet in the air before they explode.

→The Viet Cong have displayed a certain amount of discrimination in their mine warfare tactics. A document discovered by a Marine ambush party outlines specific instructions to village level cadre for the employment of mines. Local VC were forbidden to plant mines in a "disorderly" manner in hamlets, villages, on burial mounds and tombs, and on trails regularly used by the people. Mines were to be planted when patrols approached and then removed when they passed. Villagers living and working near these hidden mines were to be warned of their location. Mine fields or zones were assigned to groups of villagers who were responsible for the maintenance and marking. If mines were lost, villagers were severly disciplined.

# # # # #

Chapter IV: AVIATION

1. OPERATION YUMA

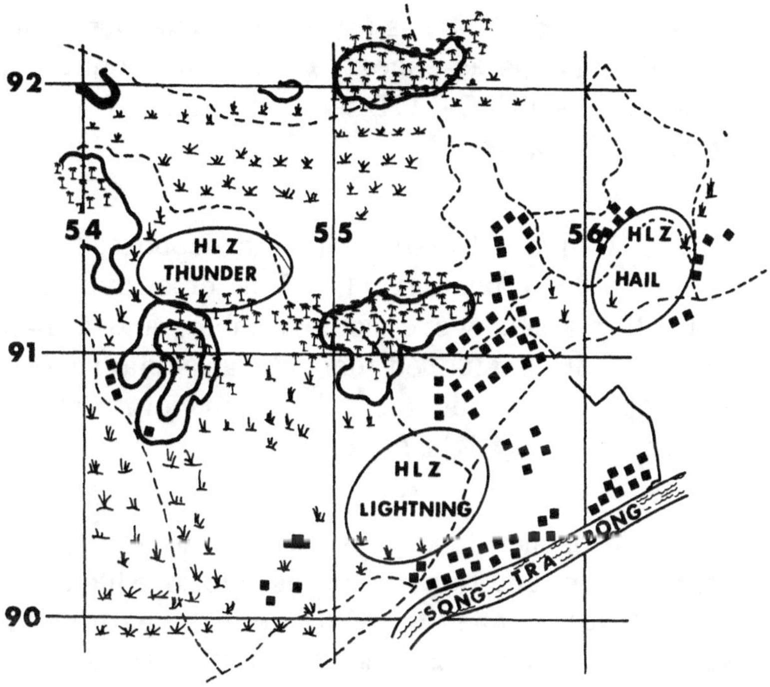

The following report of Operation Yuma, submitted by a Marine helicopter squadron, is an excellent example of a night helicopterborne assault which reaffirms many of the doctrinal techniques contained in FMFM 3-3, Helicopterborne Operations:

PLANNING

Operation YUMA consisted basically of an encirclement of a suspected Viet Cong village by elements of a Marine battalion. The helicopter assault involved the movement of 367 Marines into three closely grouped landing zones. (See sketch above.) Helicopters assigned to support the mission consisted of 26 UH-34Ds for troop transportation, 4 UH-1E gunships as escort, 1 UH-1E for command and control, and 1 C-117D as a flare ship. L-Hour was set at 0400.

On D-1 direct liaison with the supported unit was effected. As photographs of the objective area and landing zones were not available, and a map study was not considered adequate, an aerial reconnaissance was conducted for the principal troop commanders and flight leaders.

In view of the close proximity of the helicopter landing zones, and to provide positive zone identification, it was planned to infiltrate three pathfinder teams into the landing zones prior to L-Hour. The teams were to locate the designated zones, and at L-5 minutes activate a small strobe light in each zone.

As moonrise did not occur until 0329 local, and the moon was in its last quarter, continuous illumination was planned for the objective area commencing at L-10 minutes. With the prevailing wind forecast to be near calm and from the south-southeast, the flare drop pattern was placed to the north of the objective area.

Flights were designated by landing zone as a near simultaneous assault was desired. Twelve aircraft were to lift 176 troops into LZ Hail, eight aircraft were to lift 135 troops into LZ Lightning, and six aircraft were to lift 56 troops into LZ Thunder. Two waves, utilizing all aircraft in each wave, were planned for each zone. Four aircraft were to conduct a third lift into LZ Lightning. Timing was considered to be a critical factor in the initial assault wave.

For additional control and identification, each landing zone was assigned a color code--Red for LZ Lightning, Amber for LZ Hail, and Blue for LZ Thunder. Plans called for the two lead assault helicopters into each zone to place a battery operated landing zone marking light, of the designated color, at their landing point to mark the zone.

To facilitate rapid loading of troops, the pick-up zone was organized to accommodate three columns of aircraft. Each column was marked at its head by a light corresponding in color to each of the Landing Zones. Individual helicopter landing points within the column were marked with a single flare pot, with sufficient points designated to accommodate the full flight for that zone.

Helicopter approach and retirement routes were selected to afford the best control, minimal exposure to possible enemy fire and reasonable navigation check points. In view of almost total darkness existing at the time of the assault, major check points were plotted by Tacan bearing and distance from the Chu Lai Tacan.

With the number of helicopters involved and the difficulties inherent in night helicopter formation flight, the formation selected was a column of flights, column of divisions. Each flight followed the same approach route to an I.P. located three miles west of the landing zones, at which point the individual flight leaders commenced an approach to his designated landing zone. The order of flights was: LZ Hail (12 aircraft), LZ Thunder (6 aircraft), LZ Lightning (8 aircraft). Separation between flights to be no more than one minute. Retirement followed the same order with the route being to the northeast. To preclude wide divergence or bunching of aircraft, airspeeds were designated for climb, cruise and approach. Aircraft lighting was also specified, the major factor in this area being that the last aircraft of each division, or separate section, would illuminate the rotating beacon as a reference point for the orientation of the following flight leaders. Upon commencing the approach into the LZ, this light would be extinguished, indicating departure from the I.P. and final approach route descent.

CONDUCT OF THE OPERATION

Operations in the pick-up zone on the initial lift went very smoothly. The only problem noted was the tendency of hovering helicopters to extinguish the landing point flare pots.

On the initial wave into the landing zones, several minor problems developed:

→ The flare drop aircraft had difficulty in locating and maintaining station due to the fact that the Tacan facility was not operational. This necessitated voice control by the helicopter strike flight leader since the almost complete darkness precluded visual identification of geographic fixes by the flare plane.

→ Without the aid of Tacan, the flight leader had to rely extensively on DR navigation to approach the I.P.

→ Additionally, the Pathfinder teams had not been able to infiltrate to all three landing zones. Landing Zone Lightning was the only zone marked with a strobe light. With this reference point however, and the flare illumination, the other landing zones were discernible.

Subsequent waves into the zones proceeded with little difficulty. The positioning of the two colored lights in each zone was of immeasurable assistance in this build-up phase.

COMMUNICATIONS - CONTROL

The basic communications employed in the control of the various aircraft are as indicated below:

UHF - Two frequencies assigned.

→ All aircraft involved in this operation guarded a common UHF frequency. This frequency was a Tactical Air Direction frequency assigned by the Direct Air Support Center. All aircraft utilized the RIO net and were then directed to the common UHF.

→ The principal traffic on the UHF common was for the control of the flare plane. This control was exercised by the helicopter flight leader when approaching the zone. At other times the control was exercised by the HC (A) who was in a UH-1E slick in the company of the ground commander.

→ A second UHF frequency was assigned to TPQ drops after the landing was under way. It became apparent that TPQ radio traffic must have a separate net even though there was no crowding on this net during the landing.

FM - Two frequencies assigned.

→ All helicopters utilized a squadron common FM frequency for the loading zone traffic. This frequency was employed upon entering the loading area and the aircraft remained on that net until inbound to the target area.

→ At the LZ all aircraft shifted to the ground unit tactical FM net. This net has little traffic during the landing phase and provided all pilots with the ground situation commencing with the first contact with the Pathfinders when the condition of the landing zone was made known to all pilots.

→ The Command & Control aircraft monitored both frequencies at the LZ. The detailed flight briefing prior to this operation was responsible for a minimum of traffic on any one net. The primary cause of radio traffic was the failure of Chu Lai Tacan just prior to landing. This necessitated additional positioning of the flare plane by the flight leader.

COMMENTS

In this type of air operation simplicity and detailed planning are extremely vital. The many limitations imposed by darkness are sufficient without being compounded by complex maneuvers or tactics.

Continuous illumination is a necessity for a massed night helicopter assault. This operation would have been rendered extremely difficult and dangerous without such illumination.

All means of navigation must be explored and utilized. Reliance on only one could be disastrous. In this instance, dead reckoning had been computed and was the sole means available with the failure of the Tacan facility and the complete darkness existing at the time. Major topographic features were not discernible until the illumination had been initiated.

The prior daylight reconnaissance of the objective area was not only desirable, but proved vital to the successful completion of the operation.

The Marine Corps has long recognized the necessity for improving its capability to conduct night helicopter operations. To this end, thirteen Junglebuoy radio beacon sets have been provided III MAF for navigational assistance to assault aircraft. In addition, four Battlefield Illumination Systems have been provided III MAF for continuous illumination of the landing zone and battlefield area. A third development which will be under test by Commandant Marine Corps Landing Force Activities is a terminal guidance system which will provide azimuth, glide slope, and range rate information to the pilot of fixed or rotary wing aircraft. This equipment is designed for early insertion in the landing zone environment as well as semi-permanent landing areas.

# # # # #

2. HELICOPTER LANDING GUIDE

Every Marine must be prepared to act as a Helicopter Landing Guide. This job can be quickly and safely performed by a Marine if he observes the following:

→ Choose a landing zone in a clear area that will allow the helicopter to make an unobstructed approach to the zone while flying into the wind.

→ Indicate the wind direction for the pilot by using smoke, a flag or laying out a wind "T."

→ Assist the helicopter to land in the desired spot by assuming a position on the farthest edge of the zone from the direction of the helicopter approach with your back to the wind and direct the helicopter with the arm signals shown. If available, goggles should be worn to protect your eyes from the dust and dirt that will be thrown up by the helicopter rotor.

→ If vectoring a helicopter to a landing zone by radio, refer to the landing zone position by its clock position from the pilot.

The use of the green flag, as illustrated, is optional. Signals given at night are executed in the same manner except an illuminated amber director's wand is held in each hand.

→ YOU ARE CLEARED TO LAND; I AM YOUR LANDING DIRECTOR; CONTINUE APPROACH. With green flag in right hand, hold arms straight out at sides even with shoulders.

ROGER

This signal, when followed immediately by the "hover" signal and given to a pilot ready for take-off, may be used to bring him to a hover as in preparation for an external cargo hook-up.

HIGH

→ REDUCE ALTITUDE. Hold green flag in right hand. Spread arms overhead to form a "V" indicating "Reduce Altitude."

LOW

→ INCREASE ALTITUDE. Hold green flag in right hand. Position arms sloping away from shoulders in an inverted "V" indicating "Increase Altitude."

MOVE LEFT

→ MOVE LEFT. Hold green flag in right hand, with arm sloping away from body, pointing to pilot's left. Hold left hand at head level, sloping up from the shoulder.

MOVE RIGHT

→ MOVE RIGHT. Hold green flag in right hand, with arm sloping up from the shoulder. Hold left arm sloping down and away from body.

MOVE FORWARD

→ MOVE FORWARD. With hands at head level and palms toward face, make closing motions toward head.

MOVE BACK

→ MOVE BACK. Make fore-aft movements with the arms held down.

WAVE OFF

→ WAVE OFF. Hold green flag in right hand and wave arms overhead indicating "Go around or do not land."

HOVER

→ HOVER. Hold green flag in right hand. Cross palms overhead.

LAND

→ LAND. From "hover" position, move arms to a horizontal position in front of body, with hands still crossed.

DAY

NIGHT

HOLD POSITION OR STOP

→ HOLD YOUR POSITION OR STOP. Make clenched fists at eye level. Hold flat (any color) in left hand.

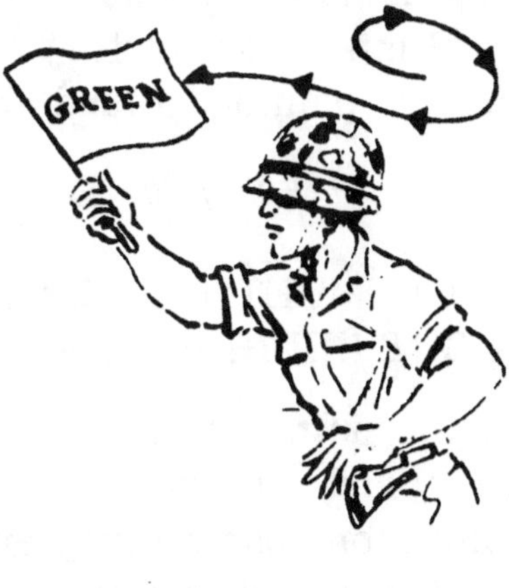

TAKE OFF

→ TAKE OFF. With green flag in right hand, make circular motion overhead in a horizontal plane, ending in a throwing motion toward the direction of takeoff.

LANDING DIRECTIONS

→ INDICATE THE POINT OF DESIRED LANDING. With green flag in right hand, place back to wind and face direction from which approach is to be made. Move arms from sides forward to horizontal position. Finish signal with green flag above head and left finger pointed to landing spot.

# # # # #

3. CONTROL OF MULTIPLE LANDING ZONES DURING NIGHT HELIBORNE ASSAULTS

Experience of units in Vietnam has demonstrated that delay and confusion occasionally occur when embarking from one helicopter loading zone at night for landing in multiple landing zones.

In order to ensure that the loading phase is accomplished with minimum delay and confusion, the loading zone should be divided into a number of different loading sites. The various loading sites should be marked in the same manner as the landing zones. If flare pots are used to marking landing points, they should be positioned far enough apart to ensure safe operations. Helicopter guides should be assigned each helicopter and briefed as to the exact location of their helicopter landing point.

If feasible, a daylight rehearsal should be held to ensure that each heliteam knows exactly where they will be positioned for loading.

Landing zones should be marked in the same manner as the loading zone. The first helicopter in each wave can accomplish this if it cannot be done before the first wave touches down. Caution, however, should be used in the way the landing zone is marked. If colored lights are employed remember that the helicopters themselves might have red, white and green lights showing and the glide indicator, if used, displays red, green and amber lights. A pattern of lights in each zone is one way of overcoming this problem.

# # # # #

4. HELICOPTER MISSION REQUESTS

During one operation in Vietnam, helicopter mission requests came to the squadron from four different sources, Battalion, TACLOG, TACRON and HDC. In some cases requests were made from one source without the knowledge of either of the other agencies or, subsequently, primary flight control.

In handling requests from three separate agencies, the squadron Operations Duty Officer is unable to assign priorities and is unable to intelligently coordinate the different missions to be handled. This results in duplication of effort, poor utilization of aircraft and lack of mission coordination by the Helicopter Direction Center.

FMFM 3-3, Helicopterborne Operations, contains the procedures for requesting helicopter support.

The HDC operates under the control of the TACC and controls the movement of helicopters from wave rendezvous to the initial point and from takeoff at the landing zone to the breakup point. It is organized and equipped to do the job. Requests outside the chain of command can only result in inefficient helicopter support.

# # # # #

5. JET PILOTS

A great deal of flying is done at night in the Vietnam area which has created a need for emphasis on prior night work training in pitch dark without a horizon, particularly at low altitudes.

In all cases, pilots in the combat squadrons were adamant that more instrument type training is required, specifically that which would be termed vertical instrument flying as opposed to smooth airways type instruments.

It was the opinion of all pilots that more instruction is needed in the reading of maps and charts together with training in low level dead reckoning in order to adequately perform current combat missions in Vietnam.

Pilots should be taught to operate their individual aircraft throughout its performance envelope because of the possibility of entering unusual flying altitudes and patterns in combat missions not normally found in routine flying.

Formation flying during combat division tactics usually finds the new aviators disoriented after the first radical maneuver. They appear to confuse basic procedures, which they usually know well, with air discipline and headwork. Pilots are good in tight formation flying but have no experience in follow-the-leader type flying for individual combat runs. Therefore, additional training is needed in loose operational formation flying known as the "loose deuce" and also tail chasing below 10,000 feet in order that pilots can learn to keep track of each other during air to ground attacks.

Division and section tactics training should include both day and night road reconnaissance and day section bombing maneuvers. Identification of targets of opportunity is as important as being able to set up a pop-up and variable dive angle maneuver to attack the target.

The primary reason given for the training of new pilots in all of the extra phases such as instruments, night time, and low level navigation was that in the combat areas there is just not enough time available to train pilots once they have joined a squadron.

Comments were received from various attack plane pilots that, since this war was not a high altitude war, air to air gunnery was not as important from their standpoint as air to ground gunnery. However, all pilots agreed that air defensive tactics are very important because one never knows when it will become necessary to use such tactics. On the other hand, all F-4 and F-8 squadron pilots stressed the fact that air to air gunnery training was vital because it taught the pilot how to get the most out of his aircraft and also gave him more confidence in his own ability.

# # # # #

6. HELO PILOTS

There is a requirement for more low altitude night instrument training for helicopter pilots. Many night helicopter flights are flown at 150 feet and below at various airspeeds down to hover.

There is a requirement for training in formation flying on instruments. On many occasions, a formation of helicopters moving in or out of a target area may suddenly encounter cloud or fog

formations around the mountains. If a pilot becomes separated, he then has to proceed individually on instruments. If he peels off the formation and tries to dive below the clouds, he can get into serious trouble in the hazardous mountain regions of Vietnam. He must be well trained in transitioning from visual to instrument conditions.

Nearly all 1st MAW helicopter flying in country is in formation and seldom does a helicopter proceed by itself. The UH-1Es use a loose type formation, whereas, the H-34s fly a "fluid four" type formation. All night tactical hops are conducted primarily on instruments.

Additional training in low level night flying would be beneficial in order to correspond with this type of flying which is currently being conducted in Vietnam.

# # # # #

7. NOTES FOR AVIATION PERSONNEL

Blinded Birds

Many night landing lights at semi-permanent helicopter landing zones are too bright and not properly shielded. Pilot/copilot night vision is impaired for approximately one-half hour each time these zones are used.

The lighting for landing zones can be shielded, in such a way, as to light the landing area while keeping the direct beam away from the pilot's vision.

Place a curved piece of sheet metal or a piece of thin lumber just above the light in such a way as to reflect the light on the horizontal landing surface. This way the pilots do not look directly into the marker lights.

* * * * *

Marking Helicopter Landing Sites

A field expedient for marking helicopter landing sites is to use discarded artillery VT fuze boxes filled with sand and diesel oil. The boxes should be buried in each corner of the site and box lids replaced when not in use. Paint the lids white to facilitate location at night.

* * * * *

Static Electricity

The electric charge generated by friction is a potential hazard in any aircraft flight. Electrical charges can be built up during taxiing, takeoff, landing and refueling. This charge is not limited to fixed wing aircraft. Helicopters, particularly the heavy transport types, can develop a charge capable of knocking a man off his feet. Helicopters hovering to pick up a pallet or other cargo, and which are carrying a cargo hook develop a static electricity charge. Ground personnel need to insulate themselves from this charge by the use of a simply constructed ground rod, leather or cloth gloves, or webbing material.

The grounding rod will discharge any static electricity into the ground, while insulation will prevent the charge from passing through your body.

* * * * *

Versatility

Rarely does a combat after-action report not mention the versatility of the helicopter. Small units are positioned in remote areas and later removed, resupply to distant positions is an accepted routine, other helicopters which are disabled have been partially dismantled and removed,

caches captured during operations are lifted to safe government storage areas, and close-in fire support where inclement weather precludes regular close air support by fixed wing aircraft have all been performed by helicopters.

There's many an infantryman who gladly tips his hat to his comrade-in-arms in a helicopter.

* * * * *

Foreign Object Damage

On many occasions in the field, foreign objects have been placed or collected in or near secure helicopter landing zones. These foreign objects have consisted of pieces of communication wire, barbed wire, various items of 782 gear, ration cans, boxes and refuse. All these items are potential hazards to both a helicopter engine and the rotor blades.

All units maintaining designated landing zones should keep them well policed and ready for immediate use. This will reduce incidents of injury to personnel and damage to aircraft.

* * * * *

Retraction of Downed Helicopters

Rapid and aggressive action on the part of both Marine ground and air units prevented the destruction of a downed UH-34 by the Viet Cong during the past year.

One UH-34 in a flight of thirteen helicopters conducting a scheduled relocation of a rifle company, experienced engine difficulty and was forced to land in a Viet Cong infested area.

Security troops were landed and almost immediately came under heavy enemy fire. Fixed wing aircraft and armed UH-1Es were diverted

to provide cover while the remainder of the rifle company was diverted into the zone to provide additional protection.

Enemy fire was received from positions 270 degrees around the area and three UH-34s were hit, but not downed.

A maintenance crew was lifted in and the downed helicopter was stripped and lifted out in three sections by CH-46 helicopters.

Within two hours of the time the helicopter went down, all Marine personnel and equipment had been removed from the area.

* * * * *

Save the Blades

Modified pilot techniques can extend the rotor blade life of the CH-46 helicopter operating in sandy areas. Studies of films of sandlanding trials showed various techniques which have a direct bearing on rotor blade erosion. During the takeoff phase, actual time spent in the sand cloud varied from 4 to 18 seconds. Pilots spending the least amount of time in the cloud lifted the aircraft vertically to a height above the center of the blowing sand before transitioning to forward flight. Pilots who stayed in the sand cloud for the longest duration lifted a few feet, then dropped the nose to effect transition to forward flight. The damage to the forward rotor blades on aircraft undergoing maximum time exposure to the sand was excessive.

* * * * *

UH-34 Engine Overspeeds and Overboosts

Engine overspeeds and overboosts experienced during operations in RVN have been in direct relation to the state of training and experience level of the pilots concerned. This is further aggravated by the tempo of operations under combat conditions.

Situations in which engine overspeeds and overboosts occur can be reduced by limiting the helicopter load to that which the helicopter is capable of lifting based on HOGE (Hovering Out of Ground Effect) charts.

The weight of the following items must be computed and subtracted from the allowable pay load of troops or cargo:

→ Crew of four
→ Two M-60 MGs and mounts
→ Machine gun ammo
→ Flak vests
→ Personal weapons and survivor kits
→ Aircraft fuel
→ Aircraft armor plate
→ Installation of carburetor air filter

Helicopter aircraft commanders have the responsibility to ensure that the helo load is within its lift capability based on HOGE charts.

* * * * *

Care of the UH-34's Engine

The maintenance crew, and particularly the pilot, influence the life of the UH-34 engine. Proper pre-oiling is a must for a new engine or an engine that has not been operated for 72 hours. When the engine is started, crank with the starter a full five seconds before switching on the magnetos. Follow this procedure for a missed start. This helps prevent high BMEP in the lower cylinders due to excess fuel or oil which may have collected. Extremely high BMEP leads to piston pin boss failure.

Proper warm-up of the engine prior to engagement prevents scorched cylinder walls and piston ring failures while overspeeds generate excessive stresses in the valves and bearings. Repeated minor overspeeds will induce valve failures.

To increase engine life on the UH-34 and ensure that the next crew has a dependable machine:

→ Pre-oil properly.
→ Use standardized starting and warm-up procedures.

→ Operate the engine correctly.

→ Try not to overspeed or overboost, but if that should happen, WRITE IT UP.

* * * * *

Helo Lift Limitations

When operations require the hasty preparation of a small landing zone in an area of high trees, helicopters are forced to land and lift vertically. Vertical lifting in conditions of high temperature and humidity permit only a minimum load. Instead of six or seven troops, a UH-34 may be able to lift only two or three troops. Plans should take such limitations, as well as helicopter capabilities into account.

* * * * *

Tire Tread Loss

The loss of an aircraft tire tread can result in damage to an area adjacent to the landing gear system. Landing gear doors, flaps, switches, fairings, and plumbing could be damaged. All these areas should be checked for possible damage after each incident of tire tread loss. Thorough inspecting for tread loss damage and double checking by supervisory maintenance personnel can prevent later interrupted flights.

* * * * *

Close Air Support

There have been many cases where units have requested armed helicopter support, when the bombs, napalm and heavy rockets of fixed wing aircraft were indicated. Ground commanders should be discriminative in their weaponeering and air commanders should guard against misuse of their weapons.

* * * * *

"MIGs, Deadbeat 3-1 Break Right"

If you're Deadbeat 3-1, your actions in the next few seconds can make or spoil your whole day. Too many after-action reports begin with "I first saw the MIG when he was at 7 o'clock firing" and end up with "The MIGs disappeared in the haze heading northeast." In this age of reliance on radar, MTDs and sophisticated missiles, basic fighter tactics tend to be de-emphasized. In a melee in hostile airspace the finest GCI in the world can't sort out the many blips in time to do any good. The best radar is still a set of keen eyeballs, and the best tactic, the ability to fly an aircraft to the limit of the performance envelope. All fixed wing squadrons, fighter and attack alike, should thoroughly train their pilots in day fighter tactics.

* * * * *

Flying Tips

The combat requirement for trained instrument pilots cannot be over-emphasized. One F-8 squadron logged 508.9 hours of actual instruments during one deployment to Southeast Asia. You can not overtrain on the gauges.

Reports continue to reach this Headquarters of severe eye injuries being prevented by helmet visors being worn in the down position. When flak hits the canopy the visor deflects the minute particles that fill the cockpit and saves your eyesight. Since this is largely a matter of habit, grow

accustomed to flying with the visor down. Be sure to have flight equipment personnel clean all visors daily.

* * * * *

Proper Procedures

In Korea, they were called "Nape Scrapes" and the connotation has carried over to Vietnam. However, prescribed delivery techniques using a ten degree glide angle, proper mil lead, and fixed release point have proven more accurate and effective than the flathatting, crop dusting delivery

method of the Korean days. Use of the radar altimeter and, in the case of the F-4B, use of the additional crewman's eyes and voice should ensure consistently accurate and safe runs. A recent instance of an F-4 scraping its underside served to demonstrate both poor pilot technique and backseat complacency.

The pilot who believes that a combat environment requires radical departures from flight procedures which were so carefully practiced at Cherry Point, Yuma, and Vieques has no place in Vietnam.

* * * * *

Fixed Wing Support

The Mark IV gun pod employed on both A-4 and F-4 aircraft has proven to be particularly effective for helicopter escort and landing zone preparation missions. This accurate gun system with its high rate of fire permits a pilot to pinpoint his target and virtually destroy it with 20mm rounds. As most targets on these missions are "soft" ones, they literally erupt and collapse under the impact of the shells. Zuni and 2.75-inch rockets are also effective on helo escort/landing zone preparation missions. The natural dispersion pattern of the smaller rocket when fired from the rocket pod provides for good target coverage.

* * * * *

Prompt Pilot Debriefings

The transistory nature of targets in guerrilla operations demands prompt reporting and quick response. All pilots and crew members play an important part in both of these operations. When flights are completed and the aircraft have returned to the base area, report promptly the results of the mission to the air intelligence section. Don't neglect any item of information no matter how insignificant it may seem. Let the intelligence specialists make the determination of the value of your reports. With each small piece of information, the big picture begins to take shape.

In one instance, reports from ground and air observers mentioned that groups of elephants had been seen in the jungle west of a Marine tactical area in Vietnam. Elephants have been used on occasion by the VC as transport animals for heavy, bulky gear.

* * * * *

Motor Convoy-Air Escort

Some difficulty has been encountered during motorized convoy escort operations in Vietnam due to ineffective communication systems between the vehicle convoy and the escort aircraft. Problem areas have been:

→ Simultaneous transmissions by radio operators resulting in faulty message interpretations and in some instances blocking out important message traffic.

→ The time interval between the moment when a vehicle receives fire and when notification reaches the escort aircraft is often excessive. This frequently precludes the determination of the source of hostile fire. Possible solutions to the problem are as follows:

Equip the convoy lead element with two radios operating on different frequencies. One radio could be utilized for air to ground communications, while the other could be used for intraconvoy messages.

• All vehicles should carry smoke grenades to be dispensed in the direction of the hostile fire in an effort to aid the escort aircraft in determining the origin of the hostile fire and to warn subsequent vehicles of the impending danger.

• Ensure that convoy operators are trained in radio discipline and the proper method of describing enemy positions.

* * * * *

Nylon Tie Down Straps

C-130 aircrews have been using nylon straps to tie down cargo. Force Logistic Command has been substituting nylon straps for link chain tie downs. These straps are lighter, stronger, less expensive, far easier to handle and they take up less storage space.

* * * * *

SERE Information

The Fleet Intelligence Center, Pacific publishes a CINCPACFLT SERE Newsletter containing valuable information of Survival Evasion Resistance Escape. The Newsletter, published monthly, includes debriefing reports and articles on SERE Techniques. Because of the nature of the material the Newsletter is classified SECRET. However, each MAG and major command receives copies of each issue. The Newsletters are worthwhile reading for every pilot.

# # # # #

Chapter V: MINE WARFARE

1. SOME METHODS OF COUNTERING VC MINE WARFARE

Mine and booby trap incidents recorded by Marine units in the Republic of Vietnam indicate that the Viet Cong are using such weapons in an offensive role. Mines are not placed as a barrier to our advance or to deny any particular area to us. Rather, they are employed to harass and lower morale by inflicting casualties and causing damage. Current VC tactics indicate an even wider use of mines and booby traps as an offensive weapon than

256-290 O-67—18

has previously been experienced. Additionally, these devices are emplaced to interrupt the supply function by denying us the continued and full time use of main supply routes. We are forced to employ a large number of personnel and equipment in daily deliberate road sweeps to clear these routes. Other targets of VC mine operations are the personnel and equipment employed in detecting operations and communications personnel and equipment. The VC have obtained information on our methods of operations and the way we react to given situations. At times they can anticipate fairly well in which direction or into which area we are going to move. Most of the local VC are too few and not equipped well enough to stand and fight even a squad sized friendly unit. Why should they stand and fight and risk almost certain death or capture when they can leave behind an explosive device that will inflict casualties more easily and a lot more effectively than a few rounds of small arms fire?

All units agree that mine and booby trap activity is concentrated within the TAORs. On operations outside the TAORs, units have found a decrease in the density of mines and booby traps. Within the TAORs, the areas most widely used for AP mines and booby traps have been:

→ Likely CP areas
→ High ground
→ Hedgerows and tree lines
→ Shady areas

→ Trail junctions
→ Fence lines and gates

An enemy document captured in the vicinity of the An Hoa industrial complex outlined mine and booby trap doctrine to be followed by all subordinate units and personnel in the area. The VC cannot afford to mine and booby trap indiscriminately; there is too great a chance for civilian casualties. Civilian casualties suffered as a result of VC action lead to a loss of support by the people, and this the enemy cannot afford. To decrease the possibilities of this happening, the Viet Cong in the An Hoa area were told when and where mines were to be employed, and what precautions would be taken to ensure that the local civilians knew of the mined areas. Specifically, they were ordered to employ the mines only upon approach of the enemy and to remove any undetonated devices on the enemy's withdrawal. Primary areas for mine activity were singled out to be the high ground, likely routes of approach, and suspected sites for CPs and bivouacs. The VC were also directed to tell the local villagers where mines and booby traps were emplaced.

In the III MAF TAORs, the majority of mines and booby traps have been found in areas and on trails that are seldom used by the local populace. There have been instances where Platoon Patrol Bases (PPB) have been evacuated for a period of 4-6 hours and upon the platoon's return, the area was found to have been mined. In other reports, engineers clearing areas have, on their return, found that mines had been emplaced behind them. Some examples of this tactic follow:

→ A command fired mine was detonated under a medium tractor resulting in one WIA, but no damage to the vehicle. The mine was fired from approximately 300 meters away using pieces of communications wire spliced together. A security squad, after sweeping the area and returning to the highway, detonated an AP mine placed in a path in a hedgerow, which the squad had used only minutes before, resulting in four WIAs. As the squad, a short time previously, had passed through the hedgerow at the same point, it was apparent the

mine had been placed after the initial sweep and in a period of one-half hour or less.

➛ An unknown type command fired mine was detonated under a truck carrying a security guard for a convoy to Quang Ngai. A sweep of the area revealed three 105mm rounds in the immediate area electrically wired by communication wire leading to a hedgerow approximately 150 meters away. The area was swept and the communication wire checked with negative results. On returning to the road, a Marine started to roll up the wire and detonated an M-26 grenade attached to it resulting in one casualty. The grenade was attached after the wire had been checked and while the security element was searching a nearby hamlet.

➛ Near a ferry crossing and under a group of shade trees normally used by troops waiting for the ferry, a Z-10 mine was found with several clay pots containing what appeared to be ammonium nitrate. The mine was found in the morning. The area was used heavily during the day, but was not secured at night.

➛ During one 10-month period, an infantry battalion, operating in the vicinity of Marble Mountain and Danang Airfield, suffered many casualties from mines and surprise firing devices. However, heavy mining was not encountered by the battalion in any specific area until after patrols/sweeps had moved through the areas a number of times. There were few exceptions to this pattern of VC mining. This leads to the belief that the VC mined these areas after they had ascertained that the unit was going to continue operating in them.

Incidents and experiences in the Republic of Vietnam up to this point have shown that mine warfare and the placement of booby traps can be carried out by almost anyone, and sometimes those least likely of suspicion. It doesn't require any high degree of intelligence to emplace such devices; just the necessary respect and caution. Anyone can be given the components and instructed how to place them. The Viet Cong do have some experts in the business, but in semi-pacified areas it is the seemingly friendly local Vietnamese who works his fields all day and breaks out his weapon or booby trap equipment at night. On a number of occasions, road sweep teams have reported explosion craters and blood stains where somebody "slipped up" the night before. Just because our units are in an area where friendly troops have been many times before or have even occupied for some time, and the people seem friendly enough, is no reason for unit personnel to feel secure from mines or booby traps.

Mines/Devices

Many of the mines being encountered are of a crude, simple type and in most cases, improvised from captured ordnance or dud rounds. The AP mines and booby traps have usually been either fitted with a pull type fuze or equipped with a trip wire. Almost all of the AT mines encountered have been improvised from artillery rounds or composed of packaged explosives and either command fired or fitted with a combination electric-pressure fuze made from a split cylinder of bamboo. This is connected to several flashlight batteries with an electric detonator. The crushing action of a heavy vehicle closes the circuit setting off the mine. It was noted in some cases that lighter vehicles, such as mules and jeeps, had passed over mines without detonating them. Also, many mines do not detonate due to faulty components or ignorance and inexperience in assembling them. Grenades, usually M-26, have been widely used both as AP mines and as booby traps. These are usually fitted with a trip wire monafilament line, communications wire or manufactured trip wire. Grenades have also been used as fuze/booster assemblies for larger charges, such as artillery rounds or packaged explosives of VC or CHICOM origin.

Some of the sources of mine and booby trap material for the VC are apparently coming from the Allied forces. Both United States and Vietnamese Army units have been making use of U.S. manufactured land mines for protective minefields. These minefields serve as a source of supply to the enemy. There are cases where mines are emplaced and then not adequately covered by observation and/or fire. The VC are able to go into these fields and take the mines for use against us. Another source of material for the enemy is our own unexploded ordnance. Artillery and mortar rounds and aerial ordnance that fail to detonate are recovered and used for highly effective mine and booby trap material.

The following chart shows the types and number of mines encountered by one Marine Battalion during a 30-day period:

Type Mine/ Firing Device	Number Detonated	Type of Detonation	Destroyed in Place
M16-A1	21	15 tripwire 6 pressure	89
M26	18	tripwire	22
Homemade (AT)	9	pressure	12
81mm mortar	4	2 tripwire 2 pressure	16
Unknown type	10	Unknown	1
105mm Howitzer	4	1 tripwire 3 pressure	16
M2-A1	3	tripwire	
CHICOM grenade	5	tripwire	4
60mm mortar	1	tripwire	8
20mm shell	2	pressure	
3.5 rkt rd	1	tripwire	1
155mm shell	0	pressure	6
57mm shell	0	Unknown	3
TOTAL	78		178

In addition to the above activated mines/devices, forty-four 60mm mortar shells and eighteen 40mm, M79 rounds were found planted in the area but not rigged with detonators.

Road Mining

Road mining is a serious problem in a counter-insurgency environment. Guerrilla forces have the opportunity to emplace mines along roads, railroads, and other well traveled routes almost at will. They are normally employed in a random manner with no prescribed pattern or density.

Plans and training in countering this type of warfare should include the following:

→ Provision for a complete and thorough investigation of all supplies, equipment, vehicles, and containers which enter areas of suspected mining.

→ Preparation and dissemination of SOPs for clearing potential mined areas.

→ Provision for trained teams for use in checking and clearing mined areas.

→ Security measures for denial of mines and firing devices to irregular forces.

→ In addition to sandbagging the flooring of vehicles, personnel riding in the vehicles must keep arms and legs inside.

→ Personnel and vehicles should stay on the well traveled portion of the road to the maximum extent possible.

Command type mines are employed both against vehicles and personnel. Against vehicles, the large majority of such mines are placed along a route where a good choice of targets would be presented to the enemy. When sweeping a road for enemy mines, a number of positive steps can be taken to combat command mines. The formation of the sweep team and its security force is important. Flank security personnel can be especially helpful in looking for wires running out from the direction of the road. The use of dogs with the point or flank security can be effective in detecting enemy personnel in cover or concealment ahead of the sweep team. In many areas, there is a good deal of communication wire running alongside the road. This makes it easy for the enemy to conceal his firing

line by camouflaging it among the mass of existing wire when he hasn't sufficient time to bury it. When communication lines run under the road, the sweep force should be familiar with the exact number of lines that are supposed to be there, and this number checked each time a team passes the location. Positive control of communication wire usage should be implemented. When it is no longer serving its function as a communication line, all wire should be removed from the field and properly disposed of, as is the policy with used batteries. Employed against personnel, command type mines are frequently directional in nature; that is, they are designed to expel a large number of fragments in a certain direction due to the configuration of the container. The Claymore mine is a good example of this type weapon. Such devices are usually emplaced facing down a trail or avenue of approach that the enemy expects us to use.

Dispersion

Dispersion is the most effective passive defense against AP mines/booby traps. Mine consciousness and keen observation can detect many mines and booby traps, and prevent their detonation; however, dispersion will minimize casualties if the device is detonated. In one incident reported on a company sweep there were 5 KIA and 23 WIA from 2 mines. In this incident there was obviously little or no dispersion. Orders have been issued directing all units to maintain a minimum dispersion of 15 meters between personnel; to follow tanks and LVTs by no less than 100 meters; that LVTs and tanks will precede

the infantry whenever the terrain permits; and that artillery and mortar fire will be used whenever possible to destroy suspected mines and booby traps. These orders are sound and if practiced will reduce otherwise potential mine casualties.

Marines, like fighting men everywhere, tend to feel that there is safety in numbers. They don't like to be spread too far apart where they can't talk with a buddy. Most mines are designed to inflict casualties by fragmentation, and it is obvious that the closer men are moving in relation to one another, the more of them that are going to be hit by fragments. Dispersion is something that must be preached and enforced on a continuous basis down to the fire team and individual level.

When units in the field come to a halt during the day, there is a widespread, and not altogether unfounded, tendency to seek shade. During the better part of the year in the Republic of Vietnam, the sun can be brutally hot. It is only natural to try to get out of it when the opportunity presents itself. In most areas there isn't much shade, and no matter how well the dispersion during movement might have been, Marines will tend to congregate in the area affording shade where they can rest more comfortably than on a trail or in a field. Recently, there have been increasing examples of mine and booby trap incidents in areas where congestion and congregation are likely.

Often, when a mine or booby trap incident occurs, there is a quick rush of nearby personnel to the scene to attempt to help. Corpsmen are probably the only ones who are going to be able to aid the casualties initially, and even they should approach with caution. The area immediately around the casualties should be checked for additional devices before other men are brought up; i.e., stretcher bearers. The VC have shown an increased use of a multiple mining technique that appears to be designed to take advantage of this tendency.

Patterns

When a company is operating in its sector of the Battalion TAOR, the platoons do most of the patrolling independently, aside from an occasional company operation. In moving out from the company base camp, the platoon will often set a pattern by taking the same avenue of approach to their objective area. Sometimes it is impossible to change the pattern because of the terrain. There might be only one avenue of approach which provides relative safety from small arms fire and a measure of concealment from the enemy. In situations where it is impossible for units to vary their routes, they should relieve each other in place. This will help screen the avenue of approach to the objective area from VC attempting to plant mines and booby traps ahead of the platoon moving into the area. It will also make the objective area (or assigned patrolling area) more accessible to the platoon entering, especially if there is a rice paddy (danger area) to cross before moving into the village.

Whenever an LVT or tank commander sets a pattern with his vehicle, he is increasing the chances of being hit with a mine. The majority of the mine incidents examined in which a tank or LVT was damaged by a mine indicated that the vehicle commander used the same road repeatedly. Whenever possible, routes should be varied, and tracks over 24 hours old should be avoided.

A lesson learned by one infantry company that set a pattern was the over-use of a base campsite. Before the company moved into the base camp for the second time in two days, the VC planted an M-16 mine that inflicted 13 casualties.

Patterns should never be set by utilizing the same base sites repeatedly. If possible, a bivouac site from which the mission may still be accomplished should be used, rather than continually trying to occupy the high ground.

In almost all operations, Marines tend to set patterns in the way they do things. The VC can easily observe this and once they determine the pattern, they act in a direct manner against it. For example, an Engineer Battalion road sweep team working a particular section of road on a daily basis, had set a pattern in the time and place they used for noon chow. Fortunately, one of them spotted an M-16 mine which had been recently placed in the particular area. Whenever and wherever possible we must avoid setting patterns. Much of the pattern setting is done unconsciously.

Positive action must be taken by all unit leaders to counter this tendency. They must be constantly aware of what they are doing and how they are doing it. If a distinct pattern is being set, efforts should be made to alter it.

Tanks

Tanks have no special equipment for the detection and/or removal of mines. They rely on their armor and weight to minimize the effects from a mine blast. Tanks have suffered no serious damage as a result of AP mines. Reconnaissance by fire is a tactic that tanks made use of from time to time to clear mines. This is employed at the tank commander's discretion when his vehicle is being canalized through a certain area, due to either man-made or natural obstacles. Both machinegun and 90mm cannister rounds have been used for this. Cases have been reported where secondary explosions have occurred. The primary limitation in this tactic is ammunition availability. When tanks are supporting infantry, the tanks should be forward with the infantry no closer than 100 meters to the vehicle. This permits the tanks ample room to maneuver and traverse their guns to bring fire on a target should the necessity arise. It also keeps the infantrymen well back from any blast or shrapnel resulting from the tank hitting a mine. The tanks should be used to smash passages through fence lines and tree lines. They can move through almost any area that is suspected of being mined or booby trapped. When infantry or other units are moving aboard tanks, tank commanders advise and prefer to have them ride to the rear of the turret. Most mines the tank detonates will explode between the first and third set of wheels, and little, if any, shrapnel should reach the men riding on the back. If incoming fire is received, the infantry should dismount from the tank immediately and allow it to move forward. The tank's greatest danger is from command or pressure type explosive devices used within the TAOR, primarily on road networks. Such devices will be packed with enough explosive to seriously damage a tank, and if not detected during the normal routine sweep of the road the tank will become a target of opportunity. Most devices encountered by tanks on other than road networks usually contain insufficient power to inflict serious damage.

Engineer Support

A number of unit commanders, while operating in the field, have shown a marked tendency to feel somewhat immune, or at least less susceptible, to mine and booby trap activity merely because they have engineer personnel attached. Some actually have the notion that engineers have mine detection equipment built into their heads. For example, requests for engineer attachments to night infantry patrols have been made "to ensure they don't run into any booby traps." Engineers are no different from anyone else. They can set off a device just as easily as an infantryman. A man specifically trained to perform a certain mission will carry

256-290 O-67—19

out an assignment in a more thorough and careful manner than another man who has an unfamiliar task forced upon him. The mission of the infantry is to close with and destroy the enemy. The mission of the engineer is to assist the infantry by rendering combat engineer support. Attached engineer personnel can be of valuable assistance to an infantry commander who makes proper use of them. One proposal would be the employment of an engineer in the double point. It would be the primary assignment of the engineer to be especially observant for signs of enemy mines or booby trap activity. This includes any visible warning signs the enemy might have left for the protection of sympathizers. The infantryman would be responsible for performing the normal security function of his position, with the additional responsibility for security for himself and the engineer. Another valuable use of attached engineer personnel in the detection of mines is their utilization when entering a suspect area, or approaching a terrain or man-made feature that appears a likely location for enemy mine/booby trap activity. When such an area is encountered (a breached fence line or a hill or village previously occupied by our troops) the engineers should be called forward to visually and electronically check it before the unit proceeds. If a device is discovered, the engineers will have the capability to destroy it in place. All that is required is the allocation of a little time and patience to ensure that a suspect area is clear.

Village gates, both around the perimeter of the village and within the village, have been and continue to be prime targets for Viet Cong booby trap activity. Upon approaching a gate, whether it is open or closed, most units usually call for their engineer support to check it and blow it open if necessary. At the same time, however, the men on line who are not near the gate will go right up to the fence line and batter it down. Indications up to this time show that most fence line breakings come off without incident the first time through! The VC usually don't have enough material to booby trap an entire fence line, so they use it in the obvious areas (the gates) where they know for sure someone will pass, and hope that someone will be careless. After our

forces move on, though, the VC have any number of choice sites to pick from. Some time later, another Marine unit moving through the area sees the fence line has already been breached in a number of places and will assume that it is free of enemy activity. Upon approaching any gate, fence line, or tree line, caution should be exercised.

We are aware that the enemy marks the majority, if not all, of the areas he mines or booby traps. He doesn't want to inflict casualties upon his own personnel nor upon local village inhabitants. Many of these signs are known to us, and the information has been published in a number of forms. Yet, there are still men operating in the field on a continuous basis that have little knowledge of these signs. If all hands cannot read the specific information for themselves, they should be schooled by their small unit leaders. Every pair of Marine eyes in the field should be looking for signs of enemy mining activity. At times, they are extremely obvious. The Divisions' engineer battalions conduct Land Mine Warfare Schools during which many of these signs are shown to personnel just as they have appeared in the field. We may not know all the signs the enemy uses, but if we know some and are looking for them, we are conscious of anything out of the ordinary, or something that "just doesn't look right."

Vietnamese Army Experience

Vietnamese units are incurring mine/booby trap casualties, although not in such high percentages as the Marines. This is the result of a combination of factors: Vietnamese units do not patrol as extensively and as thoroughly as Marine units; therefore, they are not as vulnerable to this type of VC action. When they do move, it is normally not in areas in which they have been operating for several days, and, as a result, have not set patterns of movement. When conducting sweep and clear operations, the Vietnamese usually move in columns presenting a series of narrow fronts to the VC. This tactic has the advantage of presenting a more difficult target to mines and booby traps, but has the advantage of not covering a large percentage of the

sweep area. Marine units normally sweep in assault formations, deployed with two elements up and one back, or one up and two back, making them more vulnerable to mines/booby traps, but cover the area more thoroughly as well as being deployed ready to fight. Vietnamese Army units have an advantage in their ability to communicate with the people and, do not hesitate to move villagers in front of them. A Marine platoon leader on a recent combined operation with the Vietnamese Army in the An Hoa area reported that a villager informed the Vietnamese soldiers attached to his platoon that the area to his front was mined. The platoon then changed formation, employing three columns. The area was not completely covered; however, the objective hamlet was small and the squads were able to maintain visual contact. Villagers were placed in front of the three columns as guides through the village. The villagers were controlled exclusively by the Vietnamese soldiers in this maneuver. As a result, the villagers pointed out five mines, two of which were M-16s. Supposedly, the villagers did not know the location of these mines, but found them from the VC warning markers. The Vietnamese soldier is much more aware of mines/booby traps than the average Marine and as a result is much more conscious of mines/booby traps. Vietnamese platoon leaders and company commanders still have many of the same problems that face Marine leaders; i.e., dispersion discipline and patterned behavior.

In TAORs where units are able to utilize Vietnamese military units, the capabilities and limitations of these troops must be made clear. The Vietnamese know the terrain and, if left alone on the point, will usually do a good job. The individual

Marine must have confidence in the ability of these men to lead him safely through strange areas. Units using these troops have had very few mine and booby trap incidents. If Vietnamese Army Units are not available, efforts should be made to induce the local populace to lead patrols through suspected areas.

In order to influence the local Vietnamese to provide Marines with information as to the location of explosive devices, a reward system was established in October 1965. This system has been relatively ineffective due to several reasons; primarily the fear of VC reprisals and the lack of communication between Marines and villagers. It is believed that there are many people in the hamlets and villages that would give us information were it not for fear of VC reprisals. This can be partially overcome by an interrogation system that would not pinpoint the individual. The Vietnamese Army uses a system of interrogating 20 or 30 people in private; therefore, any one of them could be the informer. In the past, it has been difficult for unit leaders to obtain money (piasters) for use as a reward for villagers who volunteer information of enemy mines and booby traps. During 1966, however, action was initiated to rectify this situation.

Counter Mine Devices

Many Marines are not wearing the "flak" jacket even though the jacket has proven its worth by saving many lives and reducing wounds. Normal operations within TAORs consist of search and destroy missions and patrols, neither of which require extensive running or extreme physical activity. In spite of this, there are many unit leaders who do not like to use the jackets, claiming it slows the troops down and tires them out.

There are a number of counter mine devices and pieces of equipment presently available and in use in the field. The engineer battalions are constantly experimenting with new devices. The more important of these items are as follows:

→ A source of controversy is the battery powered, portable, mine detector. Unit commanders, when preparing to go into the field have asked that engineer personnel "bring along a mine detector to hunt for mines." Mine detectors were not designed for use in the field on sweeps or search and destroy missions. They are intended for slow, detailed, deliberate sweeps of predetermined or specified areas. At the present time, the Marine Corps is equipped with three models of mine detectors. The AN/PRS-3 and P-153 models will react only to metallic objects, while the AN/PRS-4 will pick up any object below the surface of the ground. This equipment is quite expensive, and highly sensitive. The detectors must be carried in air-tight cases and broken out only for actual use or testing. Almost all of the serviceable mine detectors available to units in the Danang TAOR are tied up on the daily sweeps necessary on the MSRs to the forward areas. Mine detectors are not the final solution to the problem of finding or avoiding mines and booby traps in the field. In a particular area where mines are known to be or highly suspected, the mine detector can be used to clear a safe lane or passage, but adequate security and time must be provided for the team performing the sweeps. In the near future each infantry battalion in III MAF will be equipped with six P-153 mine detectors. The training of sufficient personnel (infantrymen) to operate these detectors will create minimum problems initially and a continued program of training for replacement operators will have to be implemented (at least 216 operators required for 108 P-153s). When this program is completed, the mine detection capability in III MAF will be substantially increased.

➛ The engineer battalion will be equipped with a jeep mounted mine detector that will sweep a wider lane and will be a good deal faster than the portable, hand-carried types. At speeds not exceeding 5 mph, the detector will pick up metallic objects buried to a depth of 26 inches. The search head is pushed ahead of the vehicle and is positioned approximately 8 inches above the ground by a 3-wheeled carriage assembly. The weight of the search coil and the weight of the carriage will not activate an antivehicular mine. The search coil covers a path two meters to either side for clearing road shoulders. A mine can be pinpointed within an area of two square feet by moving the coil carriage laterally. The detector will detect mines over cross-country terrain that the host vehicle will negotiate, and in all types of soil. All components of the detecting set are submersion proof to the maximum fording depth of the vehicle.

➛ In order to combat the antivehicular box mine (usually an explosive packed wooden box of 20 pounds or more with wooden dowels and aluminum blasting cap, making it almost impossible to detect by electric means) which is being employed with increased frequency on MSRs, Marines have developed a device that they term the "Road-o-Rooter" or XM-69 Mine-finder. This device, installed on the back end of a TD-15 tractor, uses scarifier teeth to dig up the shoulders of a road where most box mines are employed. A shield has been built around the driver to protect him from blast effects. The purpose of the scarifier teeth is to dig up either the mine (for a pressure type) or the contact wire (for the command type). To date, the main problem has been that the teeth have been penetrating only to a depth of about six inches. To be effective, the teeth should penetrate at least 18-24 inches. Engineer battalions are modifying the device to hold more weight and thus achieve the desired penetration.

→ To combat pressure type antipersonnel mines in the field, the Marines have been experimenting with a simple device designed to be towed by an LVT or tank. The device is made of three pieces of Marston matting attached end to end and then weighted down. Wire rope is attached to the center and ends of the weighted matting. The weighted Marston matting is heavy enough to detonate any AP explosive device that it passes over containing a pressure type firing mechanism. LVTs or tanks, thus equipped, could precede foot troops at a distance of no less than 100 meters and provide a much wider path (30 feet) for the infantrymen than just the tracks of the vehicles themselves.

→ Explosive line charges are another method of removal of enemy lines. The larger of these charges is mounted on and fired from the LVTE-1 AmTrac. Each AmTrac is equipped to carry two line charges. The smaller of the line charges, the M1E1 (approximately 95 pounds) can be carried by two men. It will fire out to a maximum distance of 170 feet and will clear an 8-foot-wide lane exposing most mines near the surface. Pressure AP mines with their pressure surface directly under the are detonated. When located within 5 feet of the line charge, mines become sensitive.

→ Many enemy explosive devices have been found on obstacles along the route of advance of friendly troops. The closed village gate across a trail is a common one and is generally regarded with suspicion. However, a bamboo bush that hangs across the trail at a height of about four feet produces a natural reaction to push it out of the way. The same reaction is produced by small obstacles lying on the trail. The use by the point of a 100-foot nylon line with a grapple on one end will make the removal of such objects relatively safe.

→ Wire cutters would aid a patrol or unit on a search and destroy mission from becoming canalized. Whenever a unit is canalized, the chances of detonation of mines and booby traps are the greatest. With wire cutters, Marines would not necessarily have to travel in the obvious places. Wire fences interwoven with thickets are as profuse as hedgerows in Vietnam. Squad leaders and fire team leaders should carry wire cutters as a standard piece of equipment.

# # # # #

2. GUIDE TO ENEMY EXPLOSIVE DEVICES

To guard against the lethal effects of enemy explosive devices, each Marine should have a sound knowledge of the external appearance and operating characteristics of all enemy mines and booby traps.

There are literally hundreds of precautions that must be taken to avoid becoming a mine or booby trap casualty. All of them are taught in Marine Corps schools, in training units and within organizations currently engaged in combat operations in Vietnam. However, the primary unit and individual responsibilities in regard to limiting casualties from these devices are as follows:

a. Unit Responsibilities

→ To recognize mine warfare is an all hands proposition, not simply a special type warfare and the responsibility of engineer personnel.

→ To indoctrinate all personnel to the hazards involved, an alertness to VC mine activity, and prompt accurate reporting. This training should be included in the unit training program, and quotas should be requested to the Division Mine Warfare Schools.

→ To train vehicle operators to recognize mined areas. The VC depend a great deal on the habits of Marines in selecting mine sites.

→ To coordinate with attached, supporting, and supported units to evaluate the VC situation at a given time in a given area.

→ To clear with individual infantry units before proceeding through their areas. This procedure will ensure timely appraisal of the VC mine situation.

→ To ensure that personnel and vehicles traveling into forward areas of the TAOR are never alone, and that safe interval is maintained.

→ To arrange for helicopter overflights to provide aerial observation of areas through which convoys or large units are traveling.

→ To control the disposing and discarding of batteries to prevent salvage by the Viet Cong.

→ To request engineer support on a timely basis so that the requesting unit may be supported to the maximum.

→ To promptly report mine activity to the next higher echelon. This includes both positive contact and suspected activity.

→ To take active and passive measures to curtail VC ability to emplace mines.

b. Individual Responsibilities

→ To alertly observe areas for signs of VC mine activity while traveling afoot along footpaths, bridges, defiles, rice paddy dikes, gates, fences, bamboo stands, overgrown areas, etc. Signs would include bamboo markers, stone markers, cans, freshly dug earth, small depressions, trip wire, etc.

→ To always employ the "buddy system" of having at least one other person in near proximity while traveling afoot.

→ To maintain proper dispersion when traveling as part of a group.

→ To advance cautiously when going to the assistance of a mine casualty. Inspect the surface for those signs enumerated above before moving into the immediate area.

→ To remain alert to detect mine activity when operating or riding as a passenger in any vehicle. Avoid disturbed earth, and puddles, lumber and other foreign objects on the road or trail surface, plus electric wires.

→ To be alert when driving through channelized areas including sand dunes.

→ To immediately report evidence of mine activity or dud ordnance.

→ DO NOT ATTEMPT TO DISARM MINES. This is work for a specialist. Merely mark in an obvious manner or use explosives to destroy the mine in place.

→ To be alert to all information disseminated on Viet Cong mine warfare.

→ To assist others in detecting enemy mine activity.

→ To understand that the employment of the standard mine detection equipment has restrictions and limitations.

c. The most common types of enemy explosive devices encountered in Vietnam are as follows:

Booby Trap Device - BLU - 3/B Bomb

Operation. A rock is placed in the bottom of a shallow hole to provide a solid base for the armed BLU-3/B bomb, which is placed on top of it. Fins on the BLU-3/B are removed prior to positioning. Judging from the sketch, enough dirt is put around the bomb to keep it upright, yet not enough to cover the striker plate. An anchor stake is driven into the ground on the opposite side of the tree trunk. The slip loops indicated in the drawing are loose, and a pull on either trip wire will cause one of the loops to slide off the short cross bar which in turn

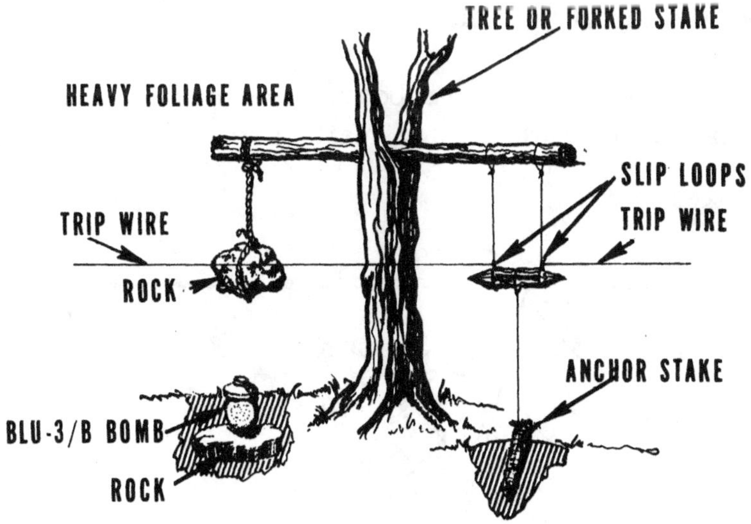

256-290 O-67—20

releases the long bar. When this occurs, the rock tied to the end of the long bar hits the bomb striker plate.

Grenade Launching Holes Against Helicopters, Infantry and Vehicles

The following information was extracted from Viet Cong documents captured by an Army unit. A series of launching holes are dug in the form of a triangle or parallelogram. Holes are approximately 24 inches in diameter at the top, two feet in depth and funnel shaped. A TNT charge weighing approximately three pounds is placed in the bottom of the hole. The charge is primed (number 8 electric cap), the lead wires extended above the ground, and the charge tamped with earth to within four inches of the top of the hole.

A 24-inch square board, two inches thick, is placed over the hole. Nails are driven into the

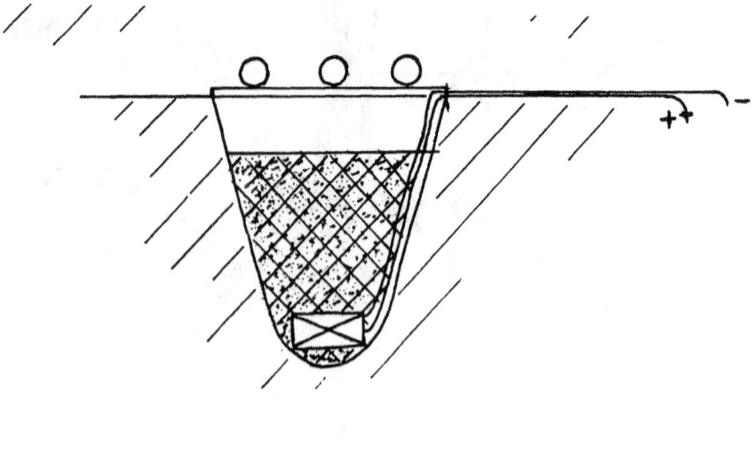

board three inches apart for the purpose of retaining the grenade arming levers when the safety pins are pulled, and also to keep the grenades in place. Stick grenades may also be employed. The arrangement is generally the same except that the grenade pull string is attached to a stake driven into the ground adjacent to the hole. BLU-3/B bombs may be used in lieu of grenades by drilling into the bottom or top of the munition and inserting either a standard grenade striker release type fuze, or a pull friction type as found in the stick grenades. The number of these devices uncovered indicates an exceptionally high dud rate. Therefore, extreme caution should be exercised when searching areas where this device has been used.

When the device is to be used against personnel and/or vehicles, the board holding the grenades is placed at a 45° angle.

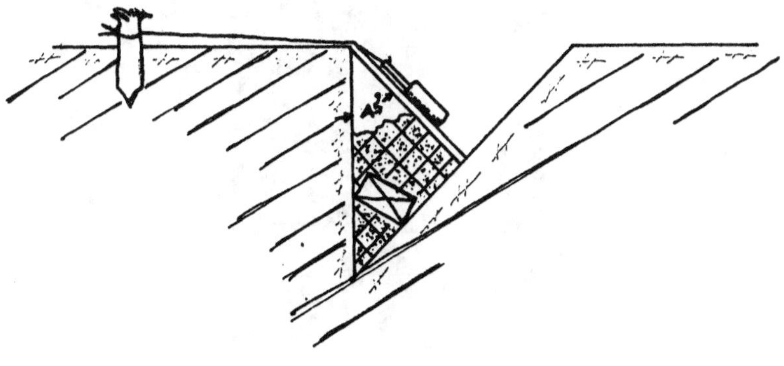

M16-A1 AP Mine

The most destructive device encountered in Vietnam has been the M16-A1 antipersonnel mine.

Until the VC received a supply of M16-A1 mines, his favorite antipersonnel mine seemed to be an M26 or a CHICOM grenade. These have been emplaced in the ground in a variety of ways. The majority have been rigged with some type of trip wire. Grappling hooks with a long length of line and a long bamboo pole thrown ahead of a man have proved

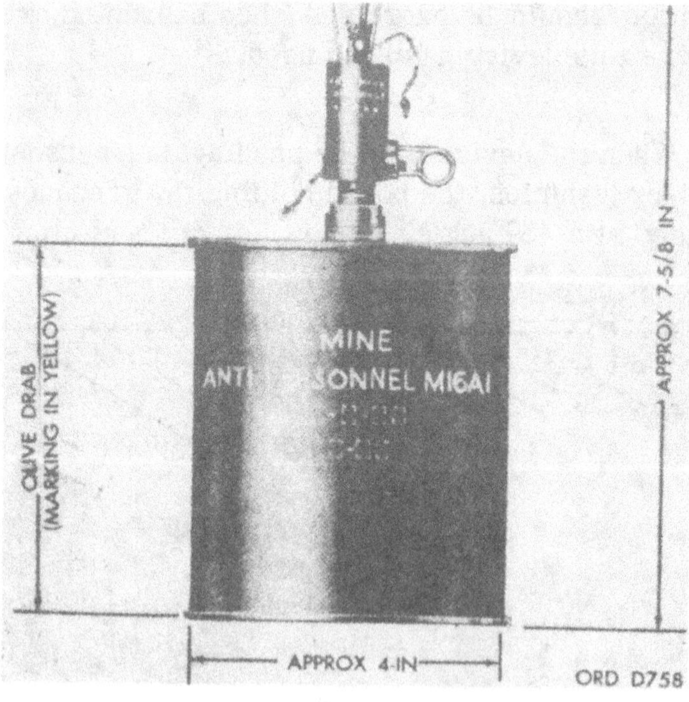

effective against trip wires. Neither of these methods has been satisfactory for the M16-A1 mine; it is too powerful to permit anyone being that close. Nor is the grappling hook or the bamboo pole effective against pressure devices unless it just happens to directly hit the release device; tracked vehicles have been more successful. Homemade devices have ranged in size and description from a small clay pot which had been packed with explosives, to a light wooden box packed with about 40 pounds of explosives and heavily laden with scrap metal. This was then suspended about six feet above ground in a tree line; the explosion was best described as devastating. Even artillery rounds wrapped with a layer of junk metal have been discovered hung in tree lines and over trails which were closely bordered by heavy brush.

VC Antitank Mine Firing Mechanism

A firing mechanism for the VC antitank mine consists of two pieces of 6-inch bamboo, one 6-inch piece of wood, four flashlight batteries and a length of electrical wire. As depicted in the sketch, the electrical wire is wrapped around one piece of the split bamboo and around a flat piece of wood. Wires are stripped of their insulation so that when pressure is exerted on the bamboo, it collapses, thus completing the circuit and detonating the charge.

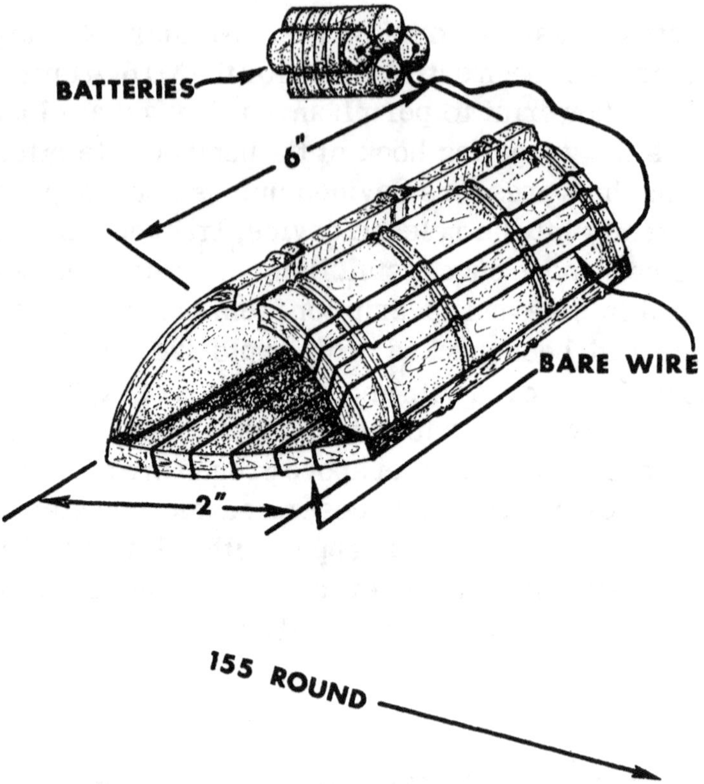

Stick Hand Grenade

The stick hand grenade, used extensively by the Viet Cong, comes in several sizes--differentiated by lengths of handle and sizes of fragmentation heads. This grenade functions by a pull string enclosed in the handle and attached to a copper wire coated with a match compound. Normally the match compound ignites a 4-second delay element, but a number of these grenades have been found with no delay element.

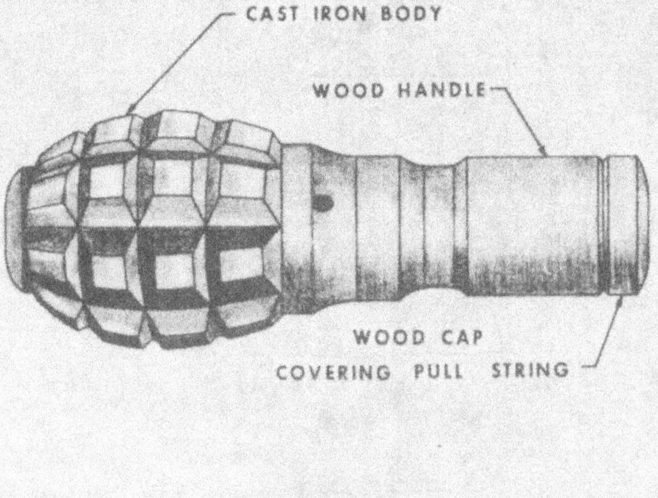

STICK HAND GRENADE

Characteristics

Type	-	Defensive
Color	-	Black
Max. diameter	-	2 inches
Length	-	6 to 8 inches
Total weight	-	3 pounds
Filler	-	TNT
Fuze delay	-	Approx. 4 sec.

Defensive Hand Grenade

The defensive hand grenade, of serrated cast iron, functions in the same manner as similar U.S. hand grenades. When the safety pin is removed and the grenade thrown, the safety lever releases the

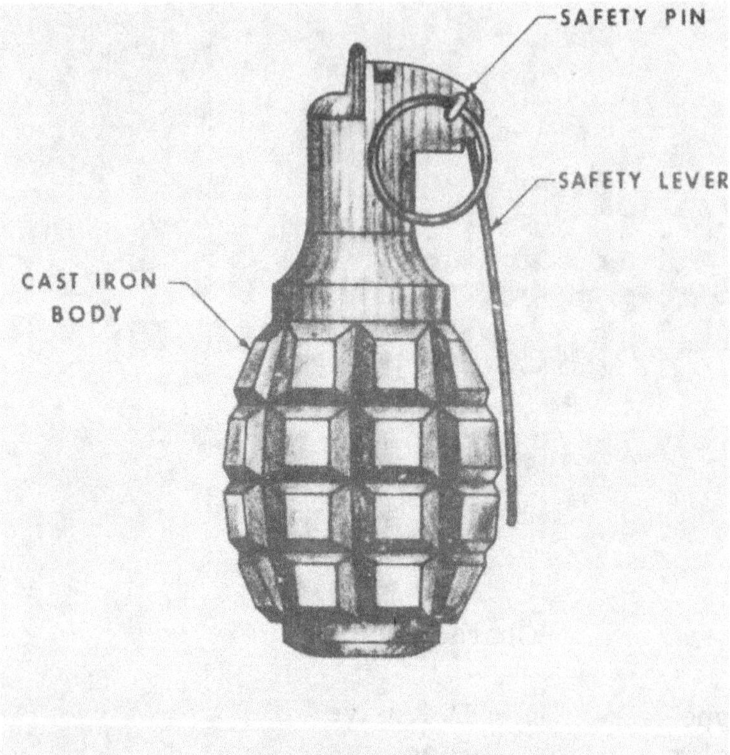

DEFENSIVE HAND GRENADE

spring of the mechanical firing device which ignites the primer and delay element of the fuze.

Characteristics

Type	-	Defensive
Color	-	Black
Diameter	-	2.5 inches
Length	-	5 inches
Total weight	-	1.5 pounds
Filler	-	TNT
Fuze delay	-	Approx. 4 sec.

Offensive Hand Grenade

The offensive hand grenade is made of explosive and sheet metal with crimped and soldered seams. It is normally equipped with a time delay fuze. These grenades must never be disassembled as a number of them have been found boobytrapped; for example, they have been found with an instantaneous (no delay) fuze, and an attempt to throw such a grenade, after pulling the pin, would prove fatal to the thrower.

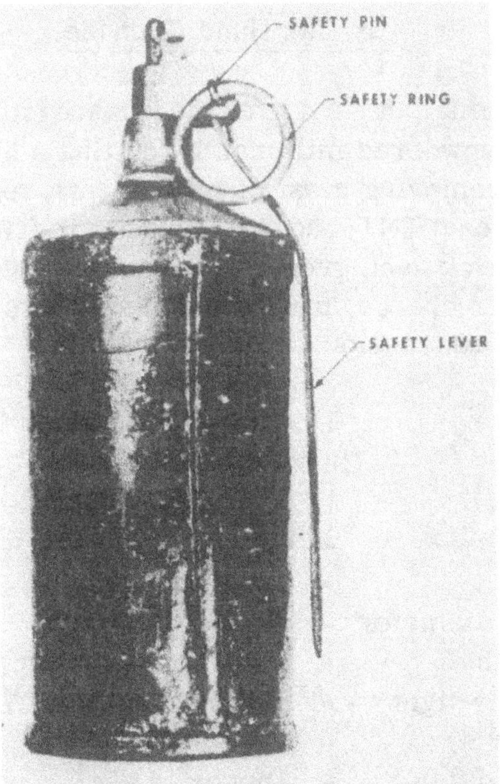

OFFENSIVE HAND GRENADE

Characteristics

Type	-	Offensive
Color	-	Generally black or olive-drab
Max. diameter	-	2.6 inches
Length	-	5.4 inches
Total weight	-	1.6 pounds
Filler	-	TNT or potassium chlorate
Fuze delay	-	Approx. 4 sec.

Milk Can Hand Grenade

The milk can hand grenade is made from a commercial powdered milk can by cutting a hole in one end and removing most of its contents, refilling the can with cast TNT, and installing a pull-friction fuze from a stick hand grenade. Because the device has no booster charge, it uses two detonators for more powerful concussion.

Characteristics

Type	-	Offensive
Color	-	Commercial label
Max. diameter	-	3.5 inches
Length	-	6.0 inches
Total weight	-	2 pounds
Filler	-	Cast TNT
Fuze delay	-	Approx. 4 sec.

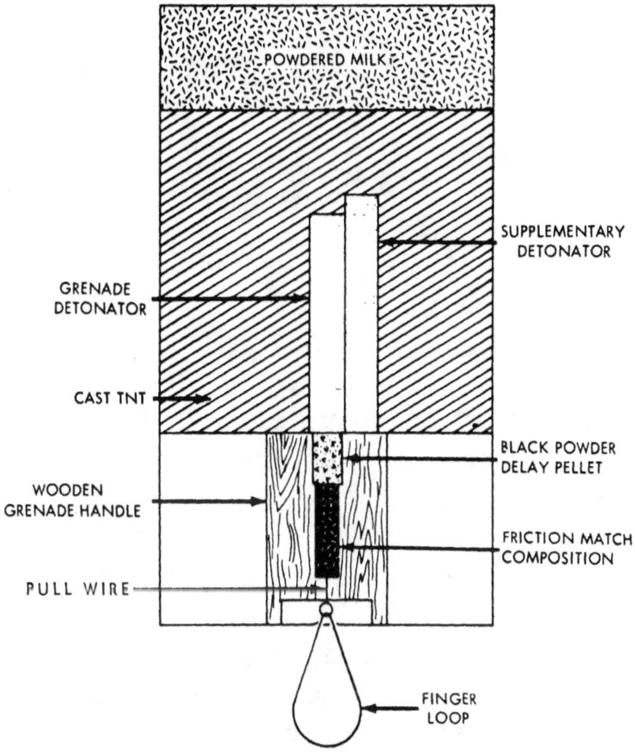

MILK CAN HAND GRENADE

Shaped Charge Hand Grenade

The shaped charge hand grenade consists of a shaped charge, a cylindrical sheet metal charge container, a conical sheet metal drag, an impact fuze mechanism, and a wood handle with a sheet metal drag lock and pin. When the lock pin is removed and the grenade is thrown, a spring forces the conical drag back over the handle to stabilize the grenade's flight (drag is attached to charge

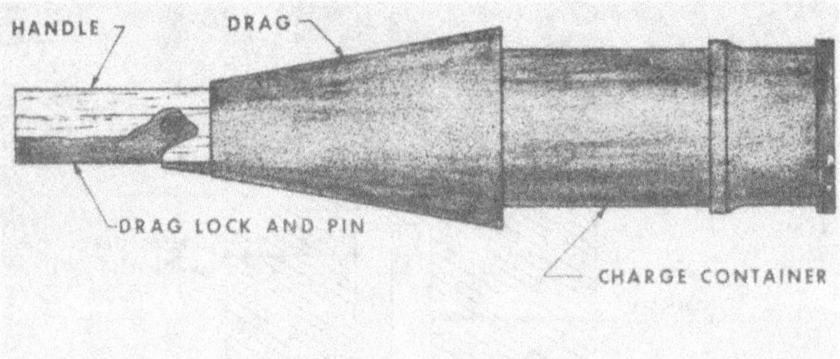

SHAPED CHARGE HAND GRENADE

container by strips of material inside the cone). When the grenade strikes, the impact fuze ignites the shaped charge.

Characteristics

Type	-	Shaped charge (HEAT)
Color	-	Black or olive-green
Max. diameter	-	3 inches
Length	-	8.75 inches
Total weight	-	Approx. 1.5 lb.
Filler	-	Cast TNT
Fuze delay	-	Time of flight

Shell Case Mine

The shell case mine has a standard artillery shell casing, mostly 75-, 105-, and 155-mm calibers. A variety of fuzing mechanisms can be improvised for this mine; the mine illustrated is detonated by the potato masher grenade inserted

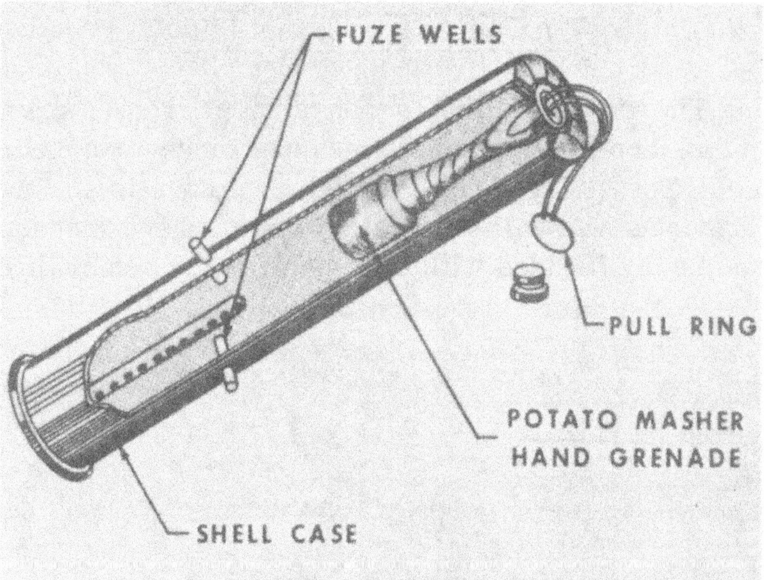

SHELL CASE MINE

into the explosive charge. Inserted into the side of the casing are two fuze wells through which electrically or mechanically initiated fuzes may be placed. The mine, generally used in an antipersonnel role, is initiated by a tug on a tripwire strung across a path.

Characteristics

Type	-	Antipersonnel
Color	-	Brass
Max. diameter	-	6 inches
Length	-	18 to 24 inches
Total weight	-	10 to 15 pounds

Filler	-	TNT
Fuze delay	-	3 to 4 sec. (with grenade)

Tin Can Antipersonnel Mine

The tin can mine is constructed from a sheet metal container similar in appearance to a beer can. The firing device for the explosive is an improvised fuze with zero delay action. A hand grenade fuze may be used with this munition by removal of

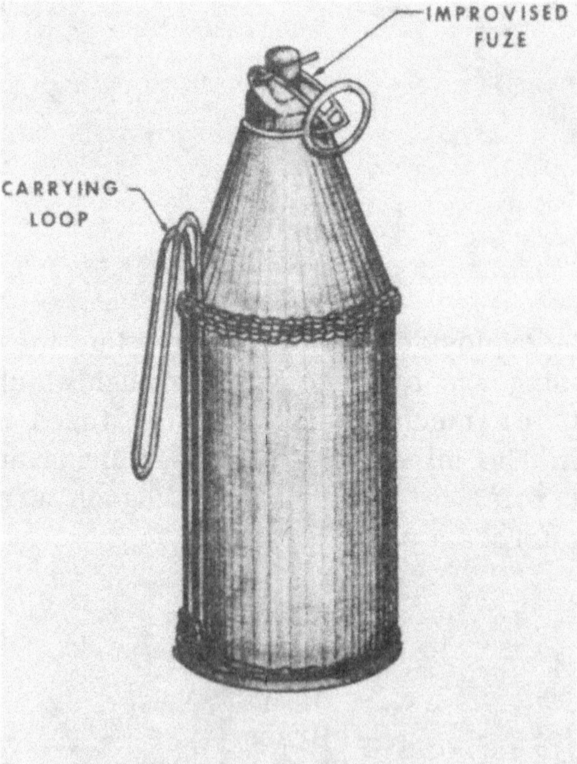

TIN CAN ANTIPERSONNEL MINE

the delay element. The mine functions by a tripwire attached to the pull ring device, which when removed allows the spring-driven striker to move downward, hitting the primer and detonating the mine.

Characteristics

Type	-	Antipersonnel
Color	-	Gray or green
Max. diameter	-	3 inches
Height	-	6 inches
Total weight	-	Approx. 2 pounds
Filler	-	TNT
Fuze delay	-	None

Concrete Fragmentation Mine

The concrete fragmentation mine is constructed of explosive encased in cylindrically shaped concrete with a flat side for stable emplacement. A 2-inch-diameter pipe on one end of the mine head serves as a carrying handle and detonator housing. The two swivels on top of the mine are used to tie it to an object. The mine's electrical detonator usually is activated remotely by means of a battery pack or hand-held generator.

Characteristics

Type	-	Antipersonnel
Color	-	Gray
Length of mine body	-	10 inches

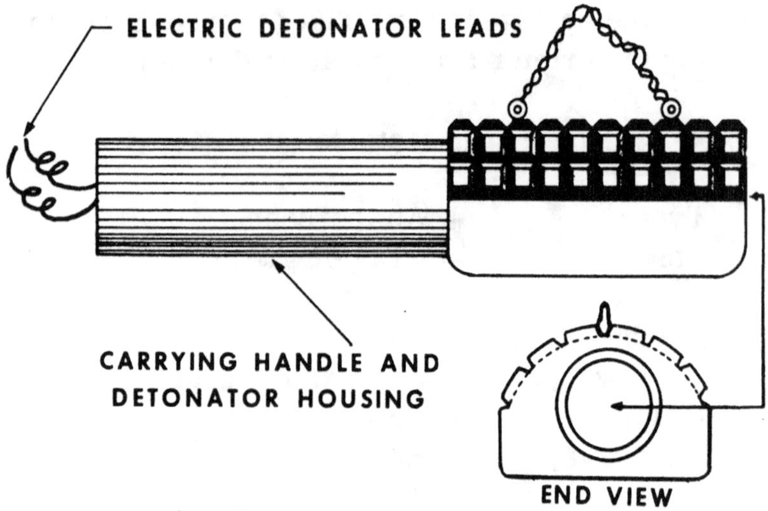

CONCRETE FRAGMENTATION MINE

Width of base	- 7 inches
Height	- 6 inches
Total weight	- 13 pounds
Filler	- TNT
Fuze delay	- None

Concrete Mound Mine

The concrete mound mine is constructed of explosive encased in concrete, but possibly a similar mine of cast iron may be encountered. The mound-shaped mine is electrically fuzed and has two fuze wells, one at each end. The iron pipe at one end of the mine serves as a pole socket, as well as being a housing for one of the fuze wells. Electric current to activate the detonator is provided by a battery pack or hand-held generator.

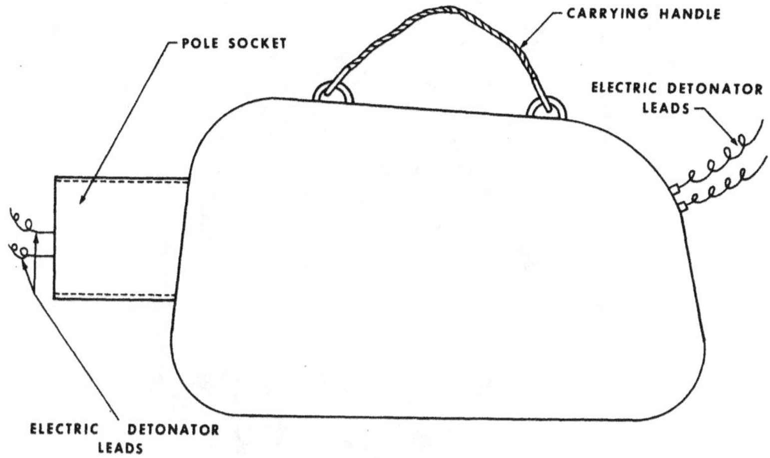

CONCRETE MOUND MINE

Characteristics

Type	-	Antipersonnel
Color	-	Gray
Max. diameter	-	5.5 inches
Length	-	14 inches
Total weight	-	13 pounds
Filler	-	TNT
Fuze delay	-	None

Betel Box Mine

The betel box mine is constructed of concrete and explosive. Its one fuze well is located on the top at the center of the mine. Used in either an antipersonnel or an antivehicular role, the mine is exploded by an electrical detonator.

256-290 O-67—21

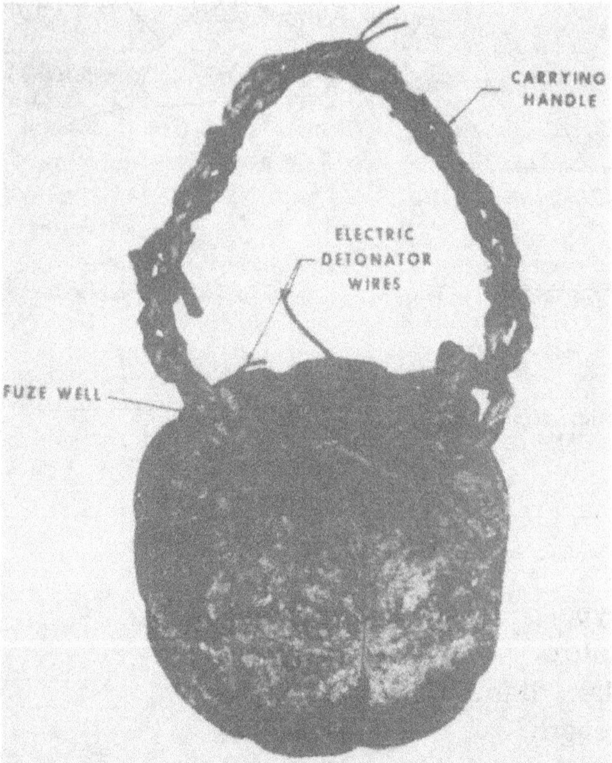

BETEL BOX MINE

Characteristics

Type	- Antipersonnel/antivehicular
Color	- Gray
Max. diameter	- 8 inches
Height	- 7 inches
Total weight	- 13 pounds
Filler	- TNT

Turtle Mine

The turtle mine, constructed of concrete with explosive inside, is used primarily as a demolition charge. It can be detonated by either an electrical or mechanical fuze (with or without delay). The mine illustrated utilizes a mechanical fuze.

TURTLE MINE

Characteristics

Type	-	Dual purpose
Color	-	Gray
Max. diameter	-	5 in. (end view is semi-circular)
Length	-	9 inches
Overall weight	-	13 pounds
Filler	-	TNT

Pineapple Fragmentation Mine

The pineapple fragmentation mine is a unique egg-shaped mine constructed of cast iron and is further identified by surface serrations and a carrying handle. The mine has a single fuze well located in one end of the body. It is fuzed with an electrical detonator which is activated by current from batteries on a hand-held generator.

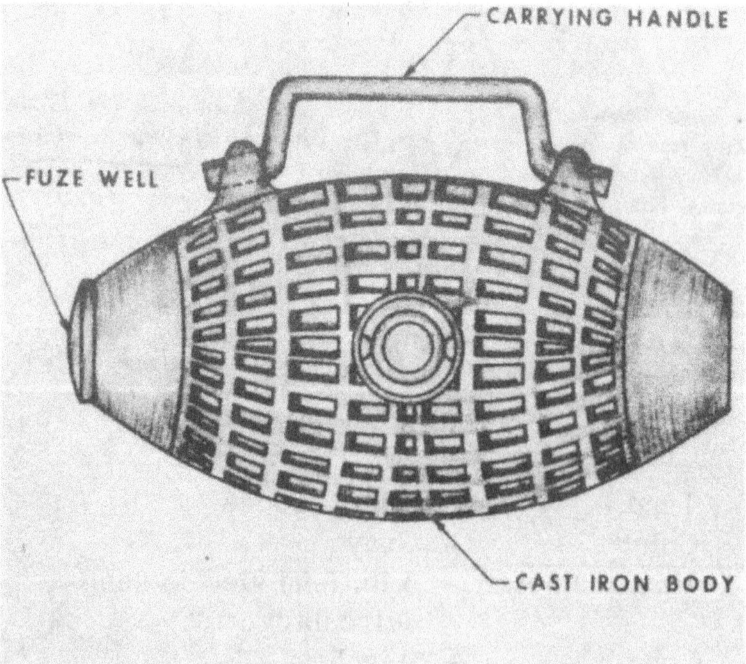

PINEAPPLE FRAGMENTATION MINE

Characteristics

Type	- Antipersonnel
Color	- Gray
Max. diameter	- 5 inches
Length	- 9 inches
Total weight	- 12 pounds
Filler	- Melinite/TNT

Dud Shell Mine

The dud shell mine is improvised from a dud artillery or mortar projectile. The mine is made by removing the fuze from a projectile and drilling a hole into the explosive for an electrical detonator. Batteries or a hand-held generator supply the current to activate the detonator remotely. The mine is usually found along roads or trails. Its effectiveness against armored vehicles and personnel varies with the type and size of projectile used.

Characteristics

Type	- Antipersonnel/antivehicular
Color	- Varies
Max. diameter	- Varies
Length	- Varies
Total weight	- Varies
Filler	- Usually TNT

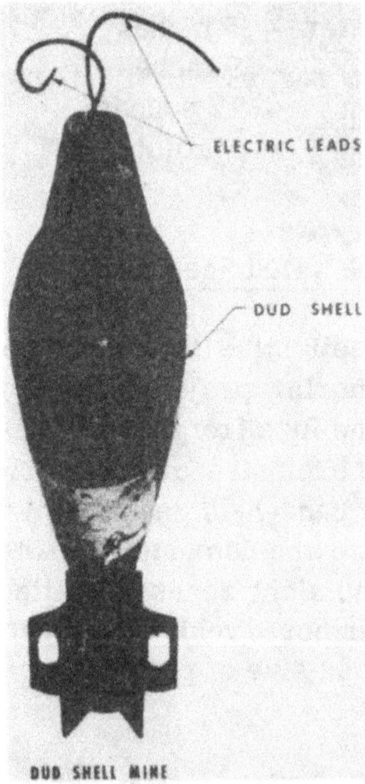

Min Antipersonnel Mine

The min antipersonnel mine, made of cast iron, resembles a stick hand grenade with a very short handle. The word, "Min," is often found cast into the body. The handle houses a pull-friction, delay-type fuze. A tug on a tripwire attached to the pull wire of the friction fuze will, by extracting the pull wire, ignite the delay element.

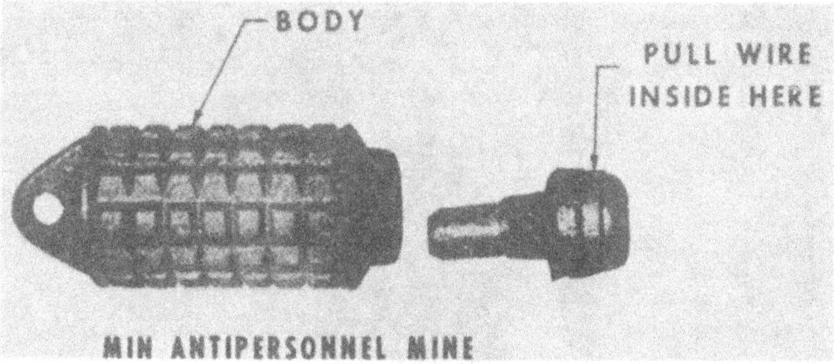

Characteristics

Type	-	Antipersonnel
Color	-	Gray to black
Max. diameter	-	2 inches
Length	-	6.5 inches
Total weight	-	2.2 pounds
Filler	-	TNT
Fuze delay	-	2 to 4 sec.

Bounding Fragmentation Mine

The bounding fragmentation mine is improvised from U.S. M2 bounding-mine or M48 trip-flare mine cases. A wooden cylinder slightly smaller in diameter than the mine case is hollowed out so that a standard grenade (frequently the U.S. M26) can fit inside. The wooden cylinder with enclosed grenade is then fitted into the mine case and the grenade's safety pin is extracted. When the mine is initiated electrically, either by a battery pack or a

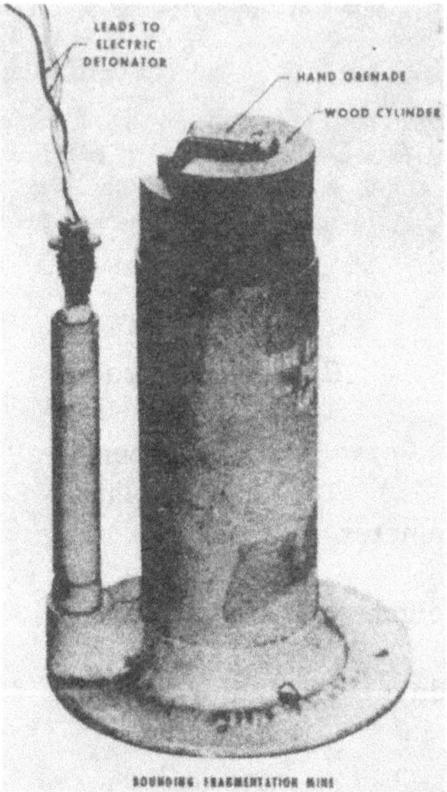

BOUNDING FRAGMENTATION MINE

hand generator, the cylinder and grenade are propelled upward. As the wooden cylinder with grenade leaves the case, the handle flies off and initiates the fuze train of the grenade.

Characteristics

Type	-	Antipersonnel
Color	-	Olive-drab or gray
Max. diameter	-	2.5 inches

Height	-	8 inches
Total weight	-	5 pounds
Filler	-	Grenade (TNT)
Fuze delay	-	3 to 4 sec. (grenade)

DH-10 Directional Mine

The DH-10 directional fragmentation mine is primarily an antipersonnel mine which also can be used against thin-skinned vehicles or similar items.

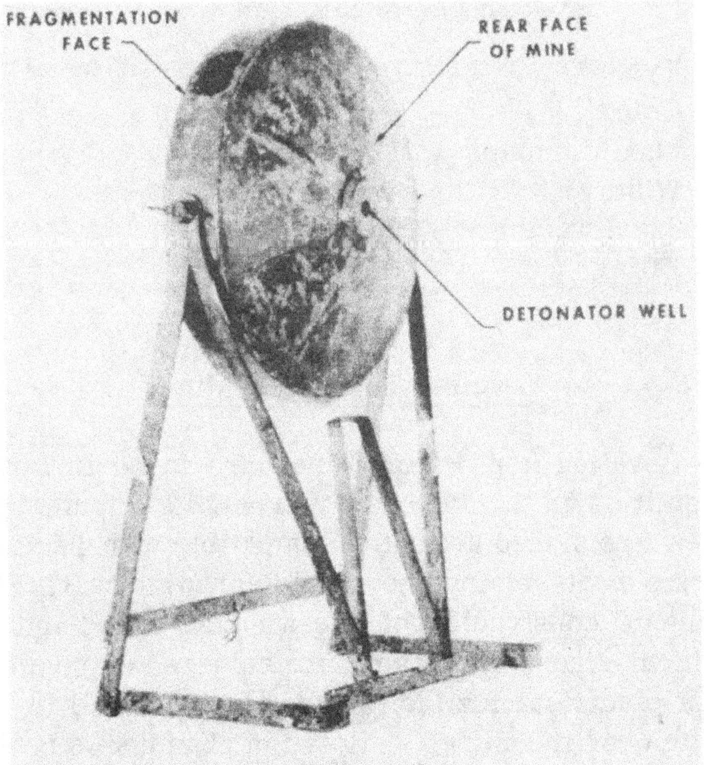

DH-10 DIRECTIONAL MINE

The concave front or fragmentation face of the mine contains approximately 450 half-inch steel fragments embedded in a matrix, and is backed up by cast TNT. Designed for electrical detonation, the mine is provided with an adjustable frame so that it can be placed on various types of surfaces and aimed in any direction. The single fuze well is centered on the convex (back) side of the mine.

Characteristics

Type	- Dual purpose
Color	- Gray to black
Max. diameter	- 12 inches
Width	- 4 inches
Total weight	- 20 pounds
Filler	- Cast TNT

Bevelled Top Water Mine

Bevelled top water mines are found in large quantities in the Mekong River and its tributaries. They are placed at depths compatible with the draft of the boats plying the particular waterway. The mine is constructed of sheet metal rolled into a conical shape; the seams are soldered or riveted. The electrical fuze is located in a fuze well in the bottom of the mine. A flotation chamber is in the end opposite the fuze well. Batteries or a hand-held generator provides the current.

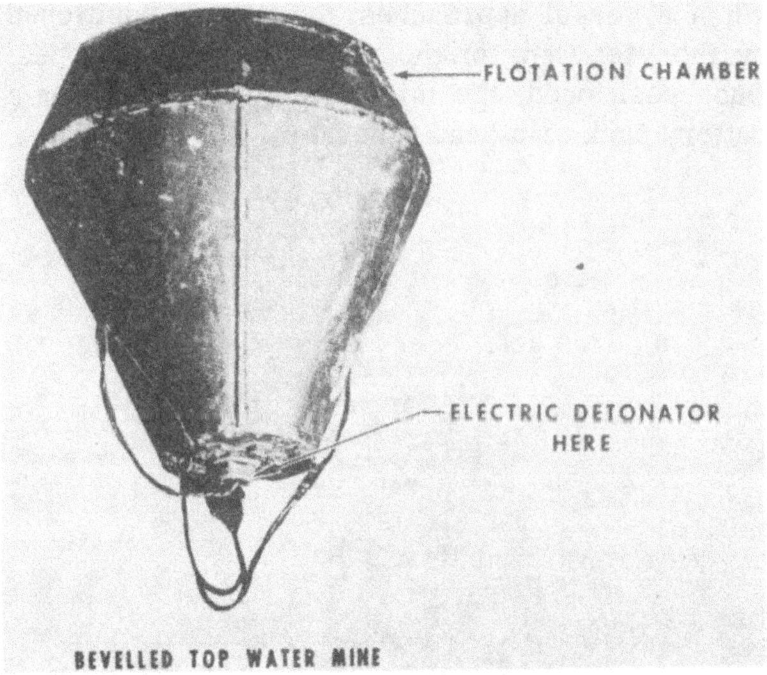

Characteristics

Type	-	Antiboat
Color	-	Black
Max. diameter	-	11 inches
Height	-	12 inches
Total weight	-	27 pounds
Filler	-	TNT

Truncated Cone Water Mine

The truncated cone water mine is manufactured from medium-gage sheet metal in two sections riveted together: the explosive section with electrical fuze (small end) and the flotation chamber. When a vessel approaches, the mine is positioned by the Viet Cong on the shore by means of ropes. Once positioned, the mine is detonated by using a battery pack or a hand generator.

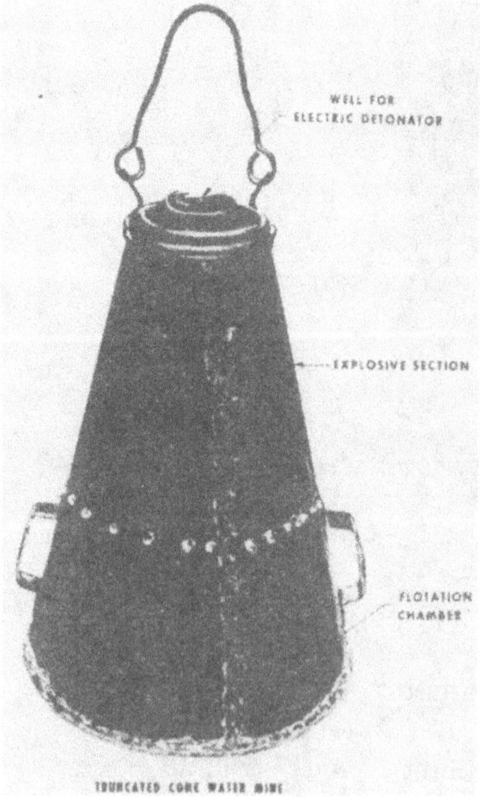

TRUNCATED CONE WATER MINE

Characteristics

Type	- Antiboat
Color	- Black
Max. diameter	- 17 inches
Height	- 25 inches
Total weight	- 83 pounds
Filler	- TNT

Small Truncated Cone-Shaped Charge

The small truncated cone-shaped charge is encased in sheet metal plates riveted together. A pull-friction fuze in the small end usually initiates the explosive charge; it contains a delay element which allows the Viet Cong saboteur to leave the vicinity before the explosion. Some charges have also been found with electrical detonators and some with booby traps in the fuze mechanism.

Characteristics

Color	- Usually black
Max. diameter	- 8 to 10 inches
Height	- 8 to 10 inches
Total weight	- 15 to 18 pounds
Filler	- TNT or homemade explosive
Fuze delay	- Approx. 9 sec. (pull-friction)

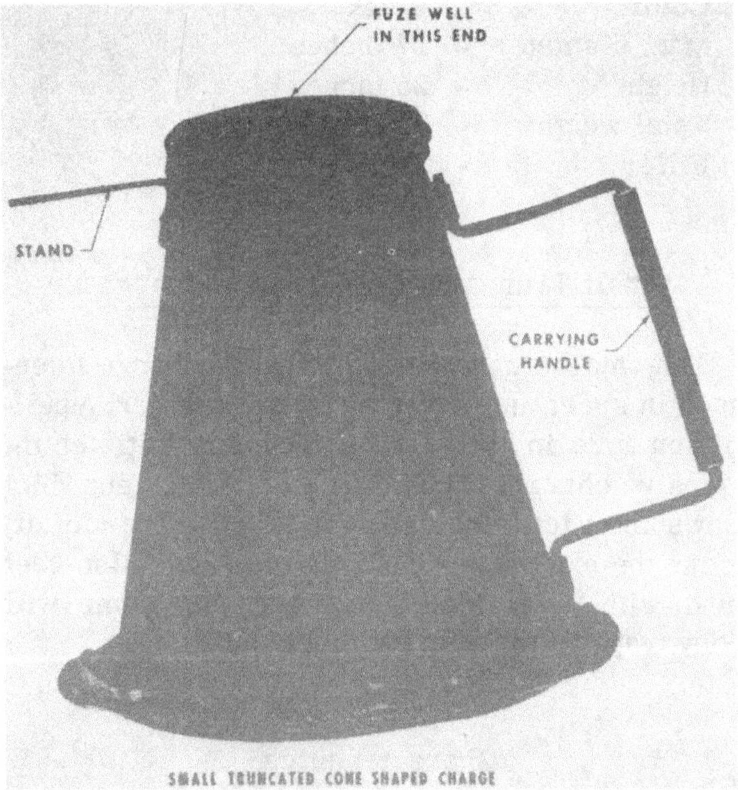

Large Truncated Cone-Shaped Charge

The large truncated cone-shaped charge is encased in heavy-gage sheet metal with welded seams. Its fuze is a pull-release or pull-friction device of unknown construction, which is initiated when a nearby Viet Cong tugs on the pull wire. This charge is also found to be occasionally fuzed for electrical initiation.

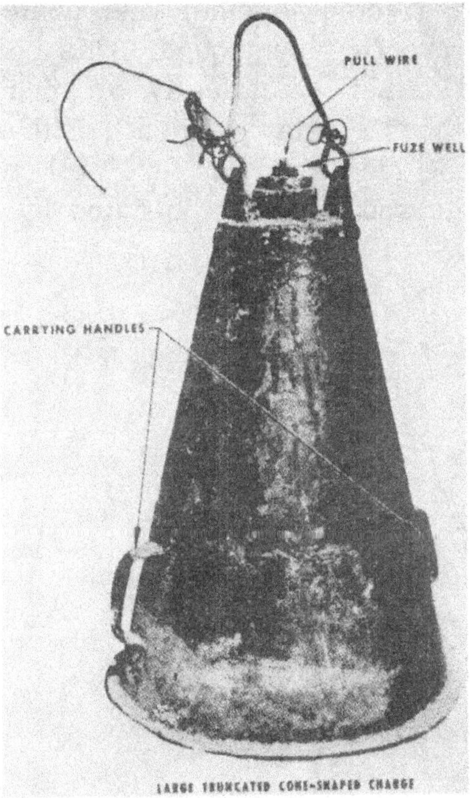

LARGE TRUNCATED CONE-SHAPED CHARGE

Characteristics

Color	-	Unpainted or black
Max. diameter	-	9 inches
Height	-	11 inches
Total weight	-	22 pounds
Filler	-	TNT

Turtle Charge

The turtle charge is encased in four pieces of sheet metal riveted together and coated with a black waterproofing compound. This charge can be initiated either electrically or mechanically (with or without a delay element). Either type of fuze would be located in the fuze well on the side of the charge and would be initiated by a nearby Viet Cong.

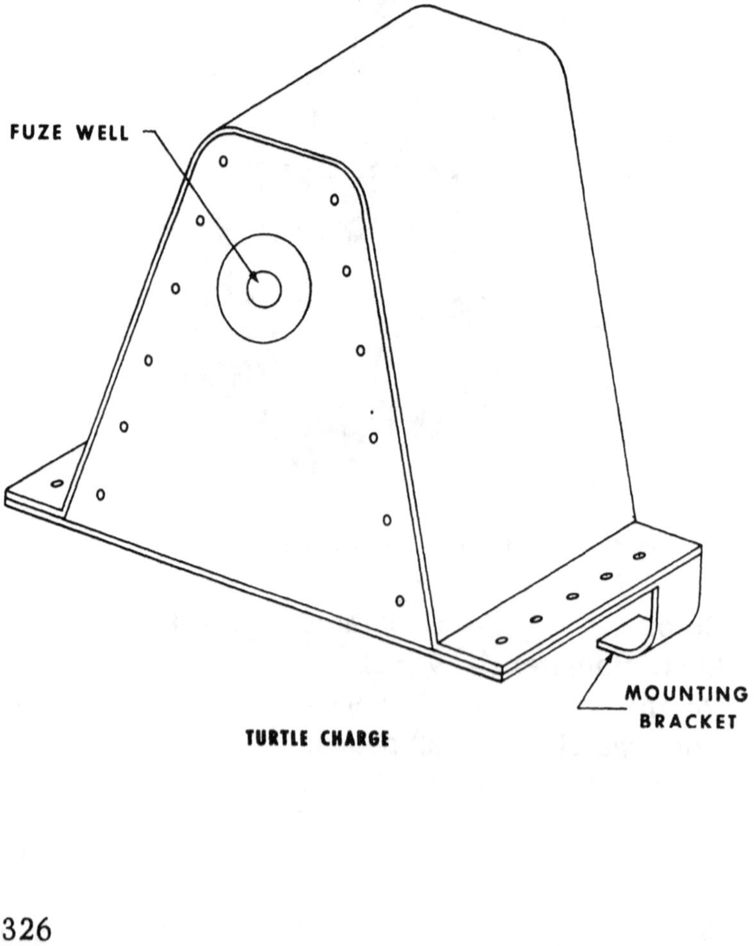

TURTLE CHARGE

Characteristics

Color	-	Black
Length	-	Approx. 4 inches
Width	-	9 inches
Height	-	5 to 6 inches
Total weight	-	20 pounds
Filler	-	Picric acid (melinite) or TNT

Cylindrical Charge

The cylindrical charge, although normally encased in sheet metal as illustrated, can also be made from artillery and mortar projectile shipping containers. The dimensions and weight vary considerably. The charge is normally fired electrically by a nearby Viet Cong using batteries or a hand-held generator. The weapon could also be fired by pull-friction, mechanical, or delay-type firing devices.

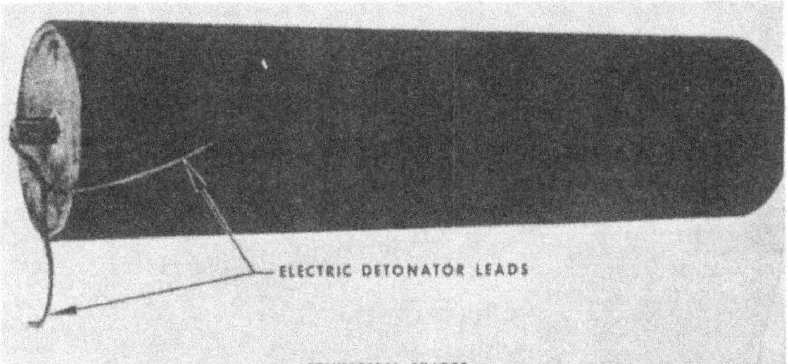

CYLINDRICAL CHARGE

Characteristics

Color	-	Varies
Max. diameter	-	Varies
Length	-	Varies
Total weight	-	5 to 25 pounds
Filler	-	TNT, potassium chlorate, or homemade explosive

Pole Charge

The pole charge consists of a quantity of explosive wrapped in waterproof material (such as a piece of tarpaulin or canvas) and lashed to a 3- or 4-foot-long pole. The explosive is initiated by a piece of time fuze crimped to a nonelectric detonator. Pole charges are generally used during assaults for destroying barbed wire entanglements and bunkers.

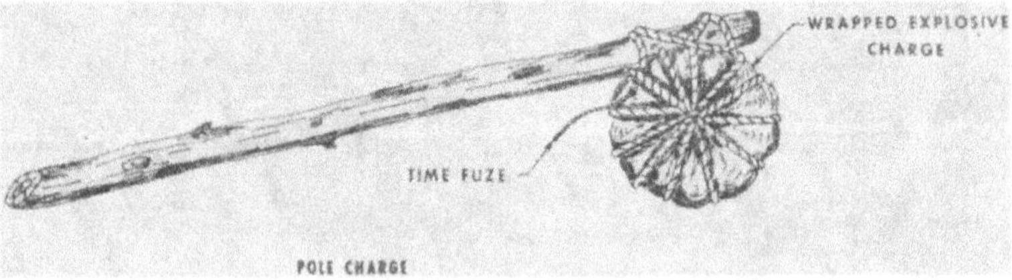

Characteristics

Color	-	Varies
Max. diameter	-	Varies
Length (pole)	-	3 to 4 feet

Total weight	-	8 to 15 pounds
Filler	-	Normally potassium chlorate
Fuze delay	-	Varies

Oil Drum Charge

The oil drum charge is made by partially filling a standard U.S. 5-gallon oil or lubricant drum with explosive and installing a wristwatch firing device (see page 333) in the bottom end. The specimen shown has two firing devices to ensure that the charge will explode if one fuze malfunctions.

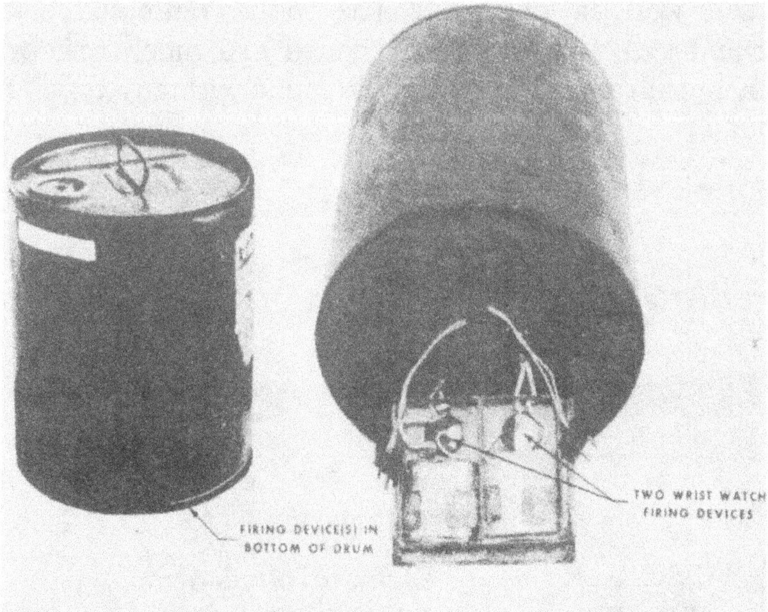

OIL DRUM CHARGE

Characteristics

Color	-	Olive-drab
Max. diameter	-	11 inches
Height	-	13 inches
Total weight	-	Approx. 25 pounds
Filler	-	Varies

Bangalore Torpedo

The Bangalore torpedo is generally made from a length of 2-inch-diameter pipe filled with explosive and initiated by a fuze. The specimen illustrated is one of the better made items and has a fuze well in one end. The most commonly encountered Bangalore torpedoes are much cruder in appearance. They may be found with any type of fuze.

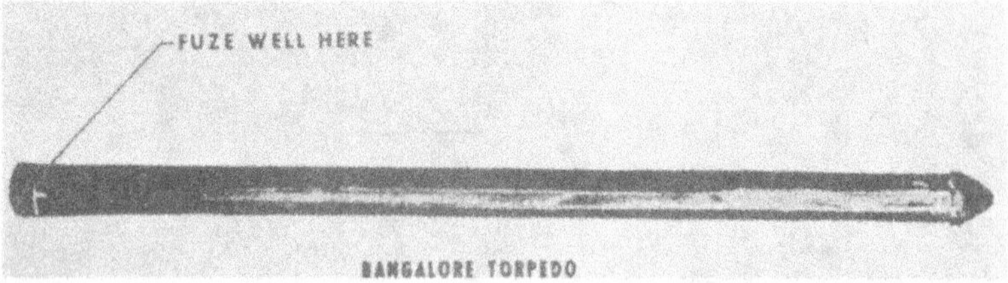

BANGALORE TORPEDO

Characteristics

Color	-	Black or olive-drab
Max. diameter	-	2 inches
Length	-	Approx. 42 inches
Total weight	-	Varies
Filler	-	TNT or picric acid

Chemical Fuze

The chemical fuze is used for sabotage. It can be attached to any mine or demolition charge. The fuze is initiated by breaking the corrosive liquid vial; the corrosive solution then gradually corrodes the wire which restrains the firing pin. When the wire has weakened sufficiently, the firing pin is released and strikes the primer, detonating the charge. The delay time provided by this fuze varies with temperature and wire diameter.

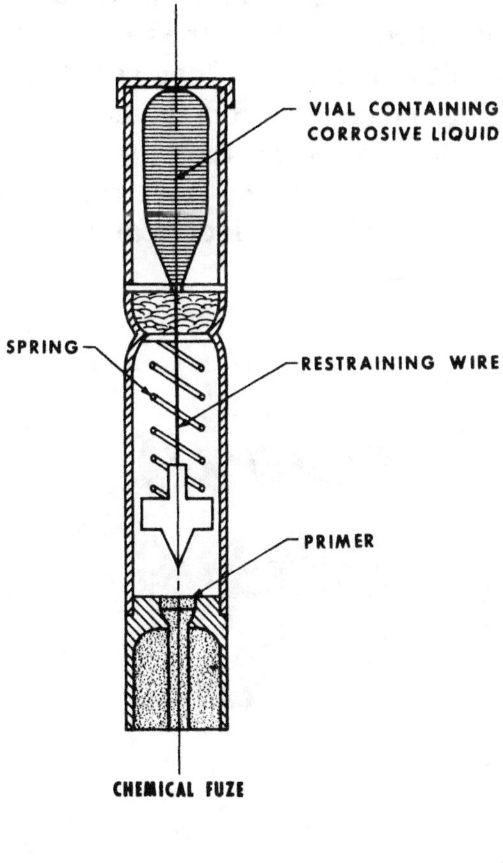

CHEMICAL FUZE

Characteristics

Type	-	Delay
Diameter	-	0.5 inches
Length	-	5 inches
Fuze delay	-	Varies; 20 to 38 min.

Pressure-Electric Firing Device

The pressure-electric firing device consists of a wood frame; a movable, spring-loaded wooden pressure piece attached to a bolt; and a length of double-strand electric wire. One strand of electric wire is attached to the bolt; the second strand (bare) is fastened to the frame. When some outside force (i.e., a person stepping on the device) pushes the pressure piece down so that the head of the bolt contacts the bare strand of wire, the circuit is completed through the electrical detonator which then fires the device.

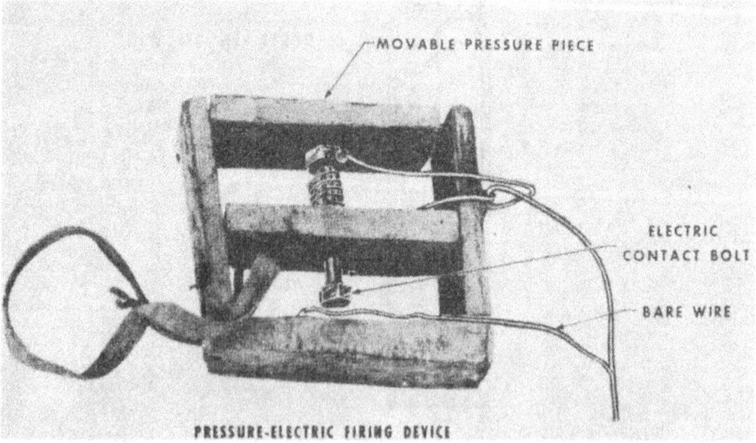

PRESSURE-ELECTRIC FIRING DEVICE

Characteristics

Type	-	Nondelay
Length	-	Approx. 4.5 inches
Width	-	Approx. 1.5 inches
Height	-	Approx. 4 inches
Operating force	-	Varies widely

Wristwatch Firing Device

The wristwatch firing device is used to provide a delay between the time an explosive charge (bomb or mine) is placed and the time it explodes. The delay period can range from a few minutes to twelve hours according to how the watch is altered and set.

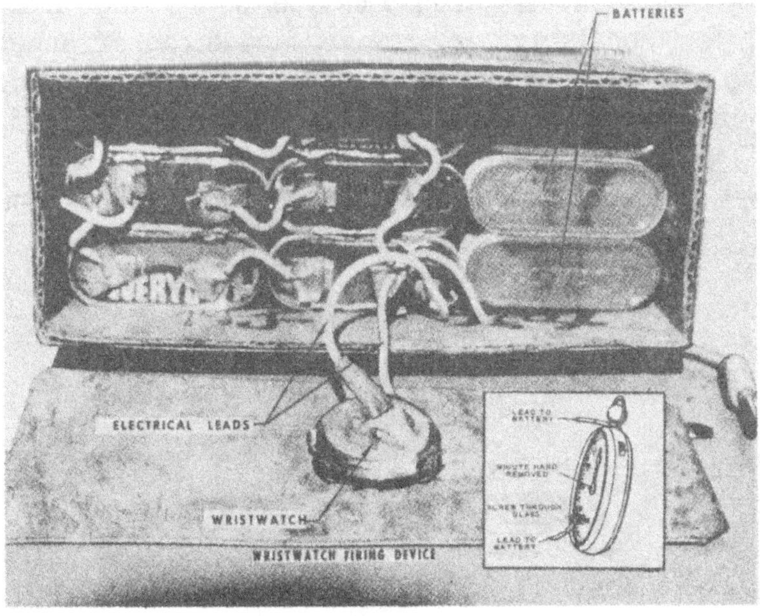

WRISTWATCH FIRING DEVICE

Either the minute hand (if the desired delay is in hours) or the hour hand (if the desired delay is in minutes) is broken off. One electric lead is connected to the stem or case of the watch and the second lead is connected to a screw passing through a hole in the watch crystal. The watch runs for a preset interval until its remaining hand touches the screw; at that time the circuit is completed and an electrical detonator explodes. The illustration shows an actual installation including the power supply; the inset shows a watch only, in schematic form.

Mousetrap Firing Device

The mousetrap firing device, as its name indicates, consists of an ordinary mousetrap, arranged so that the yoke, when tripped, will drive a firing pin (nail) into a percussion primer. This firing

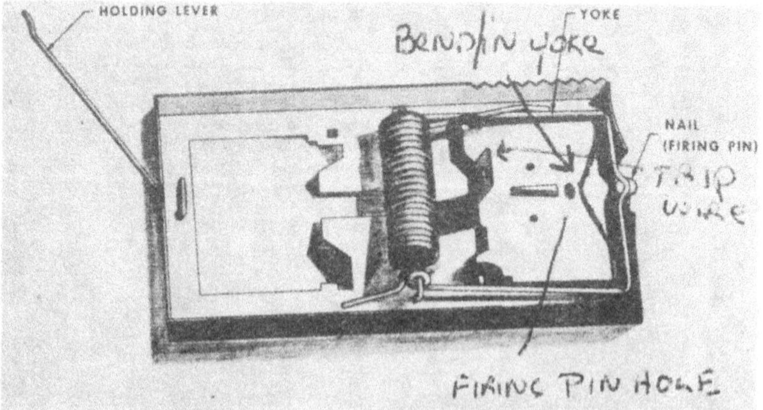

MOUSETRAP FIRING DEVICE

device has been frequently used on Viet Cong improvised guns. Its future use will probably be confined to booby trap or antipersonnel mine installations.

Angled Arrow Trap

The angled arrow trap is made of a piece of bamboo (about 1-meter long) fastened to a board, a steel arrow, a strong rubber band, a tripwire, and a catch mechanism. The device is placed in a camouflaged pit, the bottom of which is sloped in such a way that a person tripping the wire will be struck in the thorax by the arrow.

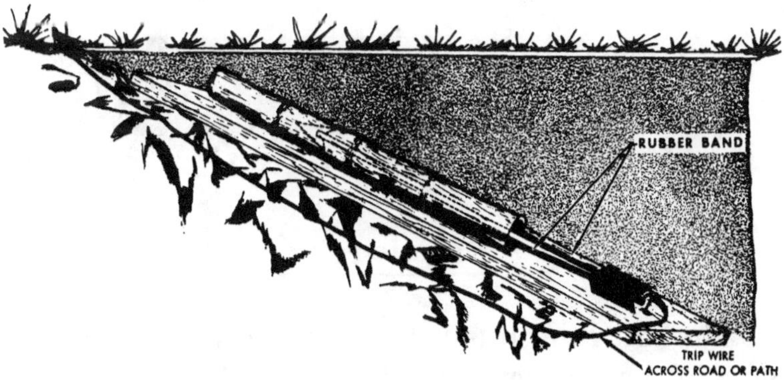

ANGLED ARROW TRAP

Whip

The whip consists of a length of green bamboo, supported by a series of posts, and three or four barbed-point arrows. The bamboo pole is bent and held in an arc position by a catch device. When a tripwire placed across a trail or path is pulled, it releases the catch device, and the bamboo pole hurls the arrows along the path at about chest height.

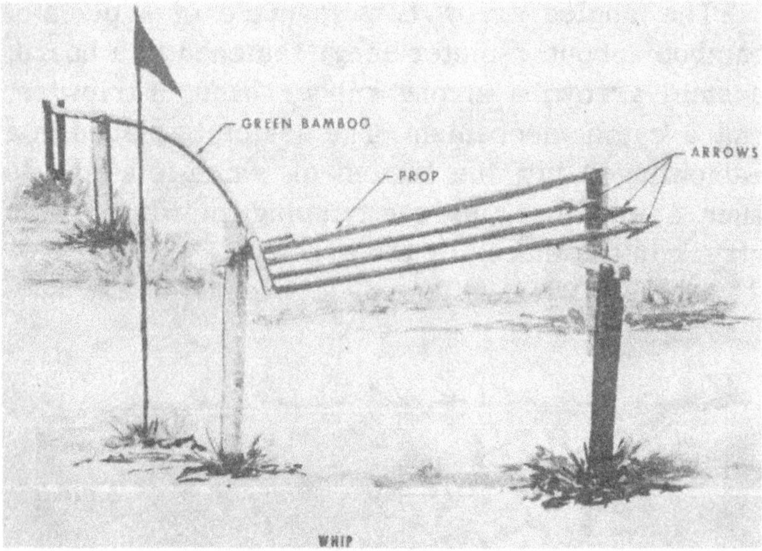

Bicycle Mine

The bicycle mine is made from an ordinary bicycle by filling part of the tubular frame with explosive, installing an electrical detonator in this explosive, and connecting the detonator to batteries and a wristwatch firing device (see wristwatch firing device, page 333) in the headlight housing. The bicycle explodes when, after a preset time interval, the wristwatch hand touches an electric contact

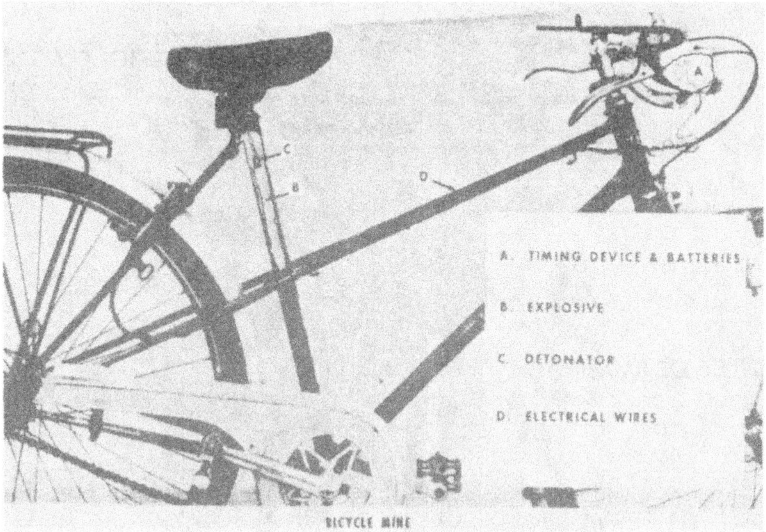

BICYCLE MINE

and the circuit through the detonator is completed. This mine can be varied by connecting the detonator directly to the headlamp power generator; when the bicycle is moved, the generator sends an electric current through the detonator to cause the explosion.

Cartridge Trap (Foot Breaker)

The cartridge trap consists of a cartridge set into a piece of bamboo fastened to a board and installed in a camouflaged pit. A nail driven through the bottom of the bamboo serves as a firing pin. The weight of a man stepping on the upper end of the cartridge forces the nail into the cartridge to

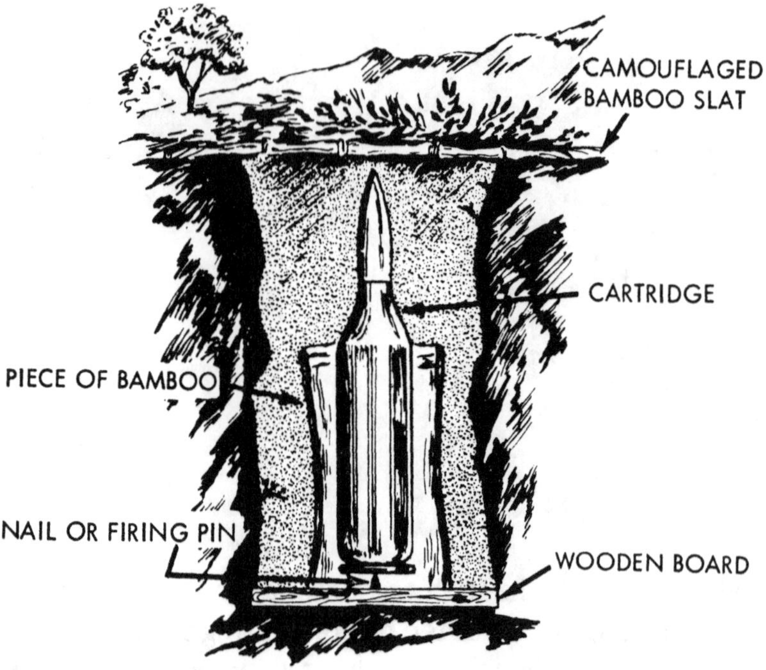

CARTRIDGE TRAP (FOOT BREAKER)

initiate the primer; the bullet is then propelled upward through the man's foot.

Spike Board Pit

The spike board pit is simply a small pit the bottom of which is lined with boards through which spikes have been driven. The top of the pit is camouflaged. A person stepping on the camouflage material falls into the pit and impales his foot or feet

on the spikes. These pits are generally about 18 inches square and 12 inches deep.

Tilting Lid Spike Pit

The tilting lid pit is substantially the same type of trap as the spike board pit described previously. The major differences are that it is much larger (about 13 feet square by 8 feet deep) and has a pivoting lid. The lid is supported in the middle by an axle; when locked in position it is strong enough to support a man's weight. When the lid is not locked, it pivots when a man steps on it and the man drops into the pit onto the boards with spikes that cover the bottom. The lid, which is counterbalanced,

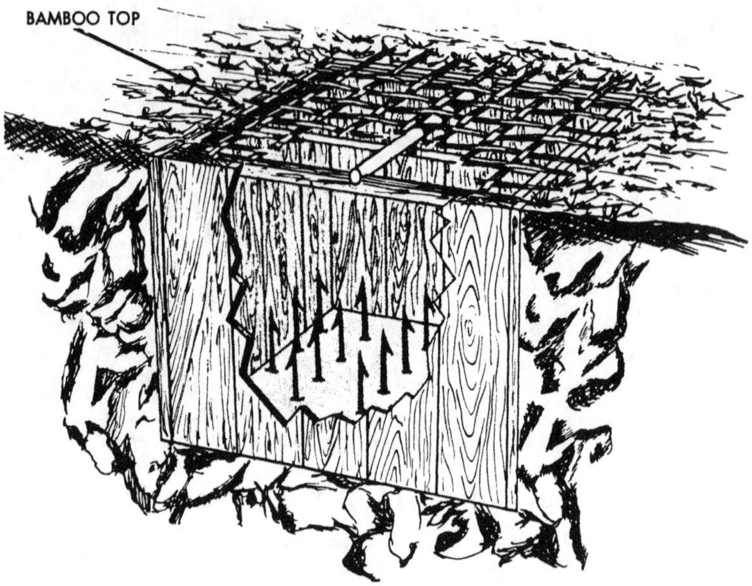

TILTING LID SPIKE PIT

then swings back to its original position. Because of the pit's depth, the walls are shored up with boards or logs to prevent cave-ins.

Pivoted Spike Board

The pivoted spike board is used with a foot pit. When a person steps on the treadle (shown in the illustration), the board with driven spikes pivots

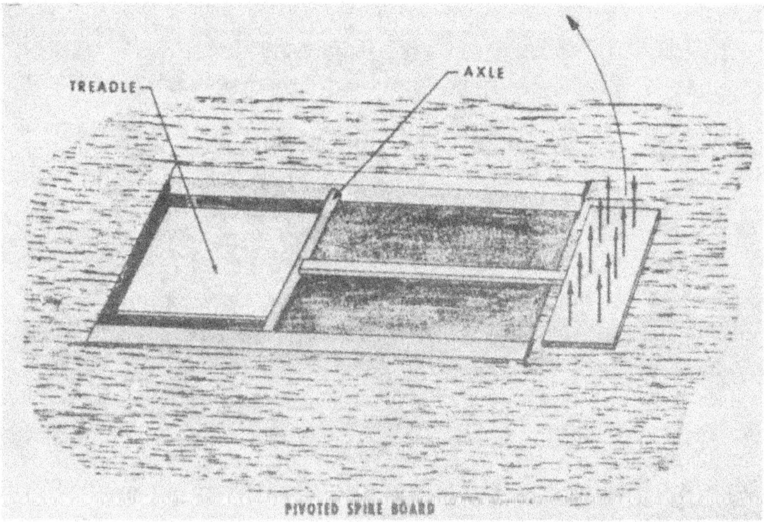

about an axle. As the victim drops into the pit, the spike board strikes him in the chest or face.

Venus Flytrap (Pit)

The Venus flytrap (pit) consists of a rectangular framework with overlapping barbs emplaced over a pit on trails or in rice paddies. The dimensions of such devices vary; the one illustrated is approximately 8 by 22 inches. The barbs are angled downward toward the pit, thus making any attempt to extract a leg exceedingly difficult. If a person steps

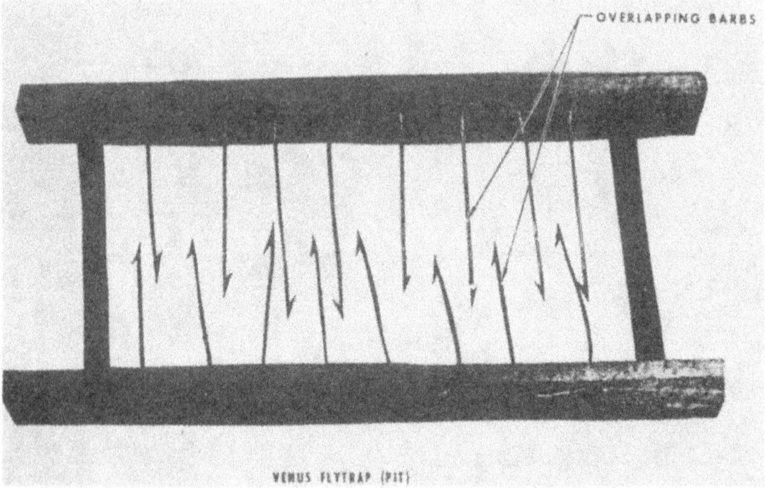

VENUS FLYTRAP (PIT)

into one of these flytraps, he should cautiously bend the barbs down or cut them before attempting to pull his leg out.

Venus Flytrap (Can)

The Venus flytrap (can) is a variation of the Venus flytrap (pit) described previously. The flytrap illustrated is constructed of a metal container. An individual trapped in one of these devices should cut off or bend the barbs downward before making any attempt to withdraw his leg.

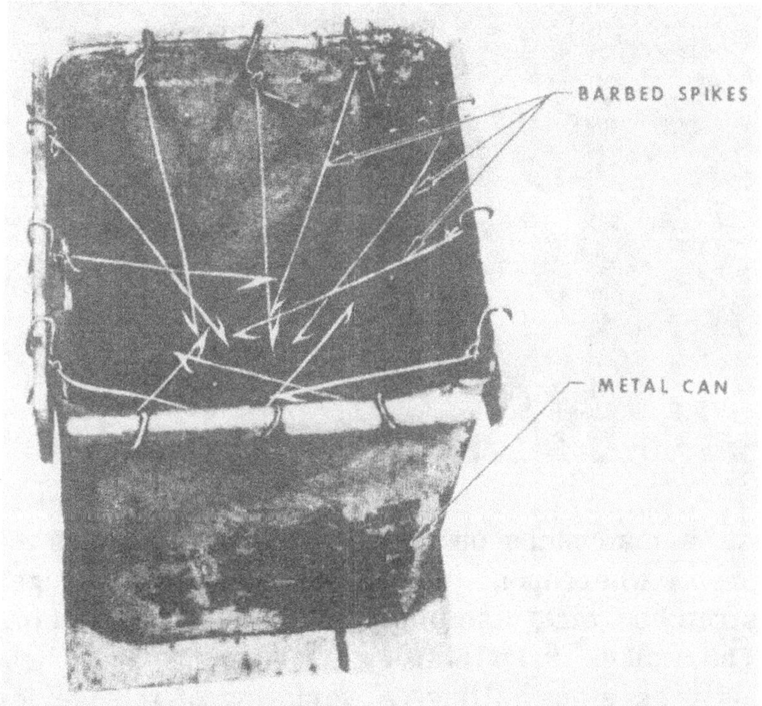

Sideways Closing Trap

The sideways closing trap, another variety of the spike trap, consists of two wood strips, each studded with barbed spikes, sliding along a pair of guide rods and sprung together by two large rubber bands cut from an automobile inner tube. A wooden prop keeps the spike-studded wood strips apart and stretches the rubber bands. The device is placed in the top of a pit (about 4 feet deep) and camouflaged.

256-290 O-67—23

As a man steps on this device, he dislodges the prop, whereupon the rubber bands, no longer stretched taut, clamp the spike strips around him. The spikes rake his legs, abdomen, and chest until he stops falling. A variation of this device consists of a length of green bamboo split lengthwise, instead of wood strips, with spikes along each side of the split.

Trap Bridge

The trap bridge is a wooden bridge boobytrapped by partially sawing through the planks and camouflaging the cut with mud. Barbed stakes are laid

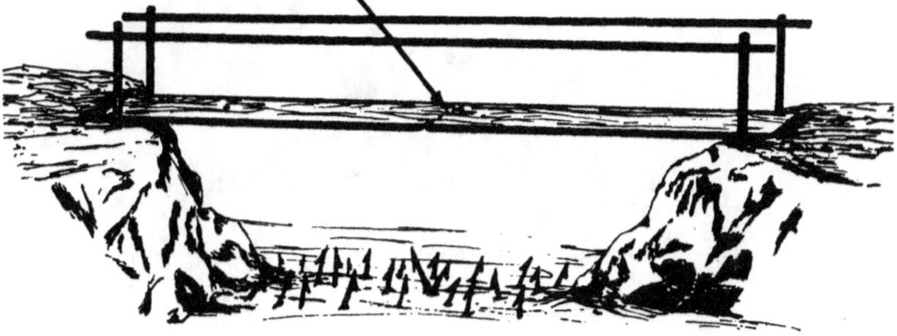

TRAP BRIDGE

underneath the bridge and along the adjacent banks; anyone crossing the bridge causes it to collapse and he or they will be impaled on these spikes.

Suspended Spikes

The suspended spikes device, also known as the Tiger Trap, consists of an 18-inch-square board with spikes. It is weighted with bricks and suspended from the branch of a tree overhanging a path. A tripwire stretched across the path beneath the spike board, when pulled, frees the device to fall on someone below.

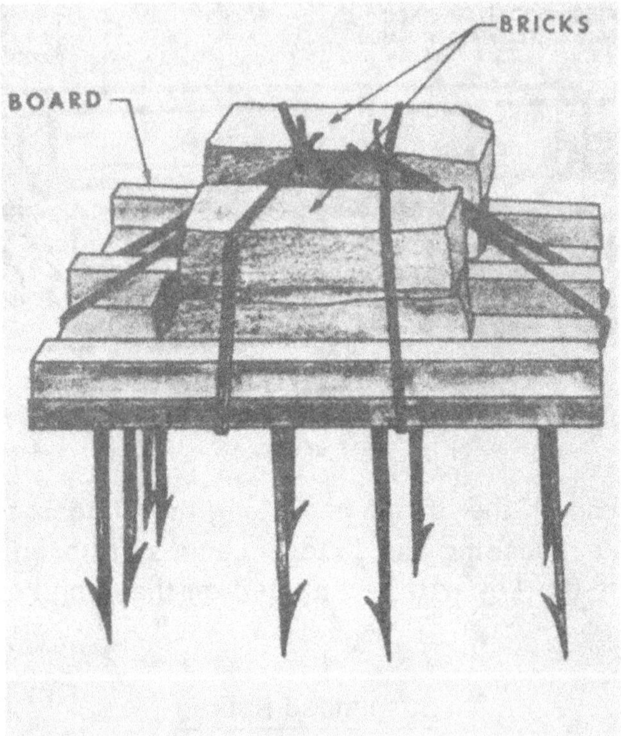

SUSPENDED SPIKES

Spike Log (Mace)

The spike log is approximately 8 to 10 feet long and studded with spikes. It is often left in roadside ditches where it is hidden in the grass. In another emplacement, called the Mace, the spike log is suspended from a tree branch in such a way that, when a tripwire is pulled, the log swings down along the path or trail--impaling anyone in its way.

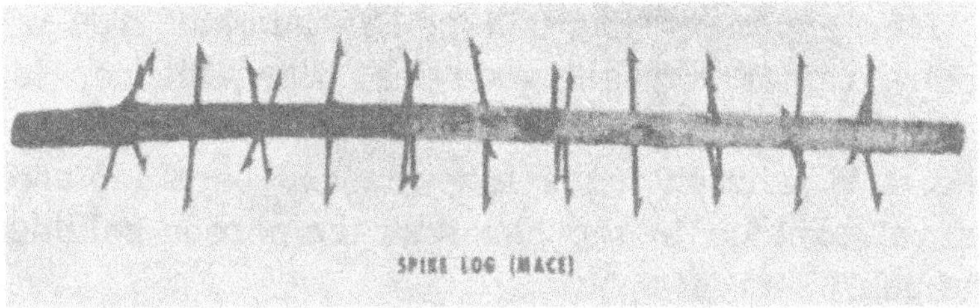

SPIKE LOG (MACE)

Cal. .22 Fountain Pen

The caliber .22 fountain pen is actually a weapon which fires a .22 caliber rimfire cartridge. It is used by Viet Cong agents for assassinations. The illustration shows the pen in the uncocked position. When the device is cocked, the round stud (part of the firing pin) will be located in the notch at the left end of the slot in the cap. If the stud is pushed out of the notch, a compressed spring will drive the firing pin into the cartridge, causing it to fire. This device can be varied as a cigarette lighter.

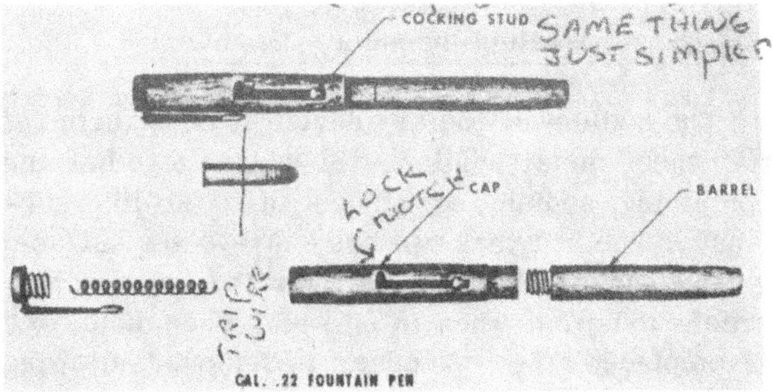

CAL. .22 FOUNTAIN PEN

Explosive Fountain Pen

The explosive fountain pen is another type of booby trap or harassing device. When the cap is unscrewed and removed from the barrel of the pen, two friction fuzes function and both cap and barrel explode in the hands of the person holding the pen.

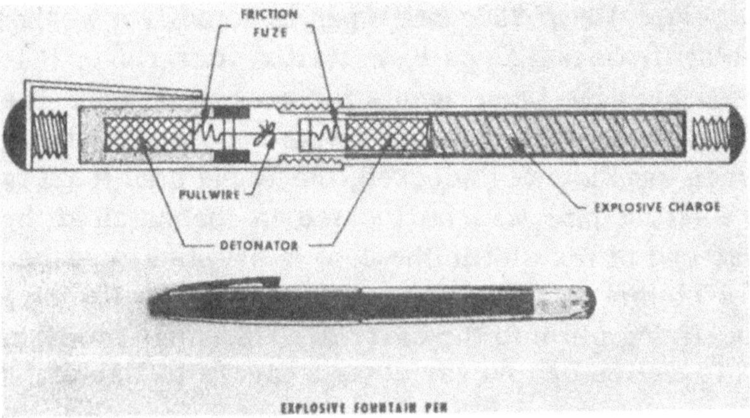

EXPLOSIVE FOUNTAIN PEN

Sodium Incendiary Device

The sodium incendiary device is constructed of two sheet metal hemispheres welded together and containing sodium suspended in a tar-like substance. The body has two holes in its outer surface. A wax and paper covering over the holes waterproofs the item when in storage. When the device is emplaced, the wax cover is removed, allowing water to contact the sodium and thereby creating heat and flame. This device is often emplaced in

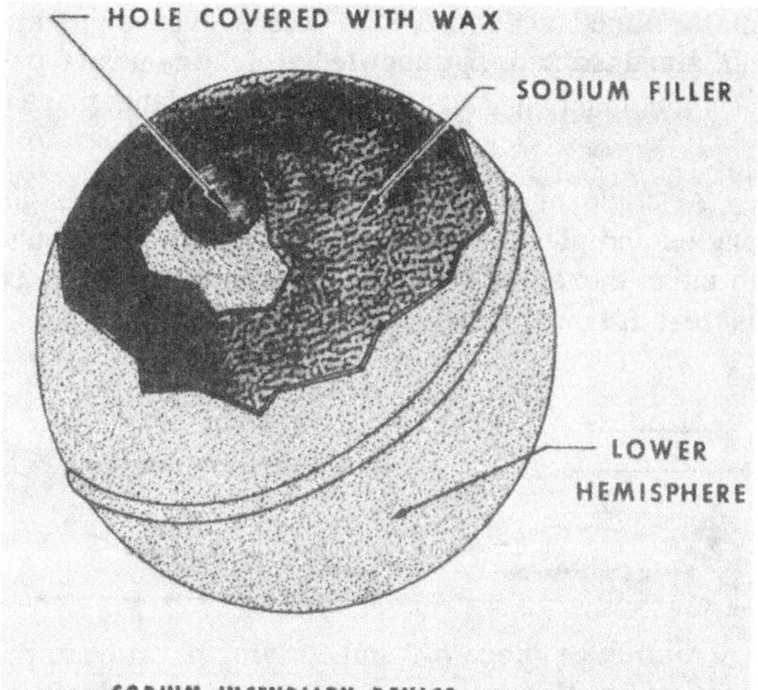

SODIUM INCENDIARY DEVICE

boat bilges and is particularly effective in any area with oil or gas seepage.

Characteristics

Type	-	Incendiary
Color	-	Black
Diameter	-	1.5 inches
Weight	-	1.5 ounces
Filler	-	Sodium

# # # # #

3. VC MINE AND BOOBY TRAP SIGNS

The VC use natural and man-made materials to mark mined and mine-free areas. The signs are not standardized, but knowledge of the general types of signs used can permit detection of a danger area.

A stick or length of bamboo broken at right angles and placed on a road or trail has been found to mean there are VC booby traps or mines 200-400 meters farther ahead.

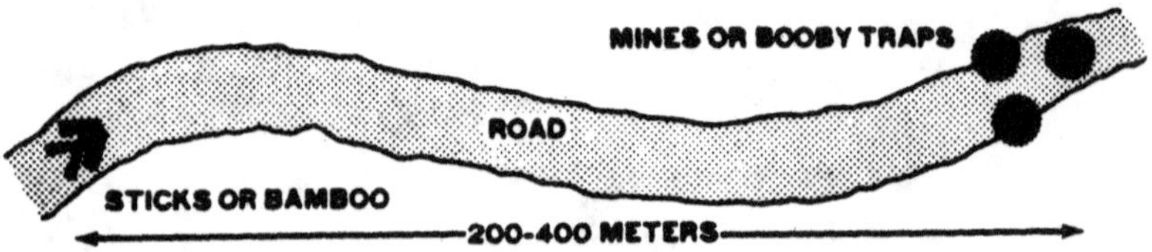

A stick or piece of bamboo lying parallel to the road or trail can mean that the area is minefree, but don't count on it.

Three sticks or three stones, one on each side of the road and one in the center means "do not use the road."

To mark spike pits, three sticks are tied together to form a tripod. These tripods are placed directly over the spike and are generally taken away upon the approach of allied troops.

Booby trapped or mined areas are marked by an arrow nailed at the top of a post one meter high. The arrowhead points to the mined or booby trapped area and the "feather" end of the arrow designates the safe area. The "arrows" are generally removed upon the approach of allied troops.

A mine or booby trap is sometimes indicated by four tufts of tall grass, tied in knots, each tuft at the corner of a meter square. The mine or booby trap is in the center of the square.

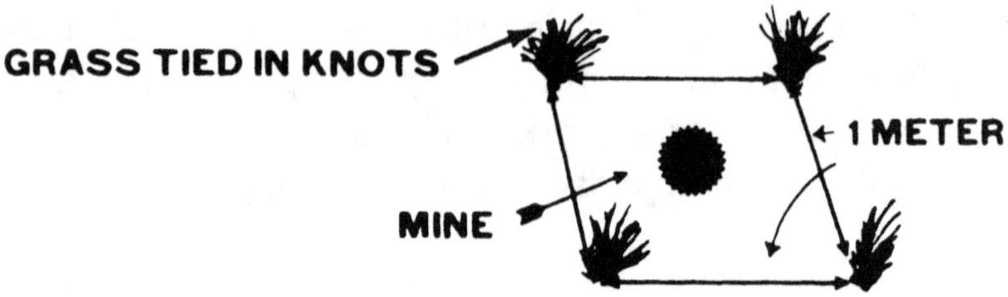

A stick, shaved flat on one side, approximately one-half meter in length, is stuck in the ground at a 45 degree angle with the flat portion of the stick facing skyward. This stick indicates that there is a mine one meter forward and on line where the flat side of the stick enters the ground.

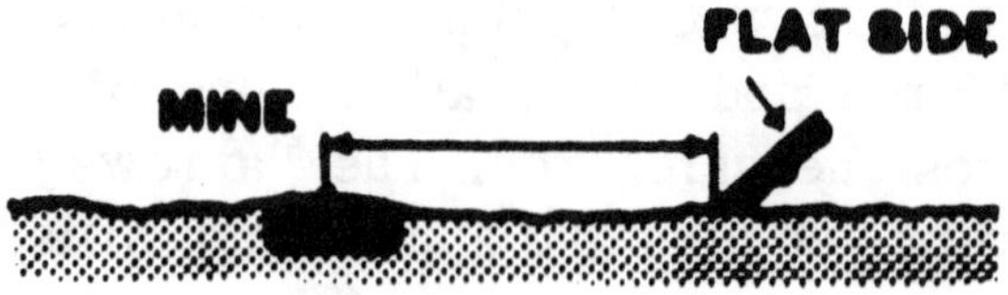

Other types of mine and booby trap indicators used by the Viet Cong are:

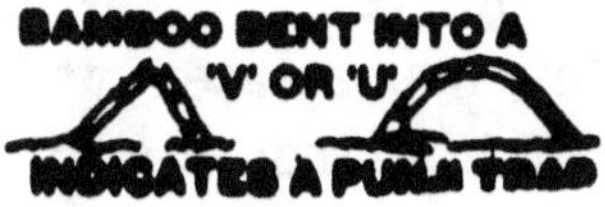

The VC may use different signs in different areas or may even change the meaning of signs, but one rule will not change:

> IF YOU OBSERVE OBJECTS IN AN UNNATURAL PLACE OR POSITION, TAKE CARE!

# # # # #

4. TIPS THAT WILL SAVE YOUR LIFE

→ When a unit moves into a new area, it is unlikely to encounter booby traps. However, if the unit leaves and then returns a few hours later, it is a good idea to conduct a thorough search for mines and booby traps. Experience has shown that the VC will have mined the area during the time the unit was away. Remember, it only takes a few minutes to rig a booby trap.

→ Whenever cutting wires leading to an electrically rigged charge, cut the wires one at a time. If both wires are cut together there is a good possibility of activating the device.

→ Interrogation by experienced Marines establishes the fact that the VC mark most mines and booby traps. The marker will normally be 200 to 400 yards from the device and will vary with the area in which the operations are taking place. It may consist of a piece of cloth, a twig bent in a certain way, a leaf tied in a knot or a pile of stones.

→ Many booby traps encountered by Marines use the U.S. M-26 fragmentation grenade. The bulk of these grenades have been supplied to the enemy by Marines who insist on carrying them "John Wayne" style on suspenders or in unbuttoned pockets.

→ Tripwires used by the enemy are often single strand (monofilament) fish line which is very difficult to see and nondetectable by mine detectors.

→ The enemy often places a booby trap so it will be easily detected. Beware! This is just a ruse to draw you into the area. There is probably another device in the immediate vicinity.

→ Two boobytrapped mines have been found on a trail which were attached to sticks three feet off the ground. Two wires were attached to each mine; one across the trail and one in the area to the side of the trail which covered any attempt to walk around the mine. Remember, when a trip wire is discovered, look for additional wires!

→ No road or trail can be considered 100% safe. Not even the road to the PX. Vigilance must be continuously exercised.

→ Unnecessary casualties have occurred in Vietnam when more than one Marine became involved in the disarming of enemy mines and booby traps. Mines should normally be blown in place. When they must be disarmed, only one Marine should perform the operation except when help is absolutely needed.

→ The LAAW (M-72) has proven to be a definite asset to the Marine rifle platoon. However, a word of caution. Destroy the expended tube to prevent its use by the enemy or it may return to you in the form of a boobytrapped mine. The enemy is extremely clever at this and takes every opportunity to use items discarded by Marines.

→ Other items normally discarded by Marines which the Viet Cong use in fabricating explosive devices are:

- Communication wire
- Batteries
- Duds
- Explosives
- Blasting caps
- Plastic waterproofing material
- Ammo boxes

→ Any Marine who approaches closely to another Marine in the presence of the enemy is doing a disservice to himself and his buddy. In one case, six men were killed and nine wounded in Vietnam by a mine believed to have been command detonated. Excessive casualties from a single explosive device can only be attributed to the tendency to bunch up. Remember, spread out and live!

→ The Viet Cong technique of placing a booby trapped 81mm round in a tree line approximately five meters off the ground has paid high dividends for them. On one occasion, a Marine patrol suffered one KIA and six WIA from such a device. The blast and fragmentation effects were comparable to a low airburst.

→ The enemy has developed two techniques to test the capabilities of Marine mine detectors. One method is to place a metal bolt in a large piece of cactus, or fill a tin can with human waste and bury it. A mine is often attached to these devices in hopes that mine clearance teams will become careless when they discover an apparently harmless piece of metal.

→ Another technique employed by the enemy is to fill ration cans with metal objects and then bury them at various depths in order to test the effectiveness of Marine mine detectors.

→ The Viet Cong have the capability of altering the M-26 fragmentation grenade so that it serves as an effective booby trap. The fuze assembly is removed and a nonelectric blasting cap with a 6-penny nail placed in the top is inserted in the fuze well of the grenade. Wax is poured into the grenade fuze well, around the nail and blasting cap to waterproof the device and hold the nail in place. The grenade is then buried upright with the nail protruding above the ground.

→ A great many enemy mines are the controlled electric detonation type. The lead wire used to detonate the mine is often Marine communication wire. It is, therefore, extremely difficult to distinguish the enemy lead wire from friendly communication lines. Suspect all communication wire!

→ All communication wire should be placed at least twenty meters from all roadways. This practice will aid in the visual detection of mines electrically detonated from locations off the roadway.

→ The Viet Cong are employing a special type of homemade grenade which incorporates a firing device actuated by acid. The grenade body is green or red and has a green safety lever. It is designed to explode when the safety lever is touched and is purposely left on the battlefield in hopes that unsuspecting troops will pick it up.

→ The Viet Cong, on one occasion, laid mines near two ramps which had been constructed to permit LVTs access to a river. The mines were laid out in a triangular pattern. A Marine demolition platoon used six charges to destroy the mines and achieved nine secondary explosions, one of which was a 155mm shell. Remember, when one mine is discovered, check for others!

→ The Viet Cong use a 10-pound shape charge with markings "MDH over L207.65 over TNT over 210" as a mine. The charge is emplaced along a road and is prepared for controlled electric detonation. Over 100 meters of communication wire is normally used as a lead. In every instance, Marines have discovered these mines by detecting the communication wire and tracing it to the mine.

→ Take the following actions to avoid contact with mines or minimize the effect of mines on the LVTP-5:

- Sandbag the deck of the cargo compartment.

- Open the hatches to reduce the pressure and diffuse the blast effect as well as to allow quick escape from the vehicle.

- The driver and crew chief of the LVT must continuously make visual inspections of the ground ahead for freshly dug areas, unusual debris, or any unusual change in an area previously traveled.

- When vehicles are in column, ensure that an extended interval is kept between vehicles and that the vehicles track each other. However, do not use the track trace made by vehicles traveling in the area before you arrived.

- Vary the pattern of employment and routes used.

- Avoid narrow routes or defiles.

- If time and conditions permit, employ mine clearance teams.

- Maintain surveillance over routes repeatedly used.

➡ Although countermeasures being taken by the III MAF have reduced the number of casualties caused by mines and booby traps, individual Marines must be constantly on the alert, particularly when physical exhaustion dulls the senses, if casualties are to be further reduced. The enemy is clever and imaginative and is continually devising new methods of employing mines and booby traps. Even handbills and election posters on the sides of trees and buildings have been boobytrapped.

→ The VC employ mines and booby traps extensively. A system of marking the emplacement of these devices is needed in order to alert their own forces operating in the area. The following methods have been used by the VC to mark the emplacement of their mines and booby traps:

- Stick or bamboo broken at right angles in road or trail indicates mines or booby traps 200/400 meters ahead.

- Three sticks or stones placed across trail indicates trail is unsafe.

- Sign on side of road or trail saying "Chu Min" indicates mines 200/400 meters ahead.

- Sign "Cam" indicates mines or booby traps are in the immediate area or on the trail.

- One to three strings above entrance to house or cave indicates booby traps.

- Tripod of wood about two inches high indicates punji pit, tripod directly over pit.

- Triangle of sticks on trail indicates mines or booby traps in area.

- Stick or length of bamboo along side and parallel to trail indicates safe for VC.

# # # # #

5. VC MINES AND BOOBY TRAPS

During the French and Viet Minh conflict, the Viet Minh used improvised explosive mines and booby traps effectively to harass, slow down and demoralize the French forces. The Viet Cong have improved upon their predecessor's techniques and are using emplaced munitions as an effective weapon. It is evident that we must learn something of the munitions and their use by the VC.

A booby trap consists of a firing device (fuzing system) and an explosive charge. The explosive charge may be any explosive: demolition charges, artillery and mortar projectiles, bombs, land mines or grenades. Therefore, it is apparent that a land mine may also be a booby trap and that it is merely a means of employing an explosive charge.

VC Fuzing Systems. All the standard initiating principles of fuzing used in U.S. munitions can be expected to be used by the Viet Cong. These initiating actions include pressure, pressure release, pull friction, pull release, chemical delay, mechanical delay and controlled firing. The complexity of the fuzing systems, their ingredients as well as their purpose, is only limited by the ingenuity of the man who constructs them. Thus, as many of the VC fuzing systems are locally produced, it would be impossible to enumerate all of the variations of fuzing systems found. Basic systems will be discussed. It must be remembered that one or more fuzing systems may be found on any given piece of ordnance. An explosive item that is primarily designed to be control fired may also have a pressure release firing device attached. Remember: CAUTION OR COFFIN!

Pressure Type Fuzes. Pressure type fuzes are probably the simplest to produce locally. The basic components are a firing pin, primer and detonator. A pressure type fuze can be made from a nail, a rifle cartridge, and a block of wood. It may also be more complex with a firing pin retained in a cocked position by a key slot which, when depressed, releases the firing pin (Sketch V-1). The Viet Cong make extensive use of modified mortar and artillery fuzes as pressure firing devices.

Pressure Release Type Fuzes. Pressure release type firing devices, normally called "mouse traps," can be easily made from commercial mouse traps. The principle behind this type is that the removal of the weight releases a compressed spring which forces the striker to fire the device. The most common pressure release type used by the Viet Cong is the grenade fuze (Sketch V-2). The VC make extensive use of grenade fuzes for booby traps. Normally, the delay element is replaced with an explosive relay to obtain an instantaneous detonation.

Pull Type Firing Device. The most common pull type firing device used by the Viet Cong is the pull friction fuze, similar to the ones found in VC and CHICOM stick grenade (Sketch V-3). When used as a mine or booby trap fuze, the delay element is usually removed and replaced with an explosive relay to obtain an instantaneous detonation after ignition. The pull type firing device is characterized by a slack trip wire. Although mechanical pull type fuzing devices have not been recovered recently, many were used against the French, and it is believed that mechanical firing devices are in the VC supply system. A CHICOM or VC version of the Russian firing device is most likely to be used in Vietnam because these were widely used in Korea after CHICOM intervention.

Pull Release Type Firing Device. Pull types are designed for actuation by either an increase (pull) or decrease (release) of tension in a taut wire (Sketch V-4). Pull release firing devices are also called tension release devices. Extreme caution must be observed when encountering a taut trip wire, as a cocked striker is always used in this type of fuze and any movement of the wire or ordnance may activate the striker. To render a pull release device safe, the striker must be blocked with a positive safety between the striker and the primer. Many straight pull devices can be used as a pull release firing device by attaching the trip wire to the striker. Pull type devices rigged for a pull release normally activate when the trip wire is broken.

Control or Command Fired Fuzing Systems. All the firing devices mentioned previously can be command fired by a person lying in wait. The fuzing system is activated by an extension of the trip wire when a suitable target presents itself. The most common method of controlled firing by the Viet Cong is by electrical means. This is accomplished by inserting an electrical blasting cap into the ordnance, laying a firing cable to a concealed position and connecting an electrical source (battery or blasting machine) when the target comes within range. The Viet Cong use this method in all types of ordnance--including underwater mines (Sketch V-5). The Viet Cong have also been known to use radio controlled triggering devices that are activated by signal transmissions on selected frequencies.

Delay (time) Firing Devices. A clockwork delay type and a chemical delay type have been encountered in Vietnam. The clockwork delay is the most common. One type of VC clockwork delay firing device is made from commercial watches. Two contacts are added; one to the hands and the other to the face of the watch. When the set time runs out, the circuit is completed to an electric blasting cap. Small alarm clocks have also been used, utilizing the clock's alarm system to complete a circuit. Chemical delay devices were used by French forces in Vietnam and may still be encountered. These are similar to the U.S. firing device, demolition, delay type, M-1.

Grenades. Many small explosive items normally used as grenades and which give the appearance of grenades are used by the VC as antipersonnel (AP) mines. Both the striker release and the pull friction grenade fuzes with the delay element removed are used in these small items. Some examples of how these small items have been used are (Sketch V-6):

As a booby trap: A grenade was placed under a rice bag in a VC safe haven. When friendly forces picked up the rice bag, the grenade exploded (Sketch V-6, Illustration No. 1).

As an AP mine: A small AP mine was attached to the side of a tree with a trip wire across the trail. The trip wire was a monofilament cord resembling fish line leader and difficult to see. Unfortunately, a friendly patrol didn't see the trip wire until it was too late (Sketch V-6, Illustration No. 2).

As an AP mine: A grenade with its pin removed was placed in a hollow length of bamboo. A trip wire was attached to the grenade. A pull on the trip wire would have pulled the grenade from the bamboo releasing the handle and allowing the striker to make its run. Fortunately, this device was discovered before it could do any damage (Sketch V-6, Illustration No. 3).

As a booby trap: Grenades or small AP mines are attached by trip wires to such items as fence gates, doors, VC flags or flag poles or any other object that friendly forces may move or destroy (Sketch V-6, Illustration No. 4).

As a booby trap: Grenades were placed in the thatched roof of a house. The pins were pulled and the handles were tied down with string or rubber bands. When friendly forces burned the house, they were surprised by grenades exploding in the area. Nobody was injured (Sketch V-6, Illustration No. 5).

Artillery and Mortar Ammunition. All sizes of artillery and mortar ammunition are used by the VC as mines. They use the smaller projectiles for AP mines and the larger ones as antivehicular mines. Both types may be equipped with any of the firing devices previously mentioned. Electrically controlled firing is often used to detonate these types of main charges. A few methods of employment are listed below (Sketch V-7):

A 155mm artillery projectile was buried in a dirt road and wired to be fired electrically. The charge was detonated under a U.S. officer riding in a 1/4 ton vehicle. Many incidents are recorded of larger artillery shells having been planted in roads and control fired when a prime target presented itself (Sketch V-7, Illustration No. 1).

During a recent operation, a large number of mortar and artillery rounds (75-105mm) were suspended from trees and control detonated when U.S. troops came within range (Sketch V-7, Illustration No. 2).

A 105mm round was found under the floor of a building in a VC area. It was prepared to be detonated by a pressure type fuze under a loose board.

Any application used with the grenade type mines can be used with mortar and artillery ammunition. 60mm mortar rounds have been recovered with grenade fuzes attached and undoubtedly were intended for use as mines - the delay element had been removed from the fuze (Sketch V-7, Illustration Nos. 3 & 4).

Bombs. The VC consider the 20 lb. fragmentation bombs to be excellent antipersonnel mines. The larger bombs (from 100 to 1000 lbs.) will stop and destroy any vehicle on the road (Sketch V-7). The VC are using more and more bombs as mines and are known to use excessive amounts of explosive to do a job. Bombs are usually used in VC safe havens, preplanted on likely avenues of approach, and are control fired when friendly forces advance.

Locally Manufactured Mines

The most famous and fast becoming the most widely used VC locally produced mine is their directional mines (Sketch V-8). These items have been found in sizes ranging from approximately eight inches in diameter to 12 inches in diameter. The principle behind these mines is that a large amount of fragments are propelled in a given direction by an explosive force. The effective range is approximately 200 meters with a dispersion area of 16-20 meters at this range. The VC directional mine has been used against troops, helicopters in landing areas, light vehicles, and as a terrorist weapon. This item is normally control fired but has been found fuzed with other firing devices to include delayed fuzing.

Any type of container may be used as a mine. Two very simple and easily manufactured explosive items were discovered during a recent U.S. operation. One item consisted of a bamboo tube filled with explosive and a standard VC pull friction grenade fuze altered for instantaneous detonation (Sketch V-9). The other was explosive wrapped in black plastic with a cocked striker mechanical grenade fuze (Sketch V-10).

VC Terrorist Explosives

A footlocker addressed to a U.S. officer was delivered to a BOQ. This footlocker contained over 100 pounds of explosive material with a clockwork activated fuze. Personnel working in the BOQ were about to deliver it to the room number indicated in the address, but became suspicious when they realized that the name in the address was not the same as that of the officer occupying the room. The footlocker was opened and the bomb was disarmed minutes before it was to detonate.

A hand grenade was placed in the front suspension system of a jeep in such a way that any movement of the vehicle would dislodge it, thus releasing the handle and causing it to explode.

A fountain pen was left on the floor of a vehicle to be picked up and examined by some unsuspecting person. When X-rayed it was found that the pen contained sufficient explosive to blow a man's hand off. It was rigged to explode when the cap was removed.

Cigarette lighters of the Zippo type have been delivered to U.S. advisors and left where they would be easily found. These lighters are explosive booby traps that detonate when the unsuspecting person attempts to light it.

Grenades have been camouflaged in bread, bricfcases and baskets of fruit. On a recent occasion, a loaf of bread containing a grenade was thrown into the back of a U.S. Navy truck. Personnel riding in the truck bed were able to throw it out before it exploded. Although two individuals received wounds, more serious injury and probable death were avoided.

Directional mines (Claymore type) have been hidden in the saddlebags of bicycles and motor bikes. Automobiles have been made into large bombs by filling door panels, seats and trunks with explosives. These type bombs or mines need not be within close proximity of the target to cause death and destruction.

# # # # #

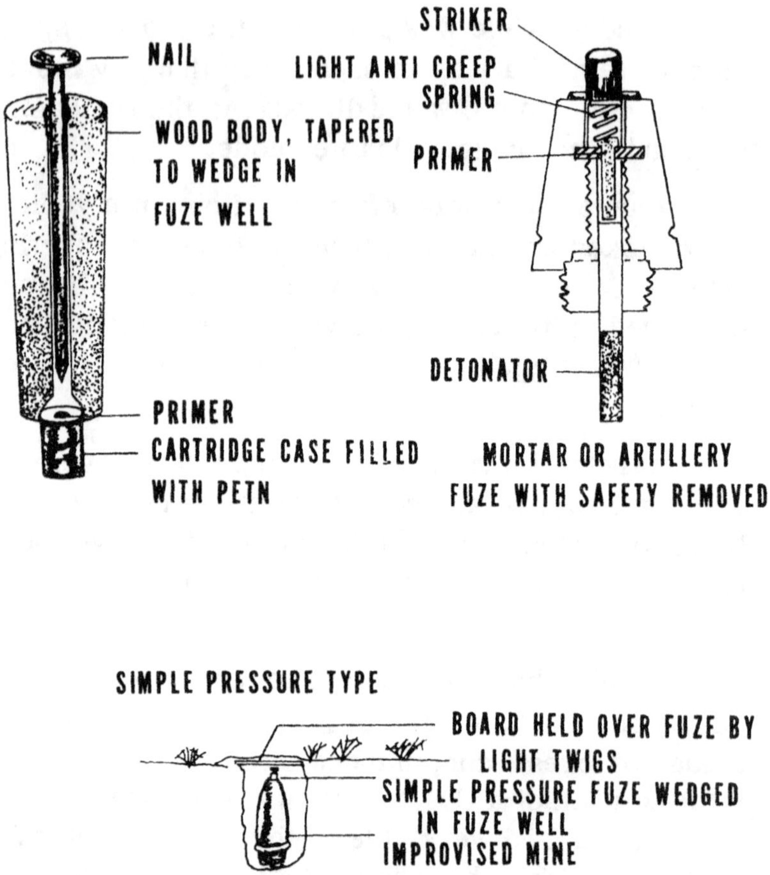

Sketch V-1. PRESSURE TYPE FUZES

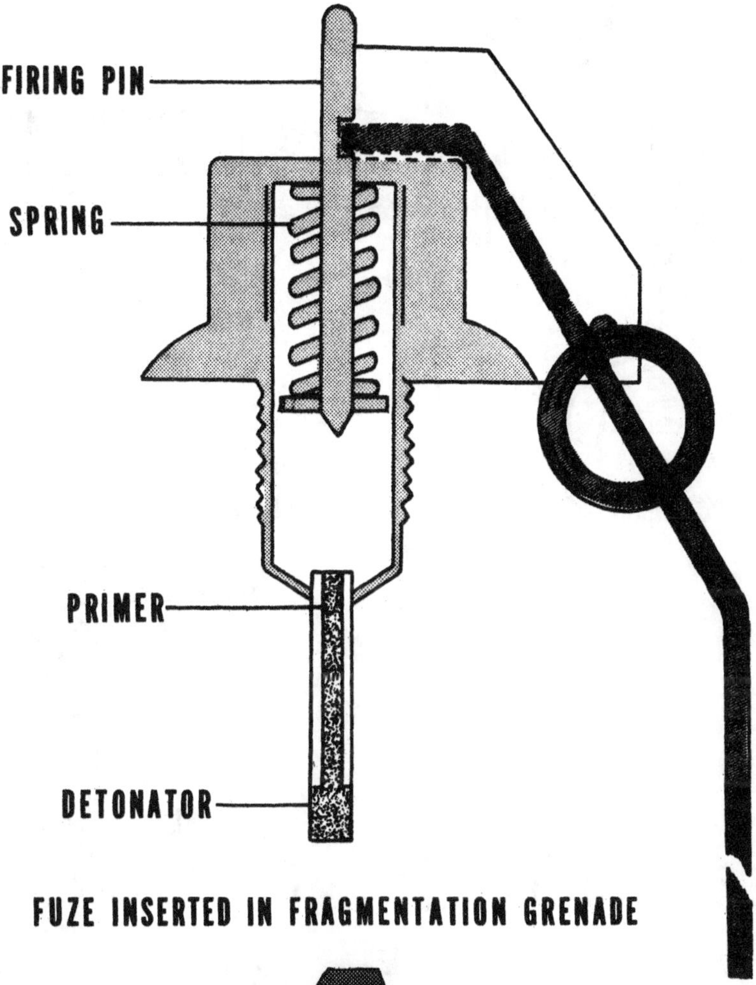

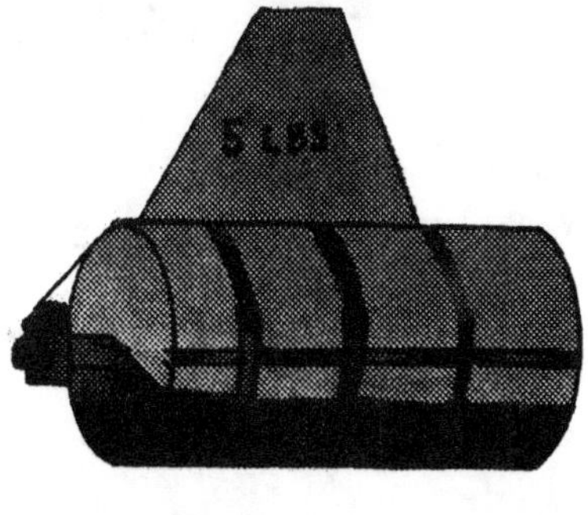

Sketch V-2. PRESSURE RELEASE TYPE FUZES

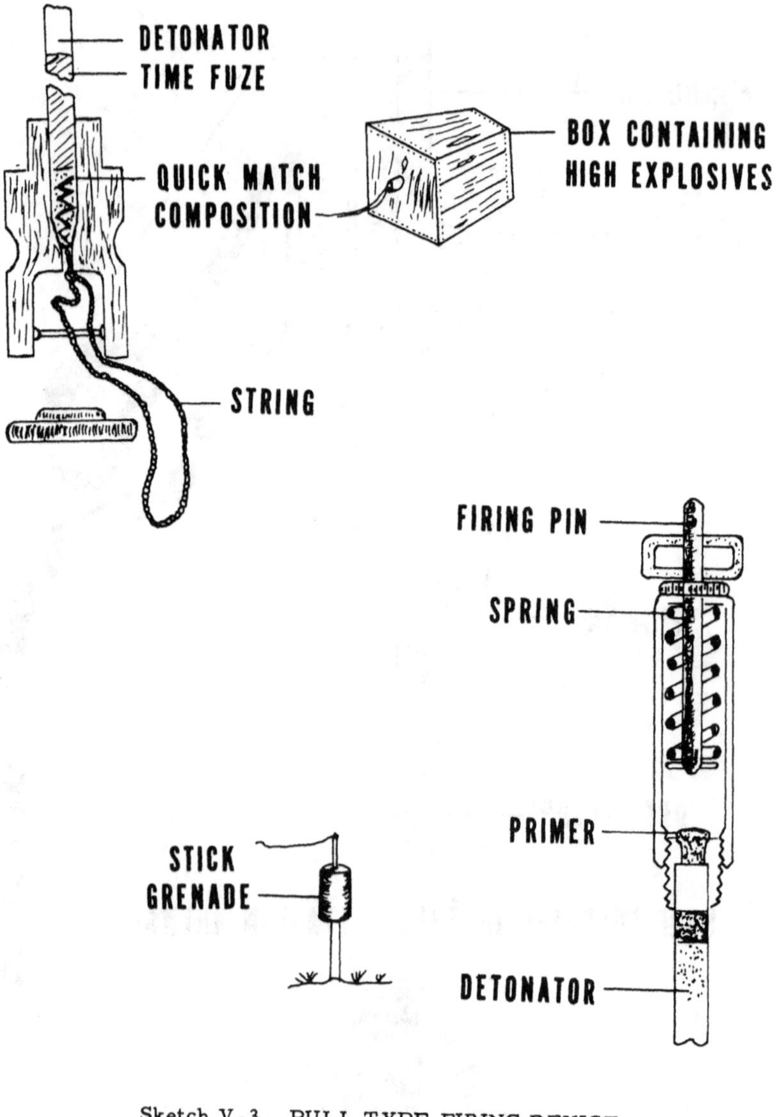

Sketch V-3. PULL TYPE FIRING DEVICE

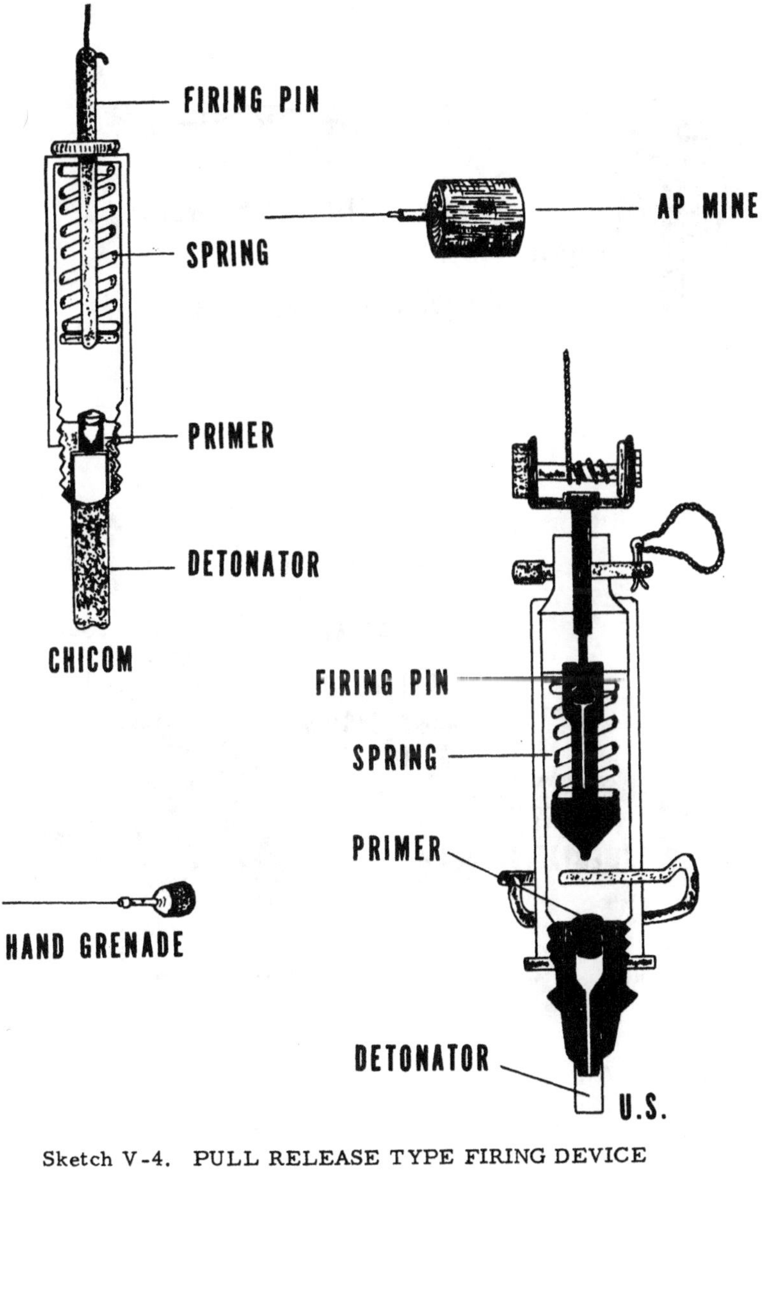

Sketch V-4. PULL RELEASE TYPE FIRING DEVICE

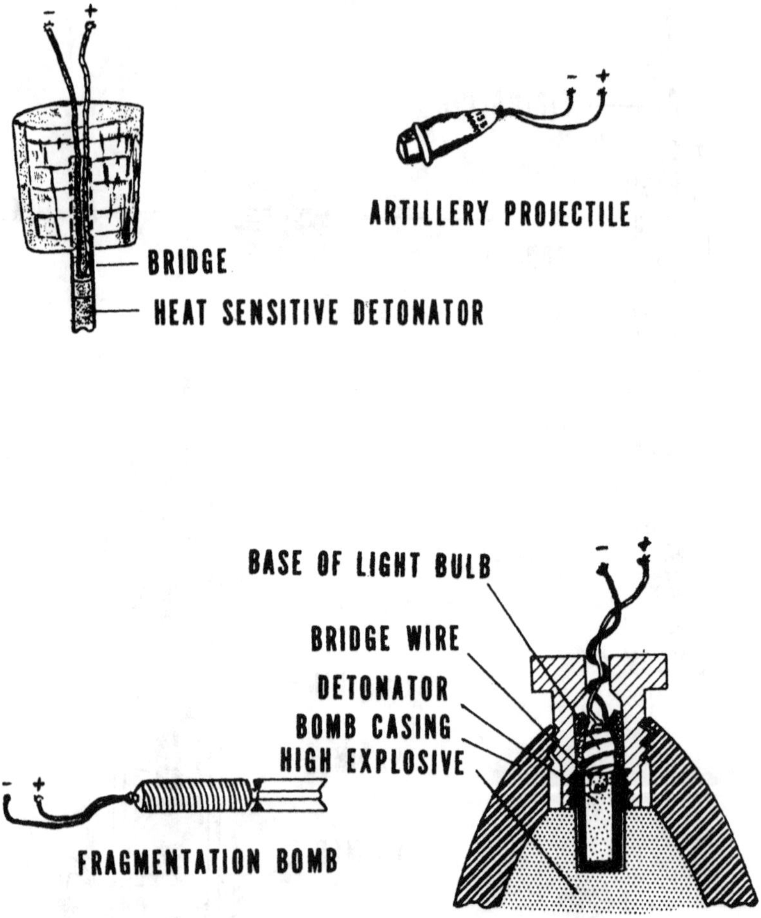

Sketch V-5. CONTROLLED FUZING SYSTEMS

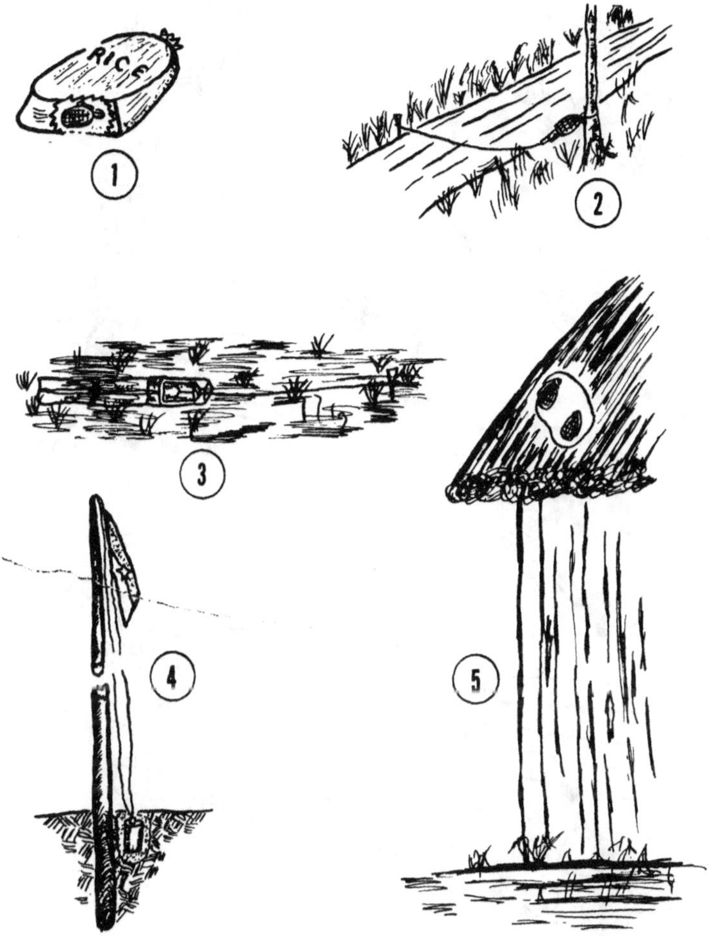

Sketch V-6. SOME METHODS OF EMPLOYING SMALL EXPLOSIVE ITEMS

256-290 O-67—25

Sketch V-7. SOME METHODS OF EMPLOYING IMPROVISED MINES

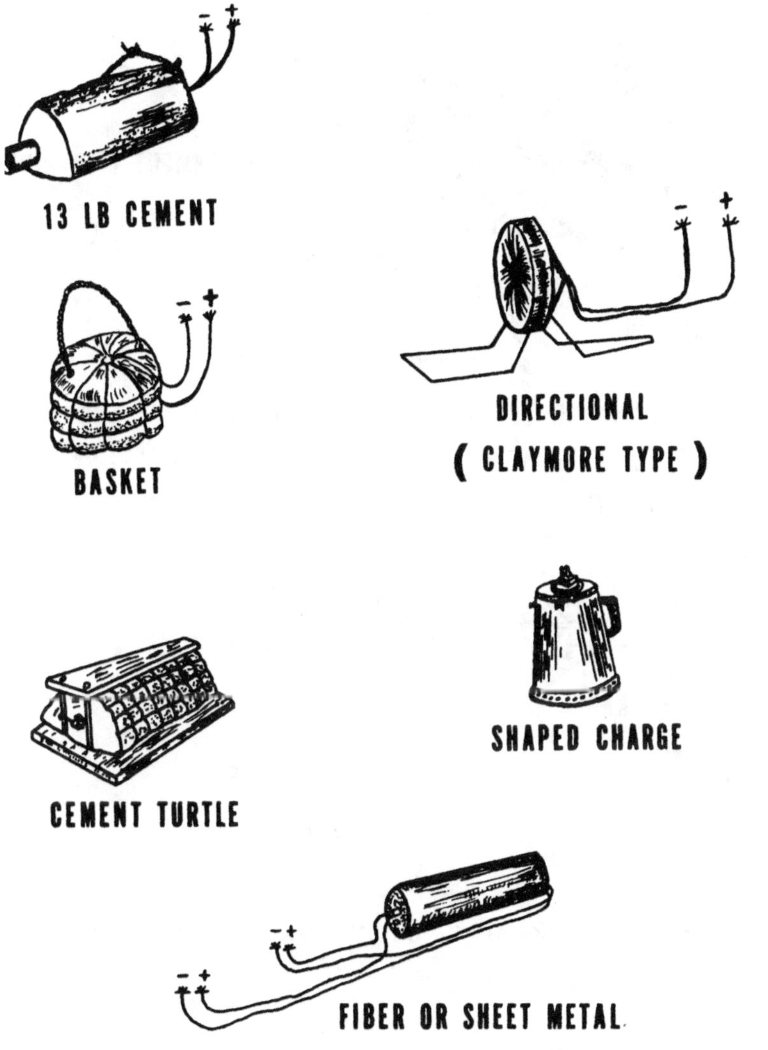

Sketch V-8. SOME VC LOCALLY MANUFACTURED MINES

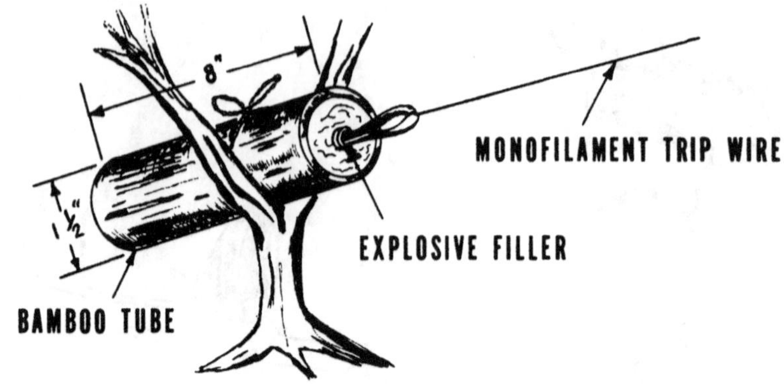

MINE TIED IN CROTCH OF BUSH RIGHT OFF OF TRAIL AND MARKED WITH BROKEN SAPLING APPROXIMATLY 3 FEET IN FRONT OF MINE.

Sketch V-9. VC LOCALLY MANUFACTURED EXPLOSIVE ITEM

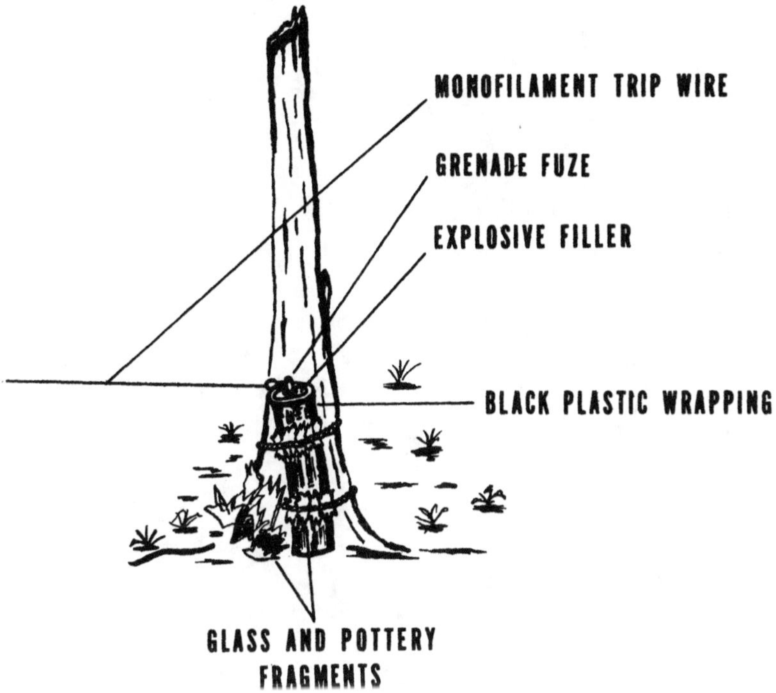

Sketch V-10. VC LOCALLY MANUFACTURED EXPLOSIVE ITEM

Chapter VI: COMMUNICATIONS

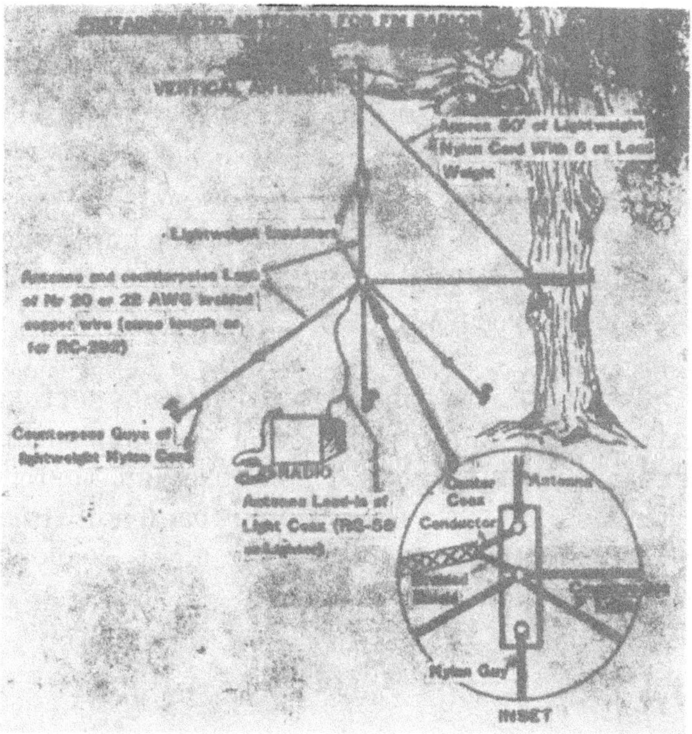

1. VERTICAL LONG WIRE ANTENNAS

The use of vertical long wire antennas for radios on battalion tactical nets has not only increased the radio operating range, but it makes available additional RC-292 antennas for the more mobile stations operated by rifle companies and artillery batteries. The materials required to install vertical long wire antennas are a coaxial cable for the RC-292 antenna, 15' of #12 strand copper wire, and 3 insulators.

# # # # #

2. ABBREVIATED RC-292 ANTENNA

The RC-292 antenna is often needed when conducting fast moving operations, however, the weight and bulk of the complete unit make it impractical to handle. To solve this, the following method has proven effective in Vietnam:

Only the antenna base (MP-68), antenna sections, coaxial cable, one mast section (AB-35) and the antenna bag are carried. This abbreviated antenna is then tied in a tree or to a pole (bamboo) without loss of effectiveness. A saving of 30 pounds is realized.

# # # # #

3. ANTENNAS FOR COMMUNICATIONS CENTRAL AN/TSC-15

Units holding AN/TSC-15 communication centrals have been experimenting with field expedient antennas for the last several years in order to improve communications up to one hundred miles.

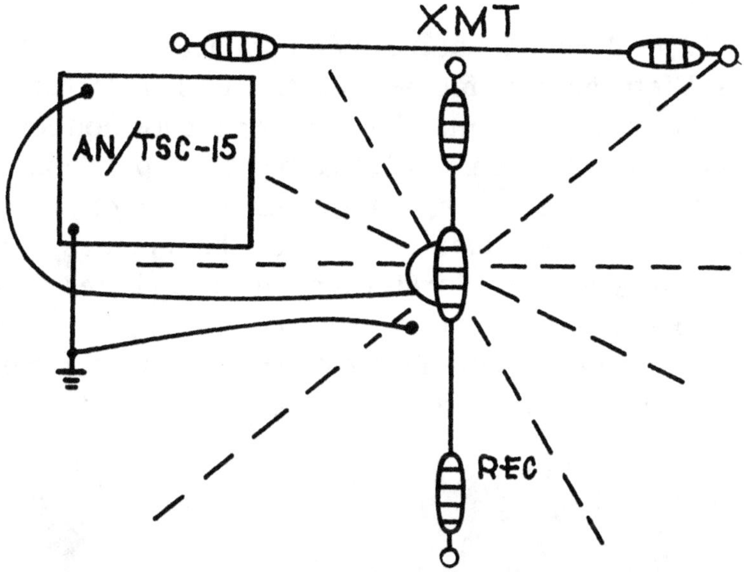

Communications Battalions in Vietnam have had satisfactory results with the following two types of antennas:

→ Receiving antenna: 1/4 wavelength above ground using WD-1/TT or AWG #8 copper wire. If the ground is poor, a counterpoise should be used with each leg 1/4 wavelength long and constructed on the ground directly below the antenna.

→ Transmitting antenna: Properly oriented 1/4 wavelength inverted "L" with approximately 1/6 vertical and the remainder horizontal.

# # # # #

4. INFANTRY BATTALION COMMUNICATIONS

The dynamic nature of amphibious operations in Vietnam has focused on the BLT level communications system. The need for a battalion command net has been highlighted by separation of units, the distances and terrain encountered and the close coordination between helicopters, the Amphibious Task Force Commander and the Landing Force Commander. This command net can be used to pass administrative traffic and periodic reports, and to control and coordinate helicopter

resupply thus reducing the volume of traffic on the battalion tactical net. One item of equipment which plays a significant part in battalion communications is the AN/PRC-25. Its light weight dependability, relatively long battery life, wide frequency band, and transmission range are all features in its favor. Integration of additional PRC-25s into battalions engaged in amphibious and semidetached operations has allowed the other organic radios (AN/PRC-6, AN/PRC-10) to be more widely distributed. Operations over extended areas relying on small unit patrols and ambushes require an extensive radio control system. The PRC-25 is the keystone in the infantry battalion communications system.

# # # # #

5. EXTEND EQUIPMENT LIFE

When communications equipment is not to be used for a day or more, remove the batteries. Damage to the equipment and interior of the battery cases can result from battery expansion and corrosion, especially in high temperature areas. Keep the inside of the battery case clean and dry. Radios such as the AN/PRC-6, PRC-10 and PRC-25 should be dried out following exposure to rain or high humidity.

# # # # #

6. OVERHEATED EQUIPMENT

Temperature, dust conditions, and high humidity all contribute to equipment overheating and subsequent failures. The following comments from Marine units in Vietnam concern this situation:

→ The S.A.E. 30-weight lubricating oil, normally used in the PU-78 generator, breaks down at high temperatures and loses its lubricating qualities. Generator life can be extended by the use of S.A.E. 50-weight oil.

→ The life of small items of equipment, modules, and components can be prolonged by placing them in a hot locker for a few hours to dry out accumulated moisture. A wooden box with a light bulb will serve as a satisfactory hot locker.

# # # # #

7. WATER DAMAGE TO RADIO EQUIPMENT

During the monsoon season, many radios of the AN/PRC-6 and AN/PRC-10 series are being turned in for repairs due to water damage.

Waterproofing bags issued initially with the equipment are being lost or destroyed and replacement items are sometimes unavailable.

The solution to this problem is "equipment discipline." If the waterproof bag is lost, a satisfactory substitute is the plastic bag which covers the BA-279/U batteries. Care must be taken when removing the plastic bag from the battery case so that no tears or holes result.

# # # # #

8. IN THE RIGHT POSITION

Frequently, unit after-action reports comment on inconsistencies in FM communications. Much of this can be directly attributed to the improper location of one of the station's antennas. On one occasion, a battalion conducting an operation well within PRC-25 range of the regimental headquarters had no communications link for four

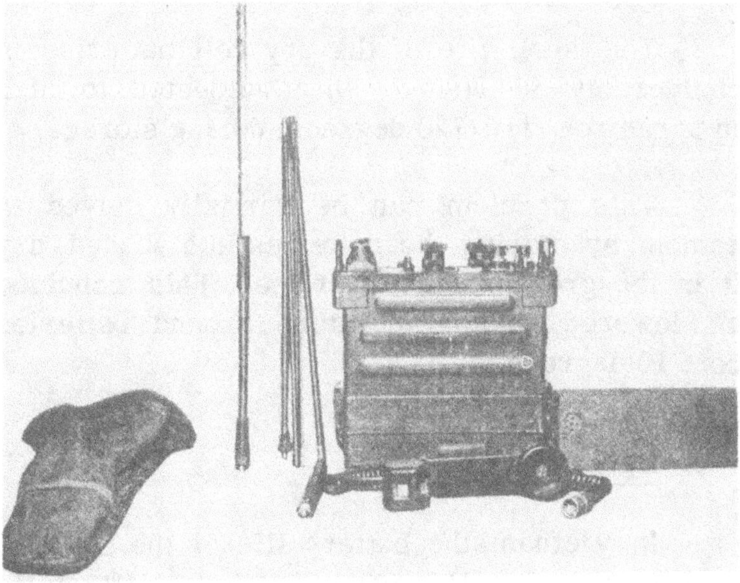

hours. As it turned out, the regimental equipment was located behind a hill that was in direct line with the battalion equipment. A communications masking chart prepared in advance could have prevented that situation, and radio relay points could have provided an alternative means of communication.

# # # # #

9. BATTERY LIFE OF DRY CELL RADIO BATTERIES

a. Shelf Life

The shelf life of the dry cell batteries is considerably shortened when subjected to high temperatures (110–120 degrees) during storage.

This problem can be partially solved in Vietnam by storing the batteries in a shaded, dry pit in the ground 3 to 6 feet deep. This technique has lowered the temperature around batteries about 10 degrees.

b. Operating Life

In Vietnam the battery life of the BA-270, BA-279 and BA-414 used in the AN/PRC-10, AN/PRC-6 radios and remote control unit AU/GRC-6 may be limited to as little as eight hours of operation.

By setting these batteries aside in a cool, dry area for twenty-four hours, another eight hours of service may be obtained. This rotation process, repeated three and four times, has resulted in obtaining as much as thirty-two hours of battery life in some batteries. Rotate batteries in order to ensure longer battery life and timely communications.

# # # # #

10. COMMUNICATIONS WIRE INSTALLATION

Much of the thousands of miles of communications wire needed to support operations in Vietnam is readily accessible to the VC for cutting or tapping. Communications wire on the ground is especially vulnerable; overhead wire much less so. Troubleshooters should travel in teams of three or four and guard constantly against sniping or ambush. A shotgun has proven to be a valuable weapon for troubleshooting teams.

# # # # #

11. OVERHEATED RADIO EQUIPMENT

Reports from field units in RVN state that the heat conditions are having adverse effects on radio equipment. Radios exposed to direct sunlight become overheated, battery life is sharply reduced, and radio components fail after a short use. Tactical man-packed equipment can be covered with canvas

material to reduce the temperature inside. Any shade or covering will serve the same purpose. A tent fly can be rigged over vehicular mounted equipment and the tenting packed up with the vehicle for each displacement. Ensure that there is a free circulation of air around all radio equipment.

# # # # #

12. RADIO CAMOUFLAGE

The position of man-pack radios such as the AN/PRC-25 is advertised when its long wire antenna is extended. Radio operators rate high on the list of targets for trained snipers. The size of the PRC-25 lends itself to being carried in

a haversack with the antenna (AT 892) bent at an angle of about 135 degrees to the rear. This will conceal the radio from the enemy, avoid snagging the antenna in overhead projections, but still permit good communications.

# # # # #

13. WIRE COMMUNICATIONS FOR A RIFLE COMPANY COMMAND POST

In a static defensive situation, wire is the primary means of communication within the battalion. Lines to platoons, outposts and OPs, as well as lines within the battalion create a need for many telephones. This causes confusion at the company CP because of the large number of phones which terminate there. The following methods have been used to solve this problem:

→ Install an SB-22 at the Company CP.

→ When the SB-22 is not available for company level use, install a TA-125 jumping the terminals so that one phone is on the battalion lines and another on the company local lines. This limits the number of phones within the company CP to two and allows an incoming call from battalion to be routed to any platoon outpost or

forward observer. Utilizing one EE-8 and TA-312/PT aids in determining which phone is ringing at the company OP, thus eliminating the troublesome chore of answering the wrong number on an incoming call.

# # # # #

14. DESTRUCTION OF COMMUNICATION BATTERIES

Used communication batteries must be completely destroyed to prevent their reuse by the Viet Cong. Burying or smashing them is not always sufficient to prevent them from falling into Viet Cong hands. If possible, burn expended batteries when excess powder increments are burned. If this is not possible, deliver them to a safe area for proper disposal.

# # # # #

15. TELEPHONE EE-8

During prolonged inclement weather periods, it has been necessary to conduct daily second echelon maintenance on all telephones exposed to the elements. Phones may be placed in the sun or in a hot locker to dry during the day. When reassembling the telephone, the receiving and transmitting elements should be tapped lightly to ensure that the carbon granules are loose and not

caked. Care should be taken so that excessive maintenance does not materially affect the performance of the equipment.

# # # # #

16. POWER SUPPLY FOR THE AN/MRC-83

If the vehicular power supply for the AN/MRC-83 is used over extended periods of time, engine failure will result. This can be remedied by alternating between the vehicular power supply and a PU-587.

# # # # #

17. FILTERS

Keeping filters clean and rotated on the TRC-75 is a must. Dirty filters keep air from circulating and thus burn out transistors and fuzes on the PP-2352.

# # # # #

18. DIRECTIONAL ANTENNAS

The use of directional antennas has increased the effectiveness of the frequency modulated radio equipment within the rifle companies. The directional antenna employed is commonly known as the "wave antenna." It consists of a length of field telephone wire (WA-1/TT) cut to the wavelength of the operating frequency and terminated by a 600 to 800 ohm carbon resistor leading to ground. The antenna utilizes a counterpoise which is also constructed from field telephone wire. A short length of coaxial cable with connector is used as a transmission line with the braided shield soldered to the counterpoise. This antenna is normally employed in static positions but has worked well for ambush teams equipped with an AN/PRC-6 radio operating at distances up to three miles. Long range patrols can carry the wave antenna in lieu of an RC-292.

# # # # #

Chapter VII: LOGISTICS

1. LOGISTIC SUPPORT AREA CONCEPT PROVEN

For years administrative plans have included directions for the establishment of a Logistic Support Area (LSA). In amphibious exercises the LSA has normally been located in the beach area. The centralization of stores and materials within a secure area has worked well in all Marine training exercises and now it's working equally well in operations in Vietnam. Distances from base area to battle however, are extended and the intervening countryside can be controlled by the Viet Cong. To support field operations, LSAs have been established at distances of up to 35 miles from base areas.

By establishing the LSA near the objective area, supplies are available to the using unit within minutes. Emergency resupply has been accomplished on several occasions in as little as 15 minutes. The availability of supplies in the objective area permits assault units to carry a smaller prescribed load, an important consideration in view of the oppressive heat and rugged terrain in which operations are conducted. Another advantage of a nearby LSA is the reduction of helicopter turnaround time.

The location of such a support area has to be carefully selected. Security and access are two

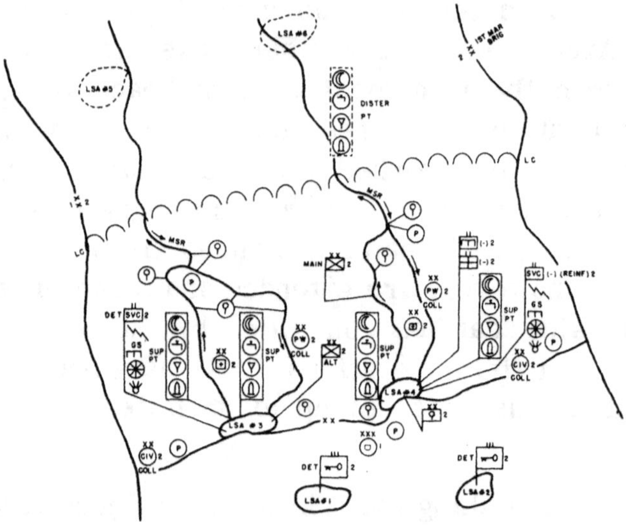

major considerations. The LSA cannot operate with one eye cocked over its shoulder for a guerrilla lurking nearby; it must have security. Support personnel have to share a considerable portion of this security requirement, although a reserve unit can provide assistance while it is positioned in or near the LSA.

A comment on helicopter control near the LSA is pertinent here. Helicopter pilots should check their radio to ensure they are on the LZ control net. Too much traffic on the tactical net makes coherent communication extremely difficult.

The LSA concept is well founded and now it's been proven in Vietnam. Use it, it's a good one.

# # # # #

2. EMBARKATION DATA

In recent deployments and in several past amphibious operations, lift requirements have not been accurately stated. In one case, the requirements for shipping actually doubled by the time loading was scheduled to commence.

Carelessness in planning can lead to inadequacies in shipping, or they may mean that equipment, supplies, and even units have to use follow-up shipping. Accurate statistical data prepared and maintained in accordance with the current embarkation SOP means just one thing; the job is done

once, done correctly, and you get the proper amount of cube and square feet.

# # # # #

3. SUPPLY SUPPORT

The basic foundation for good supply support is a timely requisition for the correct item and quantity. This requisition must also be assigned the appropriate priority consistent with the urgency of the need.

Requirements which cannot be foreseen, such as repair parts, lack of which will deadline the equipment, should be placed on priority 02 requisition immediately. Items which have a fairly constant rate of consumption should be replenished on a routine basis.

Supply support is directly related to your ability to forecast requirements. Pyramiding of supplies will not only create excesses, but deprives other units of sorely needed supplies.

# # # # #

4. SUPPLY SUPPORT UNDER MILSTRIP/NAVSTRIP

Under the procedures established by Milstrip/ Navstrip, all requisitions of a high priority or for material not carried are passed to the next higher supply activity in the supply chain. To prevent excess NORS (not operational ready supply) or deadline time of aircraft and aviation equipment, the status of requisitions is of the utmost importance.

The procedures outlined in NAVSANDA Publication 437 establishes time frames for receipt of status or material. In order to be well informed on the status and location of your requisitions within the supply pipeline, updating of status received, and the timely submission of follow-up by the requisitioner is mandatory.

# # # # #

5. TERO LAYETTES

A Vietnam-based logistic support unit has overcome unsatisfactory accounting and control of spare parts by the establishment of a shop store system. This provides a small store of spare parts in support of each maintenance commodity area (motor transport, engineer, communication/electronics, ordnance). From these shop stores, a layette of parts necessary to support each Tactical Equipment Repair Order (TERO) can be maintained. A direct control and accounting system is now in effect with the establishment of the shop store system and TERO layettes.

# # # # #

6. AIR MOVEMENT

The frequency of unit air movement brings to mind some embarkation guidelines which can be useful, whether the movement is an administrative airlift or a tactical operation. These guidelines are applicable to both:

➔ Obtain the services of a qualified loadmaster a couple of days before the move.

➔ Stage each aircraft load individually just as for ship loads.

➔ If a large lift using several aircraft is involved, establish an embarkation headquarters close

by the loading area. From here the embarkation officer and his staff of experienced men can direct the loading and be available to aircrews. A sound-powered megaphone is a handy piece of equipment to keep available in the landing area.

→ Plan on providing a small working crew for each aircraft. Once the loadmaster has put them to work keep all other nonessential personnel away.

→ Accurately compute the weights and cubes of equipment to be moved. Don't guess; weight can be critical to airlift, so weigh everything after the containers are filled. And make the containers strong enough to withstand cinching down.

→ Strong Marine backs can be used just as successfully as a forklift truck for light loads. Don't hesitate to use them rather than wait for the forklift.

→ Debarkation is just as important as embarkation; a good plan provides for getting the gear unloaded just as efficiently as it was loaded.

# # # # #

7. CONVOY SPARE PARTS

Mechanical breakdowns do occur during convoy operations, so be prepared to repair the vehicles and continue the mission. A minimum amount of time will be lost if the part is on hand in the convoy

to accomplish the repairs. A convoy spare parts kit containing high usage items has been devised by a Vietnam-based organization. This list contains over 35 spare parts ranging from fan belts for M-54 trucks to carburetors for M38A1 vehicles. Such a spare parts kit is not the complete answer to convoy breakdowns; nothing has yet taken the place of a well supervised preventive maintenance program; but rapid repair of a vehicle with readily available spare parts may enable you to avoid an ambush.

# # # # #

8. THEY'RE YOUR WHEELS

When necessary to move through sand, remember to deflate tires to provide better support.

Never reduce tire pressure so low that the tire slips on the rim. Keep valve caps on at all times. Mark the steering wheel for the straight ahead position. Safe driving is just as important in Vietnam as in the United States.

# # # # #

9. VEHICLE PREVENTIVE MAINTENANCE

Vehicles and equipment operated in Vietnam require special emphasis on operator preventive maintenance.

→ Washing facilities should be sought for daily vehicle and equipment cleaning to prevent dust and mud from working into fittings and movable parts.

→ Air, fuel and oil filters and cleaners should be cleaned and changed often to prevent engine damage and reduced engine performance.

→ Fuel water traps should be drained daily.

→ Operation over rough terrain also requires continual tightening of nuts and bolts to prevent parts from working loose and becoming damaged.

→ Brake life will be increased if a "Salt water PM"is performed after vehicles have been operated during long periods of wet weather.

→ The air breathers on the M-422 vehicle become clogged very quickly in the extremely dusty condition of Vietnam. A daily cleaning in lieu of a weekly one is required.

# # # # #

10. DON'T MISTREAT YOUR MULE

In order to conserve the M-274-(A1) vehicles now on hand and to preclude unnecessary repair/ replacement of engines, the following procedures are suggested:

→ Inspect exhaust pipes frequently. An exhaust leak may force hot exhaust gas over an already heated engine.

→ The blower assembly should be free of contamination; a fresh water flush will help clean it. See that the blower belts are properly adjusted.

→ Keep the engine clean; a dirty engine causes overheating.

→ Set the engine governors properly and then seal them.

→ Close the fuel valve when shutting down the engine.

→ Rotate the use of vehicles assigned to daily runs. This will help to equalize the number of hours of use for each vehicle.

256-290 O-67—27

→ When starting the engine, stand close to the vehicle. Keep one foot on a tire and let the starter cable return slowly. Check the alignment of idler and crankshaft pulleys. When these two are not parallel the drive belts fail prematurely.

# # # # #

11. SPARK PLUG WASHERS

A recent technical inspection in Vietnam of M-422A1 vehicles revealed that cracked spark plug washers ("o" rings) were contributing to spark plug fouling. These rings should be inspected carefully for any cracks, flattening or distortions prior to installation. Replace the washer if there is any doubt as to its serviceability.

# # # # #

12. LIGHTWEIGHT STRETCHERS

An item of equipment which can be of great value in evacuating casualties, especially during a patrol action, is the canvas stretcher. Compact and lightweight, it can be quickly employed to move a casualty to a helicopter evacuation zone. It has six cloth carrying handles sewn on the canvas stretcher and can be folded to fit under a packflap or a cartridge belt. This item is available in the Navy medical supply system.

# # # # #

13. ONTOS TRACK

Antitank unit experience in Vietnam has shown that the serviceable life of Ontos track is about 1000 miles. Beyond that the steel cables in the track bands begin to pull apart and the crossbars begin to wear thin and crack. The one thousand mile mark has proved to be a sound planning factor for track replacement.

# # # # #

14. WEAPONS CARE

Maintaining your weapon in Vietnam is a never ending job to ensure that it will operate properly when you need it. Metal parts should have a light coat of oil to prevent rust, and wooden stocks should receive liberal amounts of linseed oil to prevent cracking and splitting. In an emergency situation, No. 10 weight motor oil may be substituted for rifle oil, and salad oil may be used on stocks in place of linseed oil.

# # # # #

15. SMOKEY THE BEAR SAYS

Large generators of the PU-239, PU-482, and Stuart Stevenson group, emit sparks from their exhausts which may start fires. Recently several small fires have been started by these generators. Had the fires not been discovered and extinguished quickly, the generators and nearby equipment could have been destroyed.

Each unit using these generators should take at least three CO_2 fire extinguishers with them when deploying to the field and maintain a fire watch in the area of the generators when they are operating.

# # # # #

16. PROLONGED GENERATOR LIFE

Base camps and field logistic support areas of a permanent nature require electrical power. This means that expeditionary generators, which are designed to provide emergency power for limited periods, are going to be running around the clock to provide for the demand of power. This extended operation calls for the extreme in preventive maintenance. More frequent attention is mandatory for air cleaners and lubricating oil. A bi-weekly oil change is a minimum; air cleaners should be cleaned daily. Overall equipment cleanliness reduces the amount of dirt inducted as well as the engine temperatures. Fuel strainers and filters also need daily cleaning. Fuel tanks should be drained periodically to prevent an accumulation of water in the system. When an auxiliary tank system such as a 55-gallon drum or similar container is used and it is continually refilled by draining other containers into it, contamination of the fuel system is likely. Accumulated water from this constant refilling process is a major cause of diesel injection failures.

# # # # #

17. OVERHEATED EQUIPMENT

Temperature, dust conditions, and high humidity all contribute to equipment overheating and subsequent failures. The following comments from Marine units in Vietnam concern this situation:

→ The S.A.E. 30-weight lubricating oil, normally used in PU-78 generator, breaks down at high temperatures and loses its lubricating qualities. Engine generator life can be increased by the use of S.A.E. 50-weight oil. Oil should be changed at least once daily.

→ The life of small items of equipment, modules, and components can be prolonged by placing them in a hot locker for a few hours to dry out the accumulated moisture. A wooden box with a light bulb will serve as a satisfactory hot locker.

→ TH-5 terminal telegraphs can be arranged in a tunnel-like area, with their covers removed to help cool them. A fan covered with a fine mesh screen can be directed on the equipment. The exposure to dust and dirt necessitates a stepped-up maintenance program.

# # # # #

18. BETTER CHOW

The Force Logistics Command (FLC) in Vietnam reports that chilled and frozen subsistence stores have been partly thawing between the time they are unloaded from the reefer barge and the time they are put into the reefers ashore. This condition is especially true of shrimp and seafood. Investigation by the FLC revealed that the use of a reefer van won't solve the problem because of the short distance from the barge to the reefers, and the extended periods of time the doors of the van would have to remain open to complete loading and unloading.

.To solve the problem, loading and unloading of such stores is being done at night, or during the coolest part of the day. Additionally, more trucks are being used to haul the food and vehicle loads reduced in order to reduce the time the stores remain out of refrigeration.

It doesn't sound too important until the effect of poor food on morale is taken into consideration. Every little bit counts.

# # # # #

19. AMMUNITION CHAIN HOOK

The ammunition section of the Force Logistics Command in Vietnam has fabricated a chain/hook assembly that is used in conjunction with the 6,000 pound rough terrain forklift when handling pallets of 105mm and 8-inch artillery projectiles. The chain, approximately 40 inches in length, has a hook attached to each end. One hook is secured to the lift and the other to the pallet which enables the entire pallet to be moved. By using this method, sixteen 155mm or six 8-inch projectiles can be moved at one time.

Prior to this time, the Command found that by using only the forklift blades, many pallets were being dropped and damaged.

# # # # #

20. SUPERVISION

Truck Company, Force Logistic Support Group Alpha has established a Preventive Maintenance Booth in the motor pool area where drivers perform their weekly inspection and preventive maintenance under the supervision of a noncommissioned officer mechanic.

Within two months of the establishment of this system, there was a significant drop in the number of deadlined vehicles.

21. RAPID REPAIR PROGRAM

Under normal procedures, material requiring 4th echelon maintenance is evacuated by surface transportation to the 3rd FSR, and the owning unit is provided a disposition letter authorizing requisition of a replacement item. The repaired item is then retained by the 3rd FSR for later issue.

On occasion this system has proven too slow for units committed in combat. To speed up the system a Rapid Repair Program has been initiated by the Force Logistic Command where relatively small items are periodically air transported to the 3rd FSR by courier, repaired, and returned to service within one week. Items included are test sets, optical instruments, office machines, and other essential items in short supply.

To date, the program has accomplished its intended purpose, with all but one item being returned to Vietnam within a week.

# # # # #

22. CHAIN SAW MAINTENANCE

Units in Vietnam have found that chain saws become clogged when cutting rubber trees. It helps considerably to flush latex from the chain saw every thirty minutes by running the saw with the chain end submerged in a bucket of diesel fuel.

# # # # #

23. PLACEMENT OF CONCRETE CULVERTS IN VIETNAM

Due to the lack of adequate reinforcement and low-strength, high-yield cement-sand ratios, locally manufactured concrete culvert pipe available in Vietnam has substantially less crushing strength than the product on which the cover requirements in engineer field manuals are based. Experience has shown that to avoid crushing, the depth of cover over this locally manufactured pipe should equal the culvert diameter or a minimum of 18" rather than the standard one-half culvert diameter or minimum of 12" specified in engineer manuals.

# # # # #

24. TROPICAL ROAD CONSTRUCTION

The secret of success in tropical road construction is moisture control, compaction, ditching and crowning. A major effort should be made to obtain enough road equipment to crown the subgrade before the rainy season, as tropical rains drain quickly and do little damage to a compacted, well-drained, rut-free surface. A crowned surface with laterite will hold up well with maintenance while a rutted, uncrowned area may be unworkable for the entire rainy season or require massive laterite applications. Often there are two or three days during the monsoon season which will permit a crowned area to be shaped to grade and covered

with laterite. Water pools are the biggest enemy of a laterite surface, because the area becomes soft and ruts easily. Crowns on laterite roads may be as high as 3/4-inch per foot (or 6% slope).

# # # # #

25. RECOVERY OF CRUSHER FINES

When aggregate is crushed for use in asphalt mixes, fines passing the #200 sieve may be blown away while the aggregate is being moved on conveyors or stockpiled. The aggregate fines may be saved by placing a spray bar on the primary crusher conveyor, thus avoiding the requirement to add cement filler to meet required gradation criteria. During crushing operations a small pipe placed over and at right angles to the conveyor, drilled with 1/16" holes, produces a suitable spray bar. In addition to saving cement, the spray bar considerably reduces dust at the crushing site.

# # # # #

26. GENERATOR PREVENTIVE MAINTENANCE

When a generator ceases to function, the results can be catastrophic, particularly in a combat situation such as Vietnam. Many times a generator ceases to function at a time when units employing them can ill afford to lose their precious electrical output.

The best way to avoid this, of course, is PREVENTIVE MAINTENANCE. That is, the continual type of PREVENTIVE MAINTENANCE.

The following recommendations should keep unit generators in operable condition, even in the extreme climate found in Vietnam:

→ A biweekly oil change is considered the minimum.

→ Air cleaners should be cleaned daily.

→ Overall cleanliness of the equipment is important as it reduces the induction of dirt into the machine and reduces heat buildup caused by dirt covered engine components.

→ Fuel strainers and filters should be cleaned daily.

→ Drain fuel tanks periodically to prevent the accumulation of water in the system.

The last item mentioned is particularly important if a 55-gallon drum auxiliary tank system is continually refilled by completely draining other containers into it. It has been found that the water which accumulates in the process is one of the primary causes of diesel injector failures.

# # # # #

27. STRENGTH OF BAMBOO IN CONSTRUCTION

Extensive use of bamboo as a construction material expedient raises questions regarding its comparable strength potential. Available data on the working stresses are as follows:

→ Modulus of elasticity: about $2.5x10^6$ psi. This compares to $29x10^6$ psi for high grade steel, $1.25x10^6$ psi for white oak, and $1.6x10^6$ psi for Douglas fir.

→ Modules of rupture in bending and tensile strength: about 14,000 psi. This compares to 88,000 psi for high grade steel, and 8,300 psi for white oak, and 7,800 psi for Douglas fir.

➔ Compression strength: about 8,000 psi. This compares to 225,000 psi for high grade steel, 3,500 psi for white oak, and 3,600 psi for Douglas fir.

It should be noted that these data are the result of limited testing which produced varying results. Seasoned bamboo had greater strength than unseasoned bamboo, and bamboo had its weakest points at the nodes. One of the most desirable characteristics of bamboo as a construction material is its ability to survive the tropical climate in which it is indigenous.

When working with bamboo, remember that a four-inch diameter piece of this material, for example, does not have nearly the same cross-sectional area as a 4-inch diameter piece of timber because bamboo is hollow.

Another possibility for use as a construction material is a species of rattan known by the Vietnamese name of "MAY." This plant grows one to two inches in diameter and is known to be reasonably strong for its size.

# # # # #

28. REPAIR OF VEHICLES IN THE FIELD

Repair of vehicles in the field, particularly in sandy terrain, can be a serious problem due to shortages of construction materials. To resolve this, some units in Vietnam are constructing grease pits by using discarded 55-gallon drums filled with sand to form the walls with one end left open for an entrance. This pit can be constructed in the side of a hill or sand can be pushed up around the pit to provide access. Either planks or concrete can be laid over the surface.

# # # # #

Chapter VIII: CIVIC ACTION - PSYCHOLOGICAL OPERATIONS

1. REVOLUTIONARY DEVELOPMENT

The Marine combat forces in Vietnam, in addition to finding, fixing and destroying the military forces of the Viet Cong and North Vietnamese, are participating in the economic, political and sociological transition of the Vietnamese people into a new and independent country.

What is called the "Other War"--civic action, revolutionary development or nation-building--is

256-290 O-67—28

the primary war. It is a war in which people, not terrain or enemy units, are the objective.

The Viet Cong know this. Their primary task is simple in comparison to ours, for they seek first to destroy. They try to assassinate or kidnap any leader. They try to destroy all roads and bridges or block all canals and waterways in order to isolate the people from each other. They tax enormously to take food and money from the people. They act to discredit the Government of Vietnam at every turn. They make every effort to wreck the social system, the economic health and the political machinery of the government; to bring the nation to chaos.

The methods of the Viet Cong are cruel, but effective, for they know the people must accept their form of government if there is no other choice.

The Vietnamese people are in revolt against poverty and disease, social injustice, corruption, illiteracy, and inefficiency. They want to move into the modern world as free and independent people, to better their lives and those of their children, to control their own destiny and to make their own mistakes or gains.

Vietnam is the present area where the free world can show its strength and skills and dedication, and where under cover of its armed forces a people can compare ideologies and economic theories and make their choice.

This is no easy task for us.

Our military strength, in coordination with the Vietnamese armed forces, must be used to destroy or drive off the organized forces of the enemy.

The combined efforts of the free Vietnamese forces, their allies and the offices of the civil governments must seek out and destroy the internal structure of the Viet Cong that gnaws at the vitals of the nation from within the hamlets and villages.

Together with these efforts, the nation must be rebuilt from the destruction it has suffered.

The people must be protected from raids and reprisals. Leaders must be developed and assisted in their work.

The people must be fed, clothed, sheltered and treated for their ailments.

The children must be taught.

The farmer must be given an opportunity to grow and sell his rice, and the fisherman his catch.

The carpenter, mason and blacksmith must be given tools and a means to earn his livelihood.

The flow of goods and services from hamlet to village and village to town must be reopened.

Civic Action is a part of this effort, but cannot be separated from the larger goals of protecting a people from coercion, punishment or death; of rebuilding a society that has been subjected to every means of destruction; and of restoring a once rich and self-sufficient country to its full economic potential.

This is being done today in Vietnam.

Over a million Vietnamese, in Marine areas, are now under some measure of influence by the Government of Vietnam.

A quarter of a million Vietnamese have "voted with their feet" in the five northern provinces of Vietnam and have come into Government-controlled areas as refugees from the Viet Cong.

Children are being educated, artisans equipped, farmers provided with seed and tools and fertilizer.

Most importantly, there is hope--for continued freedom, a better life and eventual peace for the Vietnamese people.

# # # # #

2. EXPLOITING VC ATROCITIES

Recently six Vietnamese civilians were killed and one was injured when a bus they were riding detonated a VC mine near Chu Lai.

Immediately after this incident, psychological warfare officials prepared a leaflet citing this incident. The leaflet asked the villagers to withdraw their support from the VC who continually kill and injure innocent civilians by such tactics.

Tape recordings were also prepared to reinforce the printed material.

Marine Aircraft dropped the leaflets and played the tape recordings in the area where the incident occurred.

# # # # #

3. CIVIC ACTION PROJECTS

Professional medical care, which we take so much for granted, can mean a continued normal

life to a Vietnamese. The lack of it often means years of pain and discomfort. During a recent operation in a heavily infiltrated coastal district, Marine helicopters and Navy medical personnel combined to save a district chief's wife who was bleeding seriously. Rapid movement to an offshore ship, and prompt medical attention restored her to a satisfactory condition. This action plus dozens of others during a period of a week, including the extraction of more than 600 infected teeth, demonstrated medical civic action at its best. Each and every person treated, and there were more than 700, were exposed to a by-product of the medical team. That by-product is human compassion--something the Viet Cong discarded long ago.

One fundamental consideration in any civic action effort is the provision for participation by local Vietnamese authorities in civic action projects. The underlying principle that must be apparent is that it is the responsibility of the Government of Vietnam to assist its own people, and the U.S. forces are willing to provide whatever assistance they can. For example, instead of Marines contributing money to pay for a nurse in a local hospital or dispensary, their efforts should be to assist in training the nurse while encouraging the local government to assume responsibility for the nurse's salary. Regional Force and Popular Force units should likewise be encouraged to contribute time and whatever materials can be spared toward civic action programs. In this way, the Vietnamese Government, officials and soldiers, show the people that they are willing and able to assume their responsibilities.

In the past year a modest pig breeding program has begun in Marine tactical areas in Vietnam. Hardy local and imported swine have been purchased through USAID and in turn sold at a minimum price or donated to various village communities. Pigs are an important source of meat for the Vietnamese whose daily diet includes few protein foods. In scores of instances, Marines have voluntarily contributed piasters to purchase a couple of pigs, usually a male and a female, and then presented them to a nearby hamlet where other civic action programs were underway. The raising and breeding of the pigs become a highly regarded job in the village and every one of the people reaps benefits from the pig program. More food is available, civic action coverage is extended and the villagers' confidence in Marines and in themselves is increased.

The simple act of providing a hamlet with a bulletin board has proven to be one effective way of bridging the communications gap in rural Vietnam. Local notices and local and national news can be displayed for all to read. Unit civic action personnel may have to persuade the hamlet chief of the value of this idea and provide him with temporary assistance in preparing the news sheets. The local Vietnamese Information Service representative should be contacted and his assistance requested.

# # # # #

4. RIFLE COMPANY CIVIC ACTION

Nothing succeeds like success. That's more true than ever in the military civic actions programs. The following is a good example of one such

success: Several months ago a Marine rifle company began a civic action program on an island inside one of the tactical areas in RVN. Before the arrival of this company, the island was completely under VC control. Initially the Marines were confronted with the same sullen resistance by day and active fighting by night as had been experienced in other tightly controlled VC areas. Counterguerrilla operations, coupled with the pacification program, soon forced out most of the VC, and it became apparent to the villagers that the Marines were there to stay. The whole island was extremely unproductive agriculturally. One look at the people, especially the children, showed that poverty and malnutrition were everywhere. A civil authority did not exist; most of the young men had left, either in search of a better place to live or as recruits for the VC.

The Marine Company Commander organized a program that would be of obvious benefit to the villagers by giving them a new, fresh start on life. A village chief was appointed by the government and he then appointed hamlet chiefs. The company commander dealt directly with the village chief and organized several committees to deal in specific areas. These committees and the company chairman were:

Business, Labor, Agriculture, Fishing-Company Officer

Education, Political PsyWar-Company Officer

Health and Sanitation-Leading Corpsman
Military Training-Company 1st Sergeant
Public Security-Company Officer

The committee efforts were coordinated by the Company Executive Officer in his capacity as the unit Civil Affairs Officer.

The Fishing Committee arranged to procure an outboard motor which reduced the time and the number of people required to check the fishing nets. More nets were used and this in turn increased the fishing catch by about 100%. USOM provided five tons of fertilizer for the Agriculture Committee, which in turn then sold it to the villagers for a small fee which they could afford. Marines demonstrated its use, and soon crop yields were increased.

A small business was established in the main village where Marines could buy small items and get haircuts. Fair prices had been mutually agreed on and these were posted for each item; there was no haggling and both parties seemed content. The Health Committee provided daily treatment to the sick and instruction to one girl from each hamlet in rudimentary nurse training, using an interpreter to relay instructions from the corpsmen. These girls were then given practical experience at daily sick call.

There are still VC in the general area today; they see the obvious benefits for the villagers in the program and want to regain their former control. A local Popular Force unit provides men for security patrols as well as for village security. Contact with the VC is lessening each week. Soon this village will be able to stand on its own feet and show its neighbors the real and tangible benefits of a well planned, organized and aggressively pursued civic action program.

# # # # #

5. CIVIC ACTION PROGRAMS CHANGE ORIENTAL ATTITUDES

Encouraging signs that the people are responding to our civic action and psychological warfare efforts are usually hard to find and measure

according to any short range yardstick. The long slow pull in the battle for the people's hearts and minds is recognized as one of the rules in this type of war. Therefore, it is doubly gratifying when concrete indices show that the people look forward to a productive future for themselves under the established government. They sometimes appear very subtly and in the most unlikely places. This was the case when a certain pig farm in Vietnam had its population decimated by cholera and the remaining infected pigs had to be destroyed. The incident involved some 96 animals and was a heavy blow to the citizenry, since the farm represented a significant step-up in their standard of living, and to the Marines who had provided the impetus and much of the materials for the construction of the farm.

Arrangements have been made through USAID to reconstitute the herd in the immediate future. But most significantly, the people are already collecting money for the purchase of new animals and planning improvements to the physical establishment. Though discouraged, the people recognize they have a future and are motivated to keep building for this future.

# # # # #

6. SELECTION OF CIVIC ACTION PROJECTS

The most intelligent and effective approach to Civic Action is one based on the theory that units

work with and through the established governmental systems to meet the needs of the local area and its citizens. Once the consent of the local authorities has been given, Marine units can begin to relieve local needs through Civic Action projects which take a variety of forms. The cooperation of and involvement in these projects by the local government and by the people themselves have the effect of building a better governmental structure and establishing a personal and real interest in the project on the part of the people. However, efforts to improve the economic, social, and medical conditions of the inhabitants must be tempered with an eye toward a proper balance of activities.

This balance can be achieved only if, first, the area in which the project is to be initiated is carefully studied and evaluated; and second, that the project is planned in detail and programmed to meet realistic goals.

Government officials on all levels have many other tasks to perform within their areas of political responsibility. Many times, the initiation of more than one community project at the village level and below often leads to confusion, schedule lags and disinterest on the part of the people. Remember, supervision and follow-through are often not the most highly developed skills of local administrators.

# # # # #

7. NEED TO KNOW

New units arriving in Vietnam for the first time often find themselves in an unfamiliar country with unfamiliar people with strange customs. The importance of briefing these Marines before they arrive on what to expect and how to act is of the utmost importance.

Included as an essential part of the briefing should be a discussion of the Revolutionary Development Program and the demands which the program places on all Marines. In many cases, an understanding of what Revolutionary Development is will mean the difference between returning or not returning from a patrol, procuring important pieces of intelligence information or being uninformed, or being fed by the people when rations are expended or going hungry.

Almost all of the problems which arise in the relationship between Marines and the local population are the result of ignorance by Marines of the customs or situation in which they find themselves. To wage a successful counterinsurgency type operation, the support of the local population must be obtained. Civil Affairs orientation on the squad and fire team level is the key to the success of the Revolutionary Development Program.

# # # # #

8. RELATIONSHIPS WITH GVN OFFICIALS

It is essential that local Vietnamese governments, particularly in the rural areas, be reinforced and supported. This can be effectively accomplished by working with district, village and hamlet chiefs in civic action endeavors. By demonstrating confidence in and respect for the chiefs and by distributing all commodities through the chiefs, the people quickly learn that their way of life can be improved through the efforts of the government. By the same token, encouraging the village chiefs to discuss community problems with the district chief helps to restore normal relationships of authority and improves mutual trust and confidence between government echelons.

Most frequently efforts to establish or improve normal government functions achieve the greatest success when both U.S. and GVN channels are utilized; the GVN channel for formalities and the U.S. channel to obtain added impetus. When the local chief formally presents his requirements to his next higher echelon, the USMACV advisor at that echelon may be notified and his assistance solicited to ensure that the request is processed expeditiously. In some cases, the advisor may be contacted prior to initiating the request in order to determine the best method for handling the request. Additional support can often be brought to bear by requesting the assistance of USAID representatives and agents of the voluntary agencies.

Working with and through local GVN channels to accomplish community improvements is an effective means of improving the functioning of the government and also serves to improve the status of that government in the eyes of the people.

# # # # #

9. IMPACT OF CIVIC ACTION

The basic objective of Marine Corps civic action and pacification programs in Vietnam is to aid in improving or restoring the strength and stability of local government, which can hold the respect and loyalty of the people. Pursuit of this goal, coupled with Marine combat operations, will

result in improved security and improvement of the general welfare of the people of South Vietnam.

In more densely populated areas, such as the city of Danang, civic action efforts have produced less of an impact on the government and the people because the functioning of the government had not been impaired to a great extent. In these areas, civic action has provided additional resources to bolster the local government and has compensated for any potential ill-will that may develop in any area where large concentrations of military personnel are stationed. However, the presence or absence of military civic action was not necessarily a major factor in improving the effectiveness of the local government.

The greatest impact of civic action programs has been achieved in rural areas where local administration has broken down and the influence of the provincial and national governments has been non-existent. Military security and civic action operations in rural areas have usually been the major factor in restoring effective local administration.

# # # # #

10. CONTINUITY OF EFFORT

The departure of units for tactical operations may produce adverse effects on civil affairs programs in Vietnam. The gap created by the movement may have to be filled by a reduced strength unit which is neither familiar with established programs nor briefed as to local civil officials with whom contact should be maintained. However, the replacement unit can continue the simplest programs, such as MEDCAP, thereby maintaining some semblance of a sustained program.

The withdrawal of units from Marine Tactical Areas for operation is unavoidable. However, by maintaining a turn-over file which can be presented to the relieving unit and by limiting the areas of responsibility assigned to these units

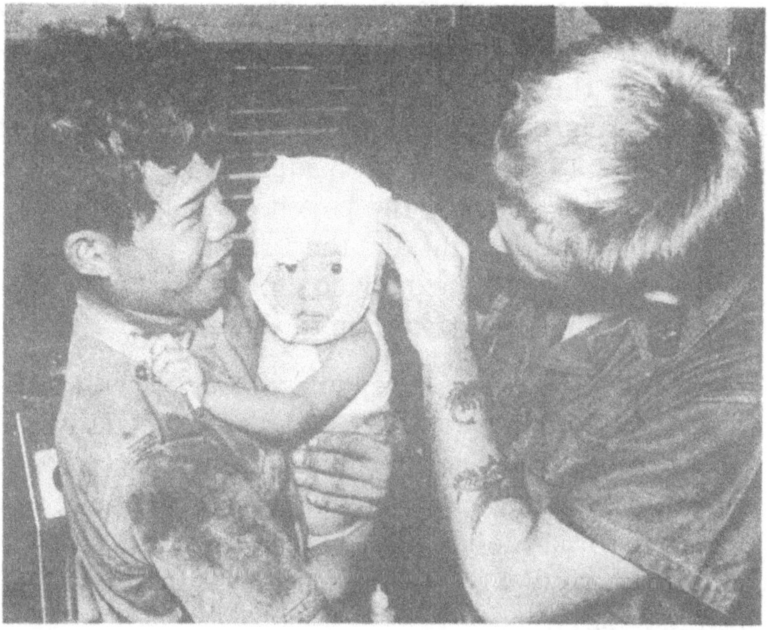

which are susceptible to being withdrawn, the adverse effect can be minimized. The turn-over file should contain, as a minimum, a listing of all completed projects, all active projects with milestone data, and the names and location of influential villagers with whom contact should be maintained. Furthermore, a representative of the relieving unit should effect liaison with the unit being relieved at the earliest so that personal introductions with officials can be arranged, security permitting.

# # # # #

11. SELECTION OF CIVIC ACTION PROJECTS

There is an occasional tendency for Marines to select civic action projects without benefit of advice from the Vietnamese people concerned. This approach has resulted in projects that neither meet the immediate needs of the people nor are desired by them. As a result, the psychological impact on the populace is slight and the return for the time, labor and material expended on the project by the Marines is not in proportion to the effort.

Too often there is a tendency to erect buildings while overlooking some of the basic needs of the people. Improvement of agriculture production and the fishing industry, development of local industries, and development of other sources of modest income are as important as medical and welfare assistance.

In order to achieve the maximum degree of success with civic action projects, the Vietnamese people and governmental officials at all levels (hamlet, village, district and province) should be consulted before embarking on a civic action program. This will ensure that projects undertaken meet the immediate needs and satisfy the desires of the people.

# # # # #

12. PSY WAR

As part of the Chieu Hoi (Open Arms) program to persuade the Viet Cong to leave their units and

join the Republic of Vietnam, safe conduct passes are distributed. These passes may be passed out by hand during pacification operations in areas of known VC control, or they can be dropped from light aircraft in and around VC bases. Shown above is a Safe Conduct Pass; should you see one later in the field you can easily recognize it. There are several distinct features to note. First, there is a color scheme which makes it easy to identify when carried by someone or when dropped by an aircraft. On one side is an illustration of the national flag of each nation represented by troops in South Vietnam. Likewise, each national language is displayed.

The other side has a drawing showing a welcoming Vietnamese soldier and a Viet Cong who decided to join the South Vietnamese cause. The spirit of friendly reception rather than a hostile attitude is presented by the smiling unarmed Vietnamese soldier. On the same side of the pass as the sketch of the two soliders is a serial number. This identifies the amount of passes printed. It also helps establish the area in which the pass was distributed and the route used by a person carrying it.

This pass entitles the bearer to retraining for several weeks at a Chieu Hoi Center where he will associate with other men who have returned to the GVN. From here he may choose to enter the Army of the Republic of Vietnam (ARVN) or be settled in a Chieu Hoi area which he can farm. The family of the returnee may accompany a man when he first returns and throughout his retraining period. If a returnee brings a weapon or ammunition with him, he is paid on a graduated piaster scale depending on the type of weapon or the amount of ammunition.

You may see several versions of safe conduct and psychological warfare leaflets; this is but one of them. Be alert for these leaflets and know how to process someone presenting one.

# # # # #

13. MEDICAL CIVIL AFFAIRS

When operating in an area with a civilian populace present and the need for civic action arises, a

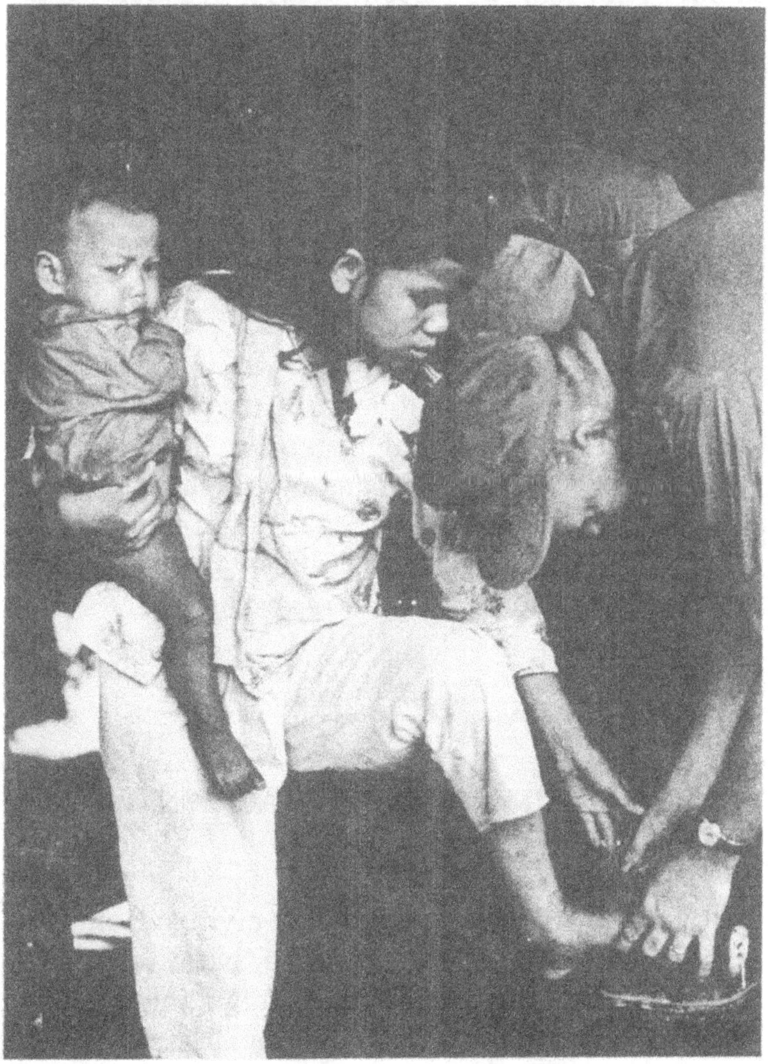

medical officer is normally called upon for duty. The need for a doctor or corpsman in a village is readily apparent, but there is also a need for semi-trained personnel to help in the village on a daily basis. This can be accomplished by seeking the advice of the village chief and asking him for nominations of two or three people who can act as nurses or corpsmen. Classes can be held in Vietnamese for selected personnel from the surrounding area. In this way, wounds can be cleansed, bandages changed, salves applied and prescribed medicines administered between visits by the corpsman.

However, the real long range goal of the program is getting the people used to helping themselves by providing a means by which they can do so and to gain the respect and admiration of the people, in addition to obtaining valuable intelligence information.

# # # # #

14. PROGRAMMING OF CIVIC ACTION COMMODITIES

Current policy requires that civic action projects be programmed in advance, but often opportunities arise for short-term, high impact civic action projects in areas recently liberated from Viet Cong control or in a recently expanded TAOR.

These projects combined with the security provided by the presence of Marine or GVN units create a marked improvement in the social atmosphere of the area, which Viet Cong propaganda cannot match.

Commodities such as food, clothes, soap, and construction materials are the critical items. Sufficient stocks of these items should be maintained, if possible, for immediate use as needs arise.

# # # # #

15. TROOP ASSISTANCE TO CIVIC ACTION TEAMS

When military units have successfully cleaned the Viet Cong from their area of responsibility, it is often possible to move some Marines to positions close to adjacent villages. A combat base might be set up in these areas and patrols conducted on all avenues of approach. In this way, the enemy is prevented from obtaining food and shelter from the villagers while the confidence of the people in the GVN cause is re-established and the shattered social structure rebuilt.

# # # # #

16. SUCCESSFUL CIVIC ACTION

Particularly successful civic action programs have been established based upon a friendly cooperative relationship between Marines and the people of villages. Here are some key points:

→ Become acquainted with the local village and district chiefs, the village elders, and other key officials. Don't short circuit their chain of command. Observe it just as you would your own.

→ Know the local security situation and the daily routine of the immediate area.

→ Establish a MEDCAP program.

→ Improve school facilities through assistance in construction and teaching.

→ Assist in organizing the self-defense forces and encourage their integration with Marine security patrols.

→ Patrol and help police the hamlets until self-defense forces achieve that capability.

→ Encourage improvements in agriculture and fishing.

# # # # #

17. A KINDLY WORD, A FRIENDLY FACE

Initially Marines were often met with suspicion by South Vietnamese but by sincerity in working civic action programs, the situation has changed. Now it is not unusual to see Marines working side by side with South Vietnamese on some project that will help a village, hamlet or the population. Playing ball with or listening to a Marine's radio have provided the South Vietnamese with a sense of trust and confidence in Marines. Efforts on the part of the Marines such as these have caused villagers voluntarily to show Marines where booby and punji traps are located, or to identify Viet Cong. This information has kept many a Marine on his own two feet. Civic action of this type requires a firm conviction on the part of each and every Marine. It is important to show by a Marine's conduct that he is in Vietnam to help and to stay in support of the village and hamlet, and to assist the RVN and its people in their efforts to defeat the Viet Cong.

# # # # #

18. DISTRIBUTION OF GIFTS

One major goal of civil affairs and civic action in RVN is to underscore the authority and enhance the stature of the local government, without overplaying direct USMC involvement. It is important to observe this principle in the distribution of gifts. Distribution at a large public gathering is desirable particularly where the impression is evident that the efforts of the local officials are responsible for these gifts. Gifts in large quantities given by Marines directly to groups of people tend to contradict this impression.

All gifts of farm implements, school supplies and other CARE and USAID goods can be made privately and without publicity to the local officials. At the same time, arrangements should be made to ensure that goods reach those who have the need for them.

# # # # #

19. DESIRABLE ASSISTANCE PROJECTS

Assistance projects that can be provided to the local Vietnamese villagers as visual, long-lasting proof of our will and determination to help the people are:

➔ Aid or advice in digging of wells.

➔ Help in repair of schools, providing school supplies and athletic equipment to schools.

➔ Help in repair/painting of hospitals/dispensaries/orphanages.

➔ Providing medical instruction to Vietnamese trainees in conjunction with the MEDCAP Program.

➔ Leveling of area for farming use.

➔ Providing English language instructors to schools or conducting classes for the Vietnamese people in the local area.

➔ Providing medical and dental aid.

# # # # #

20. HELP THE PEOPLE HELP THEMSELVES

Local improvement projects are very effective means of assisting the Vietnamese people. However, the beneficial aspects of these projects can be short-lived, unless they are accomplished in the proper manner.

➔ Emphasize equal participation by the local populace.

➔ Develop the traditional Marine "can do" spirit.

➔ Encourage the initiative of your Vietnamese co-workers.

➔ Ensure that they know how to use and care for the project, once it's completed. Examples are the construction of sanitation and medical facilities.

# # # # #

21. AREA COORDINATION RESPONSIBILITY

Upon introduction of Marine forces into RVN in 1965, area coordination responsibility generally rested with infantry battalions. Support and service support units participated in the program on a piecemeal basis, undertaking specific projects at will. This frequently resulted in duplication of effort. Furthermore, it failed to take full advantage of the inherent capability for civic action possessed by support units. This problem was recognized by CG, III MAF and assignments of specific geographic areas of responsibility for civil affairs and civic action were published.

Infantry units in the outlying areas should be relieved of area coordination responsibilities for the area to their rear. Support units are ideally suited and located to perform coordination functions in these areas.

# # # # #

22. TACTICAL BOUNDARIES

Tactical boundaries that split villages produce an ill effect on civil affairs operations. When this occurs, the village chief concerned is required to coordinate civil affairs programs and security with two separate units. Usually the chief is unable to comprehend the reason or the need for such an arrangement and considerable confusion results. This is particularly true when different civil affairs policies are pursued by the units concerned.

# # # # #

23. ASSISTANCE AVAILABLE

U.S. civil agencies and charitable institutions have provided considerable commodities support for III MAF civic action programs. Primary among these have been USAID, JUSPAO, Catholic Relief Services and CARE. In addition, technical assistance in construction and agriculture programs have been provided by USAID.

The COMUSMACV advisors at the province and district level of government have also been of assistance, particularly in the area of advice as to GVN procedures and suggestions for obtaining resources. Several sub-sector advisors have also provided financial assistance for III MAF civic action programs from the special fund provided for them by COMUSMACV.

# # # # #

24. JOINT PROJECTS

There is an occasional tendency for Marines to do all the work on civic action projects. This usually results in a completed product that, while appreciated by the Vietnamese people, has no special meaning for the people. This is well illustrated in one of the tactical areas where a dispensary was built and staffed by Marines. Not too long ago the residents in the hamlet asked for a new dispensary; after the shocked Marines asked what was wrong with the present one, the people replied that it was the "Marine Dispensary" and they wanted one of their own. This situation was further aggravated by the presence of a plaque on the front of the dispensary announcing the dispensary had been built by Marines for the Vietnamese people - but the plaque was written in English and had no meaning for the Vietnamese. Today the plaque is in Vietnamese and the dispensary is a Vietnamese dispensary.

# # # # #

25. CIVIL AFFAIRS PLANNING

In preparing for Operation Double Eagle during January 1966, a G-5 (Civil Affairs) Section was activated in the operational headquarters. Civil affairs planning for the operation conducted by this section centered around control of the civil populace in the objective area and civic action support. Medical supplies, foodstuffs, empty rice bags (for captured rice) and other materials were obtained and included in the prescribed load. In addition, a U.S. Army Civil Affairs Team (Refugee Relief) was obtained from the Commanding General, III MAF and employed on the operation. During the operation, liaison with district officials was

256-290 O-67—30

established and matters of mutual concern, such as refugee control were resolved. As a result of the civil affairs planning and preparation, units involved were prepared to cope with civil problems during the operation.

# # # # #

26. ADVERSE EFFECTS

Recently a shower was built at one of the dispensaries as part of the civic action program. The shower proved to be a very effective addition to community life. All children were required to shower before being treated; despite initial reluctance, the children began to take showers even though they were not waiting for treatment. However, the unit soon moved to another village - and took the shower with it. MEDCAP in the first village suffered a setback and, more importantly, a sure sign had been presented to the people that the Marines' presence and, consequently, the security of the area, was only temporary.

# # # # #

27. POINT OF CONTACT

A friendly face and a common language are two of the most useful tools available to the unit civic action program. Specific Marines should be assigned to maintain contact with the local leader in a single village for as long as possible. The village chief can be more effective if he deals with only one or two Marines, rather than with a different one every day. As a minimum, the Marines assigned to this duty should know the simple words and phrases of Vietnamese greetings.

# # # # #

28. PSYCHOLOGICAL WARFARE LESSONS LEARNED

The following lessons were learned as a result of a recent operation in Vietnam:

➔ Psy-War officers must have immediate access to interpreter/translators so that propaganda can be prepared quickly to exploit favorable psychological situations that present themselves during the course of an operation.

➔ The themes used during a tactical operation should be concentrated on the immediate tactical situation. Long range themes have little meaning during a combat operation.

➔ The local officials should be consulted to ensure that the propaganda used during the operation is consistent with Psy-War campaigns conducted in the past in that locality.

➔ Future propaganda should be planned to undermine anticipated counter-propaganda themes.

# # # # #

29. EMPLOYMENT OF "CHIEU HOI" FORCES

The Chieu Hoi Forces are comprised of men who at one time were in the service of the enemy and who have returned to the cause of the RVN. The use of this force in conjunction with Marine infantry units during operations has proven to be quite effective. They are aggressive and well aware of Viet Cong tactics and techniques. In several instances during a recent operation, they recruited local villagers to assist in convincing the Viet Cong and Viet Cong suspects into leaving tunnel complexes.

# # # # #

30. VC MINES INJURE INNOCENT CIVILIANS

Recently two Vietnamese boys, ages 7 and 9, were seriously wounded by a Viet Cong booby trap. On the day this happened the local Marine Psy-War Officer visited the area and distributed leaflets which stated that the VC booby traps injure curious children. The leaflets requested that villagers tell Marines the location of these devices so that children would not be exposed to this type of danger.

# # # # #

Chapter IX: MEDICAL

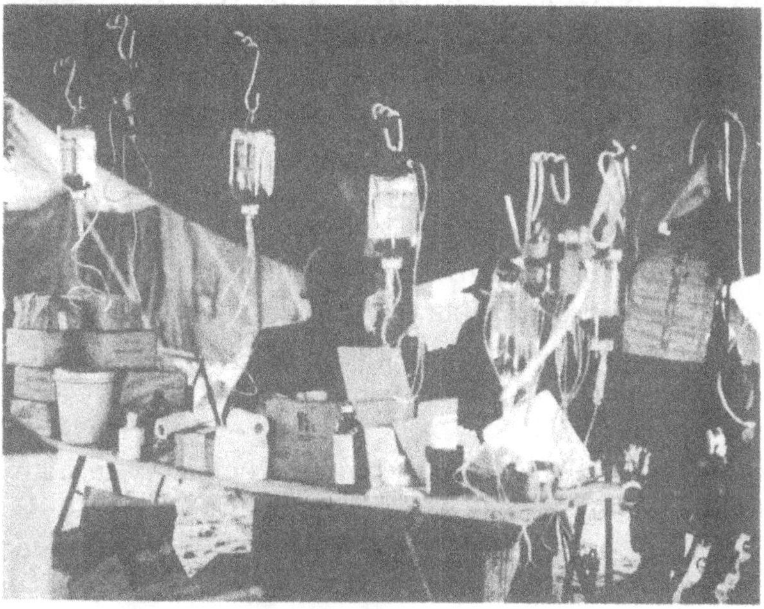

1. MEDICAL PROBLEMS IN VIETNAM

Duty in the Republic of Vietnam requires a great deal of knowledge on the part of each individual Marine. He must fully understand the problems of guerrilla warfare, the nature of the enemy, and the character of the South Vietnamese. Further, because it is a guerrilla war fought in terrain which is hostile to friendly forces, the individual Marine must know how to handle himself concerning health and hygiene. Even the simplest of activities (i.e., eating and drinking water) are complicated by health problems. Survival, therefore, requires that a Marine not only be competent in his military prowess, but also that he take special efforts to continually watch his own health to prevent illness or undue injury. This requires knowledge of a few basic rules and diligent application of them. Fortunately, most Marines adjust rapidly to the environment, abiding by established health guidelines.

Why does Vietnam present unusual or difficult problems of health? If the Vietnamese are able to live there without problems, why should we worry? The answers to these questions are fairly simple.

Vietnam is an underdeveloped country in many respects. It is especially underdeveloped medically. Because progress, as we know it, has not taken place there, the following factors result:

➛ Diseases that are almost or totally conquered in modern countries are common in Vietnam. Tuberculosis, Plague, Malaria and Smallpox are but a few examples. Hence the people there have a much higher mortality rate and suffer considerably from their illnesses. There has been no massive effort, as in our country, to eradicate these diseases. In our country all milk and food are processed to ensure health standards, people are immunized against serious illnesses and modern sanitation facilities exist. This is not true in Vietnam.

→ Many Vietnamese lack basic hygienic education. They do not understand the need for sanitation and water purification because they cannot appreciate how these things contribute to their health. Many have no idea of how diseases are contracted and spread. Thus, they are slow to accept change because they don't see where it helps.

→ There are minimal health services available to the Vietnamese population. They cannot be seen by a doctor, nurse or corpsman whenever they are ill. Only the very ill are admitted to a hospital. Folk medicine and Chinese herb medicine, which seem primitive to us, are well established practices. Further, Vietnam is a tropical country with several types of terrain. This produces diseases which are uncommon in the United States. The hot, rainy weather together with rice paddies, swamps, thick jungle and swollen rivers give rise to high mosquito populations and malaria and dengue fever. Worms that inhabit the intestines, leeches, abundant bacterial growth and certain illnesses are prevalent just because of the climate.

Specific diseases in Vietnam are as follows:

→ Diseases carried by insects are Malaria, Dengue Fever, Scrub Typhus and Plague. Malaria is the most important of these. It is a disease caused by a microscopic parasite that is injected into a human by mosquitos. High fever, headache and backache are the most common symptoms, but many others may be experienced. Untreated, it is often fatal. Most people recover quite rapidly with adequate treatment. Dengue fever causes a flu-like illness that may put a man out of action from one week to a month. It is distressing in that it may cause severe pain in the arms and legs along with chills and fever. Plague and Scrub Typhus have not been problems for U.S. servicemen in Vietnam, but affect the civilian population. Plague is a potentially fatal disease and it is important that immunizations be kept current.

➜ Illnesses affecting the stomach and intestines (amebiasis, dysentery, roundworm and hookworm). All these illnesses may cause diarrhea, abdominal pain, chills, fever and vomiting. Often they cause only a mild illness, but recurrent attacks, especially of amebiasis, may cause serious illness. Therefore seek medical attention at the first notice of diarrhea or stomach distress.

➜ Heat problems. Because of the high temperatures and high humidity in Vietnam, illnesses resulting from the heat are prevalent. Most are minor and can be avoided by simple measures. In the heat, a person loses more water and salt from the body than is normal. A loss of too much water and salt can lead to dizziness, exhaustion and occasionally unconsciousness. To counteract this, a Marine should learn to drink adequate amounts of water and at the same time, take salt tablets. Two salt tablets per canteen of water are required in very hot weather. Never take salt tablets without water, as this will cause stomach cramps. Never take water in the heat without taking salt.

➛ Eye infections. These may be caused by bacteria or a large virus (Trachoma). Anyone suffering from red, tender, painful eyes should seek treatment immediately.

➛ Rabies. There is a high incidence of rabies among the animal population of Vietnam. Any animal, such as a dog or monkey, that is retained as a pet should absolutely have rabies vaccination. Anyone bitten by <u>any</u> animal should immediately report to sick bay. Retain the animal if at all possible. Don't kill the suspect animal. Once contracted, rabies is a fatal disease. It can be prevented by proper medical attention.

➛ Infectious hepatitis. This illness, although seen in the U.S., appears to be more frequent in Vietnam. Infectious hepatitis is contacted through drinking contaminated water.

➛ Skin problems. Fungal infections and heat rash of the feet and groin are common. Increased attention to body cleanliness and use of foot and body powder are necessary to prevent these problems. Prolonged immersion of the feet in water may result in breakdown of the skin and infection. Often a Marine cannot escape exposure to the heat and water, but he can prevent the complications.

Carry extra socks in a plastic bag or under the utility jacket. Change socks frequently, when taking a break or whenever possible. Even removing the socks and wringing out the water will help. Remember to carry foot powder in the field and use it often.

➔ Any cut or minor wound becomes infected and may develop into a severe infection without proper care. Therefore have any cut, scratch or minor wound, treated as soon as possible. Often, it only takes a matter of minutes to clean and treat a small wound.

➔ Venereal disease. Syphilis, gonorrhea and several other venereal diseases are a major problem in Southeast Asia. The only way to be absolutely certain of not getting one of these diseases is to refrain from sexual association. The spread of these diseases is minimized by use of condoms and washing of the genitalia within five minutes of contact and emptying of the bladder. Soap is required when washing. Should a venereal disease be suspected, report to sick bay immediately. Modern treatment is effective, if started early.

➔ Snake bite and water buffalo. Snake bites are not a significant problem in Vietnam, but a few have occurred. Should a person be bitten, he should remain absolutely quiet and summon help. Do not panic! This stimulates your blood and aids in circulation of the venom. If possible, the snake should be killed and retained for identification purposes. Since there are more than one kind of snake, there are more than one kind of anti-venins used in treatment. Do not, however, jeopardize the safety or well-being of a group to chase a snake that crawled away. Also, remember, that all snakes will run from you unless surprised or cornered. If you leave them alone, they won't bother you. Water buffalo have injured a few Marines. When near these animals be particularly alert. If possible, avoid walking near them. Don't molest or bother them unnecessarily, as they may charge.

➛ Mental problems. At certain times during the tour of duty in Vietnam, a Marine may experience feelings of undue anxiety or depression. These are normal reactions to combat duty and most persons are able to cope with the situation. Some Marines, however, find the burden difficult and it affects their duty. If this occurs, seek help from the corpsman or medical officer. A Marine will find that there are others who have had similar problems who were able to overcome them without difficulty. Often a little rest and talking things out are all that is needed. If you notice this happening to one of your buddies, try to understand his problem and talk to him. A little reassurance in a time of need goes a long way. Marines are known to have fewer problems along this line than other units. This is due to their esteem for their buddies and the strong personal ties that are found in Marine units.

Health tips and guidelines

The majority of illnesses can be prevented by constant awareness and diligence. The following suggestions will help Marines stay healthy in Vietnam:

➔ Maintain your immunizations current. Immunizations are as important as weapons and helmets for protection. Shot cards should be checked periodically by medical personnel.

➔ Take the prescribed malaria tablets. Never fail to follow the prescribed routine. Some personnel complain of stomach cramps after taking malaria tablets. If this occurs, take the tablet after eating a meal. Minor stomach cramps once a week are nothing like the disease.

➔ Use mosquito repellent and mosquito nets. Some Marines believe that the Viet Cong can smell mosquito repellent, especially when on ambush or patrol. This is not true. The new repellent can be smelled for only a matter of inches. Remember that mosquitos come out right after dark and bite during dark hours. Therefore apply it freely during that time. Reapplication should be made every few hours. When netting is available, as in garrison, always use it.

➔ Keep clean. No one is particularly worried about their looks in Vietnam, especially when in the field. But wash and shave as often or more often, if possible, than you would at home. This will prevent most skin disorders which occur. Use medicated body powder and foot powder freely after bathing.

→ Drink purified or treated water only. Never drink untreated water. Use two iodine tablets per canteen of untreated water. In hot weather, take two salt tablets per canteen of water. Unless there is a water shortage, drink as much as you think you need. Water discipline should be discouraged except when water availability is minimal.

→ Eat only food that is authorized. Do not trust Vietnamese food or cooking.

→ Clean mess gear completely. No food should remain on trays or utensils. Any remaining food will soon develop into a mass of bacteria and your next meal may be quite upsetting.

→ Seek early medical treatment for cuts, scratches, minor wounds, diarrhea, chills and fever, vomiting, heat problems, skin problems. A few minutes spent taking care of a small problem will save prolonged hospitalization needed when the problem develops into something big.

→ Avoid stray or unimmunized dogs or animals. Rabies is almost epidemic among the animal population of Vietnam.

→ Keep feet dry and use foot powder. If prolonged exposure is unavoidable, change socks frequently and wring them out.

→ Realize that minor mental problems arise and seek treatment early. Offer help to buddies when they have problems.

Vietnam presents many hazards to health which are new to the Marine. However, most of these hazards may be prevented or minimized by diligent use of personal health measures and early treatment of small injuries and illness. Should a serious wound or injury occur, a Marine will receive the finest medical care available anywhere in the world.

# # # # #

2. THE FOUR LIFESAVING STEPS IN BATTLE

→ Stop the bleeding.

Apply pressure directly over the wound with first aid dressing in place.

If there is severe bleeding from an arm or a leg and no fracture is suspected, elevate it.

If bleeding does not slow down after a few minutes of direct pressure and elevation, apply tourniquet as a last resort.

Tighten tourniquet just enough to stop the bleeding.

Leave tourniquet exposed so it can readily be seen.

Do not loosen tourniquet until casualty is seen by medical personnel.

➛ Clear the airway.

If patient is unconscious, make sure the mouth is clear and patient can breathe.

Quickly sweep fingers through mouth to clear out mucus, blood, or foreign matter and draw tongue forward.

Position patient so saliva will drain out of mouth.

If patient is not breathing, start artificial respiration at once.

→ Protect the wound.

Use first aid dressing to keep dirt out of the wound and to control bleeding.

Support the part with splint, if necessary.

→ Prevent or treat for shock. (Symptoms of shock are pale face, cold clammy skin, rapid weak pulse, and shallow breathing.)

Stop the bleeding.

Clear the airway.

Protect the wound.

Head and shoulders lower than the rest of the body if there is no head, neck or check injury.

Make the casualty comfortable, loosen clothing and keep warm.

# # # # #

3. FIRST AID FOR BATTLE WOUNDS AND INJURIES

→ Chest wound.

Prevent air from entering wound by using an airtight dressing.

Observe the 4 Lifesaving Steps.

→ Belly wounds.

Do not attempt to replace organs.

Do not give food or water by mouth.

Observe the 4 Lifesaving Steps.

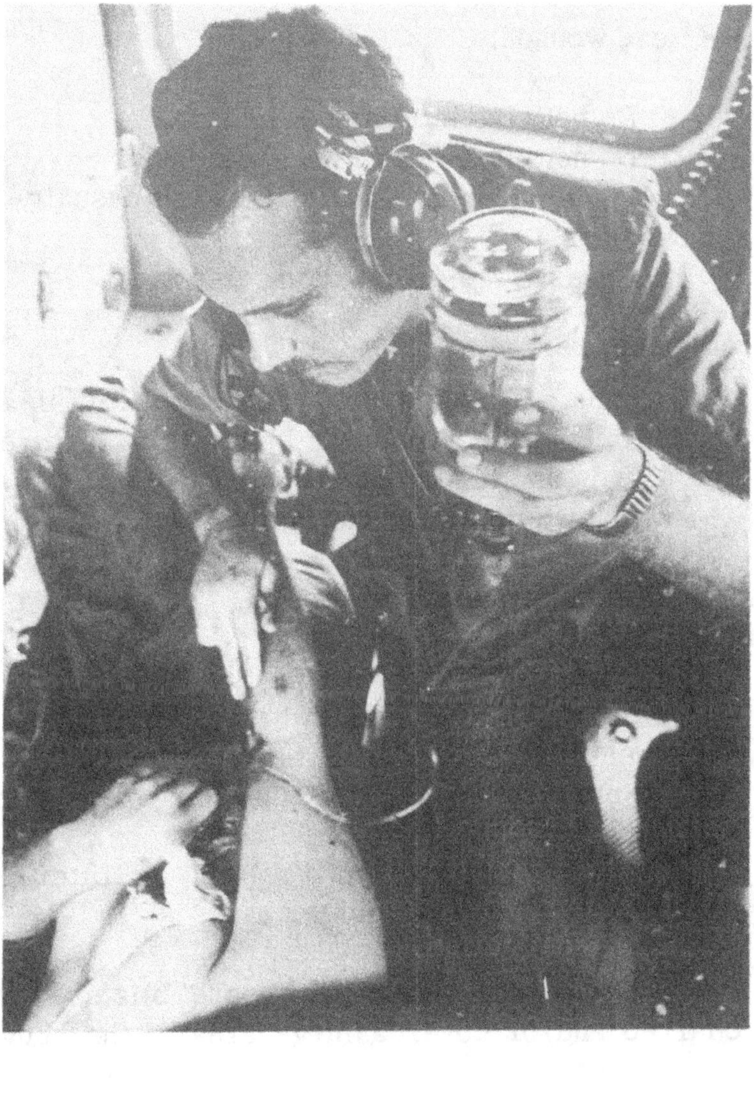

→ Head wounds.

Do not give morphine.

Do not place head lower than body.

Do not give anything by mouth if casualty is unconscious.

Observe the 4 Lifesaving Steps.

→ Fractures.

Signs: (A fracture may not have all of these signs. If in doubt, treat the injury as a fracture.)

Pain and tenderness.

Inability to move the injured part.

Deformity.

Swelling and discoloration.

Treatment:

Observe the 4 Lifesaving Steps.

Splint all fractures "where they lie" before movement or transportation is attempted.

Splint to immobilize the joint above and below the fracture.

Immobilize the entire body on litter or board for fractures of neck or back.

→ Severe burns. (Burns that are blistered or charred and/or cover a large area of the body.)

Prevent or treat for shock.

Remove or cut clothing away from the burned area only if clean dressings are available to place over the burn.

If conscious, not vomiting and there is no belly wound, give one packet of salt and soda from first aid kit in a canteen of cold water. If salt and soda pack is not available, use four salt tablets or 1/2 teaspoon of salt to a canteen of cold water.

Get casualty to medical care as soon as possible.

Apply no grease, ointment, vaseline, or lubricant of any kind to severly burned skin.

Do not try to pull clothes over burned area; cut them off.

Do not try to remove pieces of cloth that stick to the skin.

Do not try to clean burn.

Do not open blisters.

→ Heat stroke.

Symptoms:

Skin - hot, dry and bright pink in color.

Absence of sweating.

Headache, dizziness, confusion, convulsions, and loss of consciousness may be present.

Treatment:

Lower body temperature as quickly as possible by:

Removing from sun.

Removing clothing.

Keeping entire body wet by either immersing in cold water (with ice, if possible) or pouring cold water over the body.

Fanning the wet body to increase cooling.

Continue cooling during evacuation and get medical aid as soon as possible.

Give casualty cold salt water, <u>if conscious</u>.

→ Heat exhaustion.

Symptoms:
Heavy sweating.
Skin - pale and moist.
Dizziness and faintness.
Treatment:
Remove from sun.
Loosen clothing.

Casualty should drink as much cold salt water as he can tolerate (2 crushed salt tablets or 1/4 teaspoon salt to a canteen of cold water).

→ Heat cramps.

Symptoms:

Muscle cramps of arms, legs and/or abdomen.

There may be vomiting, cold sweat and weak pulse.

Treatment:
Same as for heat exhaustion.

→ Snake bite.

Immobilize the bitten part in a position that is below the level of the heart.

Improvise a tourniquet (necktie, handkerchief, or strip of cloth) and place 2 to 4 inches above the bite - between the bite and the heart. Tighten the tourniquet enough to make the veins stand out, but not enough to stop the pulse.

Start artificial respiration if the casualty stops breathing.

Get medical care as soon as possible.

→ Leech bite.

Treat as any other minor wound.

→ Predatory animal bites.

Animal bites should arouse the suspicion that the animal is rabid.

# # # # #

4. TAKE CARE OF YOUR CASUALTIES

Assistance and care for a wounded man does not end with delivering him to an aid station or getting him on a MEDEVAC flight. This is just the beginning. In cases where a man requires hospitalization, every effort must be exerted to ensure that his service records, personal effects and baggage quickly follow him. Instructions for the handling of casualties' records and gear are contained in FMFPACO P3040.2B (Policy and Procedures for Casualty Management Western Pacific Area) and in local command directives.

Every leader/commander should draw up an appropriate SOP for ensuring expeditious movement of a casualty's service records, personal effects and baggage, from his unit to the next outfit in the supply evacuation chain.

When a casualty is evacuated from the Republic of Vietnam, his records and gear move from his parent command through the supply chain to the local Force Logistics Command collection point. From one of these points, they move to Danang and are held, or are forwarded as appropriate by CO, Camp Butler (for Service Records) or CO, 3rd FSR (for personal effects and baggage). If the evacuated casualty is later returned to duty in WestPac, then his gear and records will be forwarded to his new command when he has been released from the hospital. If he is not returned to duty and is further evacuated to CONUS, then his records and gear are forwarded to the local Marine Corps Activity responsible for taking care of Marines at the hospital to which he is sent.

If a man's service records are not quickly forwarded, he may not get paid on time, his return to full duty may be delayed, and he may be otherwise inconvenienced. If he does not get his gear promptly, personal items and uniforms will not be available when he wants or needs them and will have to be duplicated at needless expense to the government and to the man.

# # # # #

5. IMMERSION FOOT

Extended operations in the flooded areas along waterways and rivers may result in a prolonged wearing of wet foot gear. Unless wet socks can be

changed frequently for dry ones, and feet are periodically exposed to the sunlight, immersion foot can result. This is an extremely painful condition in which the feet swell and take on a puffy, wrinkled look. Extra socks and planned breaks to expose the feet can avoid the worst effects of immersion foot.

# # # # #

6. LEECHES

Land leeches are encountered in the swampy areas of Vietnam. It is disturbing to discover a slimy passenger fixed securely to an arm or leg. Orientation should include information on the leech, what it is, how to avoid it, how to get rid of it, and how to treat its bite.

The land leech, like a mosquito, is a blood sucker and is found in grass and foliage from which they attach themselves to passing humans. The leech fastens itself to the skin, feeds, and then drops off. The leech bite is painless and not at all harmful, although the small wound it makes may become infected. Leeches can be repelled by applying standard insect repellent to exposed skin. They can be removed by pulling them off, by touching them with a lighted cigarette or by applying salt, vinegar, gasoline, or other strong solutions. The bite mark should be cleansed, preferably with alcohol, to prevent infection. If an infection does develop, see a corpsman for application of an antibiotic to kill the infection.

In short, leeches are nothing more than nuisances. With simple precautions, their effects can be minimized.

# # # # #

7. THE BATTALION SURGEON AND MEDCAP

When the Navy medical officer assigned to a Marine battalion arrives in the Republic of Vietnam, he will find that more than half the work expected of him involves MEDCAP (medical civil

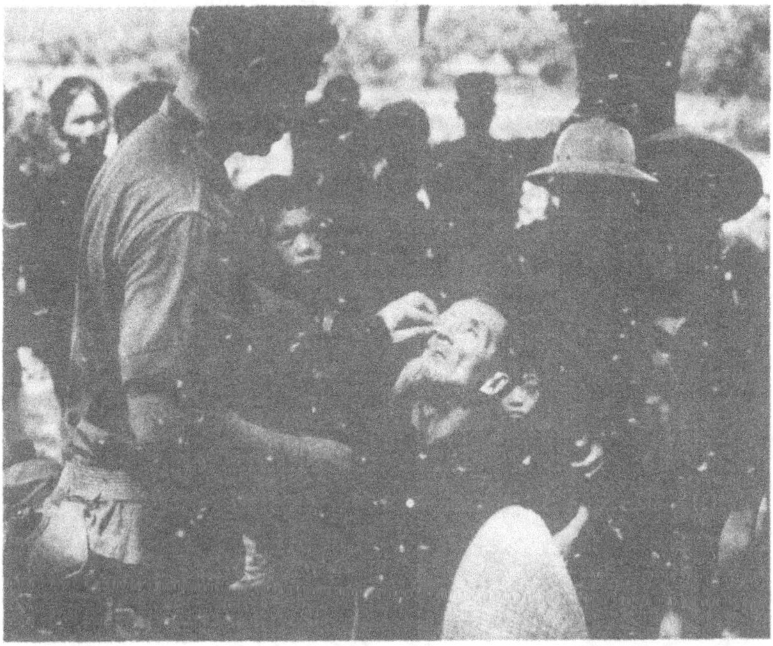

action program). He will find supplies for treatment of the civilian population readily available through his Marine civil affairs officer and he will probably find some type of MEDCAP already underway in the area. He will find himself surrounded by a civilian population greatly in need of medical treatment and instruction. MEDCAP offers perhaps the best opportunity to become acquainted with the beauties, the intrigues, the eccentricities, and the tragedies of a unique and remarkable country and people. The problems may immediately seem insurmountable and the needs so great that positive intentions may be lost in frustration at the outset.

a. The Goal

By definition, MEDCAP is an effort to help win the war. It is intended to gain the support and help of the people for the Marine units operating in the area. This is a military goal. The intention also is to help gain the confidence of the people and acquire their support for the local and national Vietnamese government. This is a political goal. Therefore, at the battalion level of MEDCAP operations the primary goal is not the idealistic, missionary appeal of improving the general health of the people. Of course, it is much more than coincidence, and certainly fortunate that this end is accomplished to some degree in following the original purpose, but it is important to make this distinction, for two reasons:

First, it explains the selection of certain "high-impact" cases for definitive treatment over cases which, medically speaking, are more deserving of further evaluation and treatment. Thus, in an insecure area, it will most often be advisable to select a child with a hare-lip and cleft-palate for surgery rather than a suspected case of congenital heart disease, megacolon, or bowel obstruction. This doesn't mean that such cases should be neglected; however, to use the last example, it may be better to treat bowel obstruction empirically for ascariasis rather than evacuating the case for surgery. Although each case must be considered of itself, two rules-of-thumb support the above suggestion. First, evacuation of cases for which a sure cure is not rather certain should be avoided. In some insecure areas more political damage can follow the return of an uncured case. Secondly, cases which will make an immediate and obvious impression on the local populace should be selected for evacuation and definitive care. Such cases are hare-lip and cleft-palates, cataracts, pterygiums, strabismus, amputees for orthopedic appliances, superficial congenital deformities for surgical repair, deforming goiters, and the like. Dental work is similarly of great high-impact value. Painless extractions produce immediate and obvious relief, as well as the tangible object of the patient's torment. In regard to the high-impact value of DENTCAP, a Navy dentist developed an inspired flourish with the needle and forceps, which, in true de Bergerac style, captured the awe and admiration of the natives who always crowded curiously around the dental stool. Penicillin is also of high-impact value, because indigenous bacteria have been found highly susceptible to the antibiotics; and impetigenous, pyogenic infections are legion in rural Vietnam.

If MEDCAP is to serve the political as well as the military goal, the method of conducting MEDCAP will be affected. Namely, on MEDCAP patrols, which will be discussed later, it is advisable to enlist the services of one or two Vietnamese "public health nurses." These are persons who, after some training, are tested in Saigon, licensed, and placed on the government payroll.

They are located in civilian aid stations in populated areas, are usually available and are usually cooperative. Their actual medical assistance is questionable; however, they help preserve the image of the Vietnamese helping themselves, and suggest that the government as well as the Marines are rendering assistance. Because they can converse more quickly with the people, it is probably best to give them liquid and tablet drugs to dispense, such as piperazine, vitamins, diarrhea tablets, aspirin, antiacids, dietary supplements, cough syrups, and others, excluding antibiotics. The major problems, then, are left to the corpsmen and M.O. Although the "nurses" are sometimes indiscriminate in the use of drugs, they probably do little harm; and they do learn to refer more serious problems to the corpsmen or M.O.

b. The Method

The following proposed method of conducting MEDCAP applies to the battalion occupying a Tactical Area of Responsibility (TAOR) and is disrupted partially or totally for the periods of time companies or the battalion are away on operations. Units left behind will carry on in the best way possible.

The conduct of MEDCAP in its phases can be broken down in somewhat the same manner as are tactical responsibilities within the battalion. The first echelon MEDCAP contact will be made by the company corpsmen in the rifle companies occupying outlying positions in the least secure areas of the TAOR.

In one TAOR the company corpsmen held daily sick call at the same time every morning in a spot close to the secure company C.P. The inhabitants of surrounding villages and hamlets quickly picked up the routine and returned on a treatment-needed basis. Thus, no pills were dispensed for future use, but individuals needing repetitive therapy returned to sick call. It is a strict rule in all phases of MEDCAP to avoid dispensing drugs for future use whenever practicable, and always with antibiotics and narcotics; for too often such drugs wind up in the hands of the Viet Cong. Exceptions can be made occasionally with drugs such as vitamins, aspirin, and piperazine which, unless they are identified, are of little value to the VC; but this is acceptable only when a case is being treated specifically, and retreatment will not be possible within the week.

MEDCAP supplies should be requisitioned through the Battalion Aid Station (BAS) by the senior company corpsman, and must be kept separate from regular organic stock. A daily report of MEDCAP activities including numbers treated, broken down into children, adult males, adult females and general types of cases treated, should be made to the BAS to be included in the daily BAS MEDCAP report to the civil affairs officer.

Since evacuation and treatment of high-impact cases is of greatest advantage when taken from the least secure areas of the TAOR, recognition of such cases should partially be the responsibility of the company corpsmen. These cases, as well as other problem cases, should be referred to the M.O.; and he should plan a weekly visit to each company CP area for this purpose. Occasionally, it may be advisable to evacuate a case to the BAS; however the previously-mentioned danger of evacuating a case to the BAS should be kept in mind.

MEDCAP patrols are set up in conjunction with the civil affairs officer with a MEDCAP team from the BAS. The patrols can also be used by the civil affairs officer for the conduct of other non-medical civil affairs business. The MEDCAP team should be composed of a M.O., two or three corpsmen, a dentist and dental technician, Vietnamese "nurses," and interpreters. Circumstances will not always allow a complete team. Necessary security ranging from a fire team to a reinforced platoon, depending on the degree of security of the area, will be provided by the civil affairs officer. Patrol routes should be drawn to cover the TAOR in the most efficient manner, taking into consideration overlapping into company areas and possible combined work with the company corpsmen. The company corpsmen are less well-equipped for MEDCAP than the patrols so the patrols should take as much of the load as possible. The routes should be retraced every three or four days when possible, often in reverse, but with a staggered schedule for security reasons. The routes can usually be arranged so that the TAOR can be covered in three or four days using daily patrols; however, it may be necessary to occasionally split into two patrols with different routes in one day. Supplies can be packed by as many of the team as necessary, and due to the lack of roads and the frequency of stops, movement will usually be on foot. It will be possible, in some instances, to use vehicles or helicopters for transportation to sections of the TAOR where patrolling will take place. Stops or checkpoints are pre-located at schools, wells or other centrally-located places. Duration of stops should probably not exceed ninety minutes, again for security reasons. While the "nurses" set up to dispense drugs under the supervision of one corpsman, who also does the necessary recording, another corpsman can set up to treat superficial skin lesions, leaving the M.O. to sort patients and treat exceptional cases with the help of the interpreter. The dental team will set up independently.

c. Treatment

In one TAOR 16,000 cases were treated in one month. Such treatment must be largely empirical, and there is a dissatisfying, discouraging quality in this for the M.O. However, it will remain this way until permanent clinics with laboratory facilities are available in rural Vietnam. So the best advice perhaps is to simply recognize this and find then a challenge in the resulting necessity for pure physical diagnosis.

Another problem which will be encountered in every area where Marines are located is that of begging on the part of Vietnamese children, and even some adults. Solicited articles are gum, cigarettes, food, candy, and soap. It is not easily recognized that the person who responds to such beggary loses the respect of the beggar. If any individual in a MEDCAP patrol responds even to the most innocent of such entreatments by a Vietnamese child, the entire patrol may be disrupted by a deluge of screaming children crowding out persons seeking medical attention. And, if this practice continues, MEDCAP may become the Vietnamese counterpart for the Good Humor wagon. In the Orient, the individual who responds to other than a professional beggar without asking some consideration in return loses face. However, this shouldn't be confused with the services freely offered by the MEDCAP team. MEDCAP offers service to the people; and, apparently, for the Buddhists at least, the provider in this case is scoring points in heaven by this good deed, and, therefore, does not deserve thanks from the recipient for being allowed to render the deed. This disposition should not be misconstrued by the members of the MEDCAP team as resentment. Indeed, the Buddhist equanimity will often be ruffled by obvious evidence of appreciation; and, in general, Buddhists make good patients.

Soap is a special problem because hygiene in rural Vietnam is lacking; the distribution of soap on MEDCAP is always greeted with utter pandemonium. Its distribution should be accomplished by relinquishing it to reliable village and hamlet chiefs for distribution. In this manner the appearance of aid from the national government is nurtured.

It might be mentioned here that one aim of the civil action program is to encourage the Vietnamese to use their own chain of command for supplies. Therefore, village and hamlet chiefs, nurses, and other government officials should be

256-290 O-67—32

vigorously implored at every opportunity to requisition their own medical and other supplies at their district headquarters. The M.O. will work with the civil affairs officer in advising and aiding local officials further in the provision and construction of aid stations, public health, and sanitation facilities. Medical and educational, as well as construction and other materials provided by USAID and other sponsors are available to the Vietnamese at any level in their own chain of command. Of course, the higher the level from which supplies are obtained through Vietnamese supply routes now, the more rapid and efficient will be the development of future economic organization and autonomy in RVN.

Specific treatment will not be discussed here at length, because seldom is it possible. Many diseases, such as relapsing fever, denque, the leptospiroses, typhus, malaria, etc., will frequently go unrecognized for lack of necessary bacteriological studies. Some confusion may be avoided by noting that, in the Vietnamese language, malaria and fever are merely synonymous. The high incidence of congenital problems among the rural population is presumably due to a relative occurrence of in-breeding over timeless generations; and the high incidence of pterygiums among young and older adults may be related to the high frequency of recurrent conjunctivitis among children and adults--itself attributed to sun, dust, contagion, and malnutrition. It is probably safe to assume that all children in rural Vietnam are infested with pathogenic parasites. Consequently, many will be anemic and malnourished. Eye and external ear infections will be seen constantly in both children and adults. Superficial fungus infections are extremely common, especially tinea capitus, which may spawn a superimposed pyogenic infection. Ulcerating fungal infections of the skin, primarily on the lower extremities, may often be confused with the ulcerations of impetigo. The lesions of yaws can usually be distinguished, unless they assume the ulcer form; in any case they respond to penicillin. Occasionally a suspected case of plague may be seen. If this happens, it is probably best to isolate the patient, notify the nearest preventative medicine unit, investigate with the hamlet chief for other cases, see that the patient is treated with the appropriate antibiotic, and stay as far away from the paticnt as possible. If it appears as the bubonic type, the bubo should be aspirated with sterile technique and as little contact with the patient as possible effected. A prophylatic course of sulfadiazine should be given contacts if the smear is suggestive. Suspected cases of meningitis should be evacuated, with or without a spinal tap, to the nearest civilian hospital with the villagers being informed of the necessity. There will be no opposition if the case is advanced.

It seems adults who survive childhood in Vietnam are fairly resistant to disease. Suspected cases of tuberculosis should be evacuated for

X-ray and told to report to the nearest civilian hospital if the chest film is positive.

The above suggestions for patient disposition are meant to be a guide only, the local situation, command policy, and professional judgment will have a profound influence in each case. Patient handling, of course, is determined by the availability of medical facilities, and this is in constant flux. The same is true for the handling of high-impact cases; however, these are important enough to obtain treatment, if necessary, by evacuation to Danang, Saigon, or the Navy hospital ship. Unfortunately, there are no existing, uniform means of transporting or treating these cases. Therefore, each case must be handled individually by the M.O. The contacts he acquires and methods he learns in making such arrangements will be good for the repetitive handling of future cases.

MEDCAP methods should constantly change to fit the military-political situation. As previously Viet Cong-controlled areas become cleared, the political aims of MEDCAP should be replaced by the public health aims. The next logical step beyond MEDCAP patrols is the establishment of semi-permanent clinics in the TAOR, with the help of village chiefs and civilian labor. In such "clinics" medicine could be kept in locked cabinets; they could be staffed by one or two corpsmen, initially, with one or two permanent Vietnamese nurses; regular clinic hours could be kept, and a referral system set up; training of one or two additional nurses could be undertaken; and health education of the people could be started with movies, lectures, and demonstrations in sanitation and hygiene. Presumably, such clinics could remain self-operating after military support has left. That such a clinic set-up is possible has been demonstrated in one Chu Lai TAOR. A corpsman associated with a squad of Marines working independently with a company of popular forces troops in a combined-action camp, set up a dispensary to train P.F. corpsmen and to treat troops and their dependents. Not only did the P.F. corpsmen receive excellent training--within the obvious limits of the situation--but the dispensary became a highly reputed treatment center to which Vietnamese people traveled several kilometers. And it became a well-organized referral center for MEDCAP cases to the First Medical Battalion.

# # # # #

8. MALARIA

Malaria is a medical problem in Vietnam. With the conduct of operations into the highlands and jungles where malaria control measures have been impossible due to Viet Cong control, the incidence of malaria has risen to the point where it is now a significant military as well as medical problem. The emergence of a strain of malaria (Falciparum) which is relatively resistant to the standard chloroquine-primaquine antimalaria drug has aggravated the problem of malaria control.

Full emphasis is being placed on use of individual protective measures for the avoidance and prevention of malaria; however, these measures are most difficult under tactical conditions. The mosquitos which transmit malaria have a habitat quite similar to that of the Viet Cong: they are found in the forested highlands and are most active at night. The Viet Cong are highly infected with malaria and constitute a reservoir of infection to be passed to forces opposing them. Thus, avoidance of malaria would require avoidance of the Viet Cong and this is not compatible with our mission. This is the real dilemma.

The malaria incidence for Marines in Vietnam during 1966 was 15.2 per 1000 per year. On the other hand, 25% of all French troops in Vietnam in 1954 contracted malaria.

The relatively low incidence of malaria among Marines in Vietnam today attests to the efficacy of malaria discipline, use of individual protective measures, and the standard chloroquine-primaquine suppressant drug.

A special word about this standard drug is indicated. Much has appeared in the press recently concerning the failures of this antimalarial compound. Chloroquine-primaquine is a good drug for the suppression of malaria. Without it, the incidence of the disease would be much higher than is actually being encountered.

# # # # #

9. DISEASES OTHER THAN MALARIA

Diseases being encountered in SEA are the same as those which have plagued field armies in past campaigns. Rare and exotic diseases have not been a problem. Rather, intestinal, respiratory, and skin conditions are the leading causes for visits to medical facilities. The attack rate of these diseases is highest among troops newly arrived in-country--prior to their becoming acclimatized to the environment of Vietnam. After a period of acclimatization, the rates fall to a reasonable and militarily acceptable level.

Acclimatization necessary for troops to regain full combat effectiveness requires approximately:

→ Five days to compensate for the significant time differential between Vietnam and the United States.

→ Two weeks to adjust to the temperature and humidity of the environment.

→ Five to six weeks to achieve immunological potency against the common infectious agents causing intestinal, respiratory and skin diseases.

# # # # #

10. IMPROVED MEDICAL EVACUATION SYSTEM

The American Marine wounded in Vietnam today has the best chance of recovery that he has had in any war to date. While it is not appropriate to make direct comparisons between wars due to the many variables involved, it is noted that mortality among wounded reaching medical channels

approximates 1%! This compares favorably with the 2.2% figure in Korea, 4.5% in World War II, and 8.5% in World War I. There are many reasons for this substantial improvement in field medical care.

Forward helicopter evacuation, which originated in Korea, has become the standard method for movement of patients from the battlefield to forward hospitals in Vietnam. With this improved helicopter evacuation capability, no Marine in Vietnam is more than 30 minutes away from a medical facility capable of initiating definitive life-saving resuscitative surgery. More casualties are reaching hospitals faster, which makes the 1% mortality figure even more significant.

Whole blood, which has been a problem in each major war to date, has not been a problem in Vietnam. An efficient blood distribution system has kept pace with the increasing requirement for whole blood. In no instance has blood not been available when and in the quantities needed.

Improved medical facilities have made it possible to utilize the most modern surgical techniques in the most forward hospital installations. Air conditioning, no longer a luxury, is considered essential to the control of the environment of the critically wounded before, during, and immediately after surgery. The most modern surgical equipment for general and specialized procedures is available in forward medical facilities.

Advanced surgical techniques are being applied, daily, in all forward hospitals--not just in selected hospitals located to the rear. Blood vessel surgery, sporadically used in Korea, is now commonplace in Vietnam and has significantly reduced the number of amputations that used to be an accompaniment of war surgery. Great advancements in the art of resuscitation, including the use of whole blood and electrolytes, have been brought to bear on the management of wounded with highly successful results.

# # # # #

11. NOTES FOR THE MEDICAL OFFICERS AND CORPSMEN

→ Make sure each man in the battalion has a complete first aid kit (jungle kit). This gives you a readily available supply of battle dressings and saves the ones in the corpsman's first aid bag (Unit One). This keeps your resupply problem down to manageable levels.

→ Most casualties are not normally seen at the BAS. It is important, therefore, that the M.O. sees that the corpsmen receive adequate refresher training in first aid.

→ There are no helicopters normally designated as ambulance helicopters in the Marine Corps. Conversely, all helicopters can be used for casualty evacuation. However, they will not come equipped with medical personnel or stretchers unless this has been specifically requested. Learn to make the best out of what's available.---"When in the field, improvise." (Ponchos make good litters.)

→ Make sure that all weapons are cleared and locked with the magazine removed before entering the BAS.

→ If you go to the field, travel light. Corpsmen should carry a Unit One, a couple of bottles of albumin, and their personal gear.

→ Helicopters have changed the whole concept of evacuation from the field and should be used to evacuate anyone who can't function.

→ Evacuation by helicopters has changed the approach to medical aid of the wounded in the field. You do a man a disservice if you delay longer than to do what is essential to keep him alive until he reaches the hospital. Stop hemorrhage, plug chest wounds, establish airways, etc. Usually there is time for this while waiting for a helicopter to arrive.

→ There is no such thing as a BAS in the field. You can't sedate and hold battle fatigue cases for 72 hours and you can't take a sprained ankle case off of his feet for a couple of days. The "garrison" BAS is the only place where you can and should have a holding capacity.

→ If a doctor is in the field his most important function is to establish a triage area. Assign available corpsmen to the casualties to dress wounds. Remove most of the WIA's clothing--it will have to come off anyway at the hospital and it is very easy to overlook multiple wounds in the dark. Don't allow red filters on flashlights in the triage area as you won't be able to see blood or wounds. Give albumin (or other fluids) if there is time and also penicillin or tetracycline. Get an idea of numbers of casualties and who you want to go first. Have some Marines collect ponchos and organize Marines in groups of fours to carry the wounded.

→ It's difficult to do in combat, but filling out the essentials on the DD-1380 card must be done. As soon as possible see the S-1 representative and give him the names of the wounded to keep the Commanding Officer informed.

→ Points to emphasize to your corpsmen in handling of any WIA's.

- Close open chest wounds.

- Stop bleeding - if a limb is gone, put on a tourniquet.

- Marines are young and tough, but they are frequently dehydrated in the field due to the heat, low salt and water intake and possibly concurrent diarrhea and this predisposes to shock.

- If the casualty is bleeding, give albumin - it really does the job, and if the evacuation is going to be delayed due to hostile fire, night, etc. and there are no other contraindications (abdominal wounds, etc.) give P.O. fluids.

- Immobilize wounded extremities to prevent pain and possible fat embolism.

- Wait a couple of minutes on morphine - once a wound is immobilized and if the patient is handled gently, he will rarely complain of pain again. We really need a better way of giving IB morphine to prevent peripheral sequestration in vascular collapse, but it can be done with a syrette. (Ed. note - Demerol and disposable syringe can be utilized.)

- Use wide roller gauze on multiple fragment wounds of extremites. Battle dressings take too long and you are only temporizing anyway.

- When stability is essential in moving a casualty, three packboards can be secured together to make a very satisfactory litter. Also, a poncho and a couple of bamboo poles make a good litter.

- Ace wraps (3", 4", 6") make effective pressure dressings, especially on large or multiple wounds. They can be quickly applied over a battle dressing or roller gauze and also used to secure a splint. Because of the corner straps on battle dressings, it is sometimes difficult to get enough pressure over the center of the dressing to stop bleeding. Crisscross tying helps.

- Each corpsman should carry a couple units of albumin taped to the shoulder straps of his Unit One.

- When an operation is begun corpsmen would be wise to stuff the pockets of their jungle utilities with extra battle dressings and roller gauze. Demolition bags (get from engineers) are good for carrying extra bandages and a few sick call items.

- Many corpsmen like packboards because they can be gotten out of quickly to allow freedom of movement in treating casualties.

- With diarrhea being such a frequent problem in the field, at least a couple of corpsmen in each company should carry a canteen of Kaopectate and/or a bottle of paregoric.

- M.O.s have been impressed with the beneficial effects of Serum Albumin as a blood substitute. Many corpsmen carry two units taped to the straps of their Unit Ones.

# # # # #

Chapter X: SPEAK VIETNAMESE

The following phrases and words are those most commonly used by Marines during combat operations in the Republic of Vietnam. The majority of the words and phrases have been taken from a list published by Leatherneck Magazine and titled, Fire Team Phrase Book. It is printed on water resistant material and designed to withstand the severe climatic conditions encountered in Vietnam. (The Fire Team Phrase Book may be ordered in accordance with the instructions contained in Section III of Marine Corps Order P5600.31.) The use of these phrases by individual Marines and unit leaders in the past has greatly contributed to the success of many operations.

ENGLISH	VIETNAMESE	PRONUNCIATION
	GENERAL CONVERSATION	
Hello, good-bye	Chào.	Chow.
Mr.	Ông.	Um.
Mrs.	Bà.	Bah.
Miss.	Cô.	Ko.
You (child).	Em.	Em.
How are you?	Ông (bà, cô, em) mạnh giỏi không?	Um mon yoy come?
I'm fine.	Tôi mạnh giỏi.	Toy mon yoy.
Thank you.	Cám ơn ông.	Come on um.
Please say it again.	Xin ông nói lại.	Sin um noy lie.
Excuse me, I don't understand.	Xin lỗi ông, tôi không hiểu.	Sin loy um, toy come hew.

MILITARY TERMINOLOGY

ENGLISH	VIETNAMESE	PRONUNCIATION
Do you speak English?	Ông nói tiếng Anh không?	Um noy tyen Ahn come?
Let's go.	Chúng ta đi.	Choong ta dee.
Where?	Ở Dâu?	Uh-a Doe?
Aid station.	Trạm cứu thương.	Trom coo thwong.
Booby trap RPT.	Bẫy nổ.	By No.
Corpsman.	Y-tá.	EE-tah.
Doctor.	Bác Sĩ.	Bac shee.
Explosives.	Thuốc nổ.	Too-oc no.
First aid.	Cứu cấp.	Coo cup.
Flare.	Hỏa châu.	Wa cho.
Grenade.	Lựu đạn.	Luu don.
Guerrilla.	Quân du kích.	Kwun you kick.
Helicopter.	Phi cơ trực thăng.	Fee cah trook tong.
Jeep.	Xe díp.	Say yip.
Jet plane.	Phi cơ phản lực.	Fee ca fun luke.
North Vietnamese.	Người Bắc Việt.	Newy bac Viet.
Propeller plane.	Phi cơ cánh quạt.	Fee ca cun quot.
Trap.	Bẫy.	By.
Truck.	Xe cam-nhông.	Say com nyong.
Pilot.	Phi công.	Fee come.
Platoon leader.	Trung đội Trưởng.	Trung doi trew-ong.
Viet Cong.	Việt cộng.	Viet Cong.
Vietnamese.	Người Việt Nam.	Newy Vietnam.
Husband.	Chồng.	Chum.
Wife.	Vợ.	Vyuh.
Chinese.	Người Trung Hoa.	Newy trung wa.
Communist.	Cộng sản.	Kong san.
Rice.	Gạo.	Gow.
Water buffalo.	Con trâu.	Con trow.
Enlisted men.	Binh Sĩ.	Bin shee.
Sgt.	Trung sĩ.	Troong shee.
Officers.	Sĩ quan.	Shee kwun.

ENGLISH	VIETNAMESE	PRONUNCIATION

(ARMED FORCES OF THE RVN)

Regular Forces.	Chủ Lực Quân.	Chew Luke kwun.
Regional Forces.	Địa Phương Quân.	Dia foong kwun.
Popular Forces.	Nghĩa Quân.	Nyah Kwun.
Army.	Lục Quân.	Luke kwum.
Navy.	Hải Quân.	Hi kwun.
Air Force.	Không Quân.	Come kwun.
Marine Corps.	Thủy Quân Luc Chiến.	Tooy kwun luke chyen.

(BRANCHES OF THE ARMY)

Infantry.	Bộ binh.	Bo bin.
Artillery.	Pháo binh.	Fow bin.
Engineer.	Công binh.	Come bin.
Medical.	Quân y.	Kwun ee.

(MILITARY UNITS)

Squad.	Tiểu ðội.	Tyew doy.
Platoon.	Trung ðội.	Troong doy.
Company.	Đại ðội.	Die doy.
Battalion.	Tiểu ðoàn.	Tyew dwan.
Regiment.	Trung ðoàn or Liên ðội.	Troong dwan.

256-290 O-67—33

ENGLISH	VIETNAMESE	PRONUNCIATION

WEAPONS

Pistol.	Súng lục. or Súng sáu.	Shoom luke.
Rifle.	Súng trường.	Shoom trew-ong.
Automatic Rifle.	Trung liên.	Troong leen-en.
Carbine.	Cạc-bin.	Cock-bin.
Mortar.	Súng cối or Moọc chê.	Shoom coy.
Rec-Rifle.	Súng không giật.	Shoom come yaht.
Gun, cannon.	Đại bác.	Die bahc.
AA artillery gun.	Đại bác phòng không or Súng cao-xạ.	Die bahc fum come.
Howitzer.	Đại bác ngắn nòng.	Die bahc ngahn nòng.

TIME

Time.	Thì giờ	Tea yuh.
What time?	Mấy giờ.	May yuh.
This week.	Tuần này.	Twan high.
Next week.	Tuần sau.	Twan shao.
Last week.	Tuần trước.	Twan troo-oc.

ENGLISH	VIETNAMESE	PRONUNCIATION

(DAYS OF THE WEEK)

Today.	Hôm nay.	Home nigh.
Tomorrow.	Ngày mai.	Nigh my.
Yesterday.	Hôm qua.	Home kwa.
Sunday.	Ngày Chủ Nhựt.	Nigh choo nyut.
Monday.	Ngày thứ hai.	Nigh two high.
Tuesday.	Ngày thứ ba.	Nigh two bah.
Wednesday.	Ngày thứ tư.	Nigh two two.
Thursday	Ngày thứ năm.	Nigh two num.
Friday.	Ngày thứ sáu.	Nigh two shao.
Saturday.	Ngày thứ bảy.	Nigh two by.

(SEASONS OF THE YEAR)

Planting time.	Mùa gieo hạt giống.	Moo-uh yeho hut yome.
Harvest time.	Mùa màng.	Moo-uh mung.
Monsoon season.	Mùa mưa.	Moo-uh moo-uh.

ENGLISH	VIETNAMESE	PRONUNCIATION

NUMBERS

1	Một.	Moat.
2	Hai.	High.
3	Ba.	Bah.
4	Bốn.	Bone.
5	Năm.	Nom.
6	Sáu.	Shao.
7	Bẩy.	By.
8	Tám.	Tom.
9	Chín.	Chin.
10	Mười.	Mooy.
11	Mười một.	Mooy moat.
12	Mười hai.	Mooy high.
13	Mười ba.	Mooy bah.
15	Mười lăm.	Mooy lom.
20	Hai mươi.	High mooy.
21	Hai mươi mốt.	High mooy moat.
25	Hai mươi lăm.	High mooy lom.
30	Ba mươi.	Bah mooy.
35	Ba mươi lăm.	Bah mooy lom.
40	Bốn mươi.	Bone mooy.
45	Bốn mươi lăm.	Bone mooy lom.
100	Một trăm.	Moat trom.
500	Năm trăm.	Nom Trom.
1000	Một ngàn.	Moat ngon.

In forming numbers above ten in Vietnamese, you say "ten-one" for eleven. "ten-two" for twelve, "two-ten-three" for twenty-three, "three-hundred-three-ten-five" for three hundred thirty-five, etc. (Except in 15, 25, 35, etc., where 5 becomes Lăm instead of Năm).

ENGLISH	VIETNAMESE	PRONUNCIATION

ENTERING A VILLAGE

This village is surrounded.	Làng này bị bao vây.	Long ni be bow vay.
Bring the village chief.	Dẫn xã trưởng.	Yan sa troo-ong.
You will not be harmed.	Ông không bị bạc đãi.	Um come be buck die.
How many V.C. are there?	Có bao nhiêu Việt Cộng?	Caw bow nyew Viet Cong?
Where are the weapons hidden?	Những súng giấu ở đâu?	Nyoong shoong yo uh dow?
Where are the tunnels?	Những đường hầm ở đâu?	Nyoong bwong hum uh dow?
Where are the booby traps?	Những bẫy nổ ở đâu?	Nyoong by no uh dow?
Come outside.	Ra ngoài.	Rah noy.
Enter first.	Vào trước.	Vow troo-oc.
When was the attack?	Tấn công xẩy ra bao giờ?	Tun cung say rah bow yuh?
I am an American Marine.	Tôi là thủy-quân lục-Chiến Mỹ.	Toy la tooy kwon luke chyen mee.
Where is your unit?	Đơn vị của ông ở đâu?	Done vee kwa um uh dow?
Where is your village?	Làng của ông ở đâu?	Lahn kwa um uh dow?
Where is your camp?	Trại của ông ở đâu?	Try kwa um uh dow?
Where are the friendly troops?	Bộ đội nước bạn ở đâu?	Bo doy nwoc uh dow?
Is this trail safe?	Đường mòn nầy có nguy hiểm không?	Doong mow night caw ngooy he-em come?
How many V.C. were killed?	Bao nhiêu Việt Cộng bị chết?	Bow nyew Viet Cong be chet?
How many villagers were killed?	Bao nhiêu người làng bị chết?	Bow nyew newy bang be chet?

ENGLISH	VIETNAMESE	PRONUNCIATION
How many people were wounded?	Có bao nhiêu bị thương?	Caw bow nyew be twong?
Draw a picture.	Xin vẻ hình.	Sin vyeh hen.
Take me there.	Xin chỉ đường đến chỗ đó.	Sin chee doo-ung den cho daw.
Point for me.	Chỉ Cho Tôi.	Chee chaw toy.
How many men have weapons?	Bao nhiêu Người có súng?	Bow knee-o newy caw shoong?
We will follow you.	Ta sẽ theo các ông.	Ta shea teo cac um.
Show me your I.D. card.	Cho tôi coi căn cước ông.	Chaw toy coy khan coo-uhk um.
What village are you from.	Ông ở làng nào đến?	Um uh-a long now den?
Trust us.	Tin vàochúng tôi.	Tin vow choong toy.
Do not be afraid.	Đừng sợ.	Dung shuh.
We are friends.	Chúng tôi là bạn.	Choong toy lah bahn.
We want to help you.	Chúng tôi muốn giúp các ông.	Choong toy moo-uhn zoop cock um.
What is the name of this village?	Làng này tên gì?	Long nigh ten zee?
Where is the village chief?	Làng trưởng ở đâu?	Long true-uhng uh-a dow?

HANDLING PRISONERS

Drop your weapon.	Để súng xuống.	Day shoom swong.
Hands up.	Giơ tay lên.	Yuh tie len.
Come here.	Lại đây.	Lie day.
Don't move.	Đứng yên.	Doong yen.
Silence.	Đừng nói.	Doong noy.
Stand up.	Đứng đây	Doong yay.
Lie face down.	Nằm xuống.	Nom swong.
Undress.	Cổi ao.	Coy ow.
Dress.	Mặc.	Mock.
Turn around.	Quay lại.	Quay lie.

ENGLISH	VIETNAMESE	PRONUNCIATION
Move out.	Đi ði.	Dee dee.
Hurry up.	Mau lên.	Mau len.
Turn right.	Rẽ tay phải.	Ray tay fie.
Turn left.	Rẽ tay trái.	Ray tay try.
Halt.	Đứng lại.	Doong lie.
Walk ahead.	Đitrước.	Dee trock.
How many people are with you?	Có mấy người với ông?	Caw may newy vuy um?
Sit down.	Ngồi xuống.	Noi soong.
Show me your hands.	Đưa tay cho tôi coi.	Do-a tay chaw toy cov.
You walk in front.	Ông ði ðằng trước.	Um dee dahng true-uk.
Surrender.	Hàng ði.	Haang dee.

U.S. GOVERNMENT PRINTING OFFICE : 1967 O—256-290

www.ingramcontent.com/pod-product-compliance
Lightning Source LLC
Chambersburg PA
CBHW070158240426
43671CB00007B/484
* 9 7 8 1 7 8 0 3 9 1 3 3 5 *